During his remarkable career David Hill has been chairman then managing director of the Australian Broadcasting Corporation, chairman of the Australian Football Association, chief executive and director of the State Rail Authority NSW, chairman of Sydney Water Corporation and chairman of CREATE, a national organisation responsible for representing the interests of young people and children in institutional care. He is the author of the bestselling *The Forgotten Children*. He lives in Sydney.

1788

The Brutal Truth of the First Fleet
The biggest single overseas migration the world had ever seen

DAVID HILL

WILLIAM HEINEMANN: AUSTRALIA

To my mother

A William Heinemann book
Published by Random House Australia Pty Ltd
Level 3, 100 Pacific Highway, North Sydney NSW 2060
www.randomhouse.com.au

First published by William Heinemann in 2008
This edition published 2009

Addresses for companies within the Random House Group can be found at
www.randomhouse.com.au/offices.

National Library of Australia
Cataloguing-in-Publication Entry

Hill, David.
1788.

ISBN 978 1 74166 800 1(pbk).

First Fleet, 1787–1788.
Convicts – New South Wales.
Transportation of convicts – Great Britain.
Penal colonies – New South Wales.
New South Wales – History – 1788–1851.
New South Wales – Social conditions – 1788–1851.

994.02

Cover paintings of the First Fleet ships the *Alexander*, the *Lady Penrhyn* and the
Supply by Frank Allen
Cover design by Christabella Designs
Internal design by Midland Typesetters, Australia
Typeset in Sabon by Midland Typesetters, Australia
Printed and bound by Griffin Press, South Australia

10 9 8

CONTENTS

ACKNOWLEDGEMENTS

In the writing and researching of this book, I was able to access an extensive amount of primary source material due to the survival of a great deal of the original documentation in archives and libraries in Britain and Australia. For this I am extremely grateful.

A wealth of official letters, records and government files exist in the Public Records Office in Kew, England, and many of these documents were published in the *Historical Records of New South Wales* in the late nineteenth century and in the *Historical Records of Australia* from the early twentieth. There are also a number of original documents and copies in various Australian libraries, including the National Library of Australia in Canberra and the State Library of New South Wales in Sydney.

In addition to having access to the official records and dispatches, we are fortunate that many of those who sailed on the First Fleet kept journals and diaries. (The unfortunate aspect is that most were written by naval officers and marines, and we have little by way of first-hand accounts from women, convicts and the Aboriginal people.) The first journals were sent back to England on returning ships in late 1788 and published the following year in London, even though many of the authors would not themselves return for some years. The last of the personal accounts was written around thirty years later by an American seaman, Jacob Nagle, when he returned to his homeland.

Also, a number of very valuable personal letters survive, and originals and copies of the originals are available in a number of libraries, including the Mitchell Library in Sydney. I would like to thank all the staff of these institutions who helped me in my research.

Increasingly, all of this documentation is becoming electronically accessible, including via the Sydney Electronic Text and Image Service (SETIS), run by the Sydney University Library, and the electronic resources of the Mitchell Library. I found both of these resources very helpful.

Finally, I would also like to register my thanks to everyone at Random House for their guidance and support, and particularly to Kevin O'Brien for his professional and sensitive editing.

NOTE ON EXTRACTS
FROM PRIMARY SOURCES

In quoting material from the primary sources consulted for this book, I have remained faithful to the authors' non-standard grammar, spelling and punctuation as much as possible. However, there are some cases where a verbatim transcription would have hampered the meaning or otherwise presented a stumbling block to the reader. The only text that I have corrected, as such, is the misspelling of people's names. I have, though, made a number of formatting decisions in my transcriptions, such as to italicise the names of all ships, to spell out abbreviations, such as 'wt', meaning 'with', to spell out numbers and to eliminate the confusing use of capital letters in the middle of sentences. I hope the reader will forgive me for taking these small liberties.

There was also the problem of conflicting dates being given by different journal writers concerning the same event. In these cases I have compared a variety of accounts, where possible, and quoted from one of the concurring ones.

1

ENGLAND

*More prisoners were destroyed by [disease] in gaols
than were put to death by all the public executions in
the Kingdom.*

At four o'clock in the morning on Sunday 13 May 1787 the signal was given by the flagship *Sirius* for the ships of the First Fleet to set sail and begin their eight-month voyage from Portsmouth to establish a British convict colony in a remote and little-known spot on the far side of the world.

There was no ceremony or fanfare, as it was still nearly two hours till daybreak when the ships were assembled outside Portsmouth Harbour at Spithead, which separates the mainland from the Isle of Wight.

So began the program of mass exile that over the next seventy years would see more than a hundred and sixty thousand convicts dispatched from Britain to New South Wales and to other Australian colonies.

The First Fleet was the biggest single overseas migration the world had ever seen at the time. Each of the eleven tiny ships – the largest was less than forty metres long – was heavily loaded with human cargo (they carried nearly fifteen hundred people between them), two years' supply of food and the equipment needed to build a new settlement once they reached their destination.

This was the Georgian era, and Britain was enjoying the beginnings of the Industrial Revolution, the expansion of the mighty British Empire and the rising affluence that went with it. Great canals, sturdy roads and giant bridges were being constructed, and, from the 1760s, labour-saving machinery was being introduced for the manufacture of cotton, iron, steel and pottery. The steam engines developed by James Watt and Matthew Boulton were being put to various uses, and there was a quickening pace of advancement in all fields of human endeavour.[1]

The Empire was expanding at a time when the earlier European powers of Spain, Portugal and the Netherlands were in decline. In 1773 the British Parliament passed the legislation that began the government takeover of the administration and control of India from the British East India Company, which was to precipitate nearly a hundred years of British rule of the subcontinent. In 1768 Captain James Cook had begun a series of remarkable voyages through the southern oceans and the Pacific in which he discovered new lands and claimed new territories for the Empire.

It was also the age of the Enlightenment. As the century progressed, new approaches and fresh currents of thought provided the setting for the revolutionary changes ahead. It was during the Enlightenment that the ecclesiastical establishment was dislodged from its central role in cultural and intellectual life, and science was emancipated from the restraints of theological tradition. Predominant figures included Newton, Rousseau, Voltaire, Kant, Hume, Locke, the Irishman Edmund Burke and the Americans Thomas Paine, author of the *Rights of Man* (which supported the French Revolution), Benjamin Franklin, scientist, statesman and writer, and the younger Thomas Jefferson. These latter two were involved in the drafting of the American Declaration of Independence. In 1776 Adam Smith's *The Wealth of Nations* was published and the first of the six volumes of Edward Gibbon's *The History of the Decline and Fall of the Roman Empire* was released.

The late eighteenth century was a period during which music, theatre, the arts and science flourished. Writers included Jane Austen and the social commentators Samuel Johnson and James Boswell, while William Hogarth was satirising British society in his highly stylised paintings and cartoons. Prominent poets included Coleridge, Wordsworth, Blake and Byron, and the painters Gainsborough and Reynolds were making names for themselves. The Georgian era had its own architectural style – made famous by architects such as Robert Adam, James Wyatt and John Nash – and its own style of furniture, which was characterised by strong, clean lines typically highlighted with vertical reeds and flutes.

Britain's king at the time was George III. He was to sit on the throne for fifty years from 1760 – at the time the longest reign of any monarch – and his rule covered tumultuous change and dramatic events. He had come to the throne as a 22-year-old on the death of his grandfather, King George II,[2] and was the third German to become the British monarch but the first of those to be born in England and to speak English as his native language.

The German kings had taken over the throne of England when Queen Anne had died in 1714 without any heirs. The English realm was offered to her nearest Protestant relative, George of Hanover, who became George I of England. Throughout the long reigns of George I, his son George II and George III,[3] the very nature of English society and the political face of the realm changed. The first two Georges took little interest in the politics of rule and were quite content to let ministers govern on their behalf, but George III became far more involved in the running of his governments.

After a rocky start, largely due to the instability caused by the Seven Years War with France, George III was to become a popular monarch, although the remainder of his reign was far from easy. He was first believed to have gone mad in 1788, the year the First Fleet arrived in Australia, and at one point Parliament debated whether he should continue as king.[4] He appeared to have recovered, but in 1811 the recurrence of the illness forced him to abdicate in favour of his son, the Prince Regent, who would later become King George IV when his father died in 1820.

King George III typified much of the enlightenment of the era. He founded and paid the initial costs of the Royal Academy of the Arts, started a new royal collection of books and later gave all sixty-five thousand copies to the British Museum (now the British Library). He was keenly interested in agriculture and earned himself the nickname 'Farmer George' for his enthusiastic work on the royal estates at Windsor and Richmond. He also studied science and made his own astronomical observations. Many of his scientific instruments survive and are now in the British Science Museum.

George III had become king when George II died suddenly in October 1760, and immediately a search began to find the new young monarch a suitable wife, so as to ensure succession. The year before George was said to have been smitten by Lady Sarah Lennox, the daughter of the Duke of Richmond. He was forced to abandon the idea of marriage with her, however, as she was not a royal and was therefore deemed to be an unacceptable match.

The following year he married Duchess Sophia Charlotte of Mecklenburg-Strelitz at St James' Palace in London. George met his wife for the first time on the day of the wedding, but they appear to have enjoyed a happy marriage and had fifteen children together. In contrast to his predecessors and his sons George III does not appear to have taken a mistress and enjoyed spending time with his family and farming on the royal estates.

The remarkable advances of the age and the rising level of affluence did not benefit everyone, of course. While the rich got richer, an overwhelming majority of people continued to live and die poor. The industrial changes brought a huge movement of people from the country to the increasingly overcrowded towns and cities. This over-crowding was compounded by the 'enclosures' of the commons, whereby landowners fenced off land that had previously been used by everyone. Hand in hand with the growing numbers of King George's displaced and unemployed subjects came an increase in crime, as many resorted to stealing to survive.

At the same time King George and his governments were distracted by a succession of foreign wars, first with France and later with Britain's American colonies. The American War of Independence would have a direct bearing on the British decision to dispatch the First Fleet and to create a convict colony in Australia. For most of the eighteenth century the British had been transporting surplus convicts to America. In 1717 the Parliament had passed the *Act for the Further Preventing of Robbery, Burglary and Other Felonies and the More Effective Transportation of Felons etc.*, which marked the beginning of the large-scale removal of criminals to foreign shores. Over the next sixty or so years about forty thousand convicts were sent to America, until the practice was halted when the American colonies rose up in revolt against Britain.

Unlike the later transportation to Australia the system of transporting convicts to America was entirely privately run. Convicts committed to transportation were sold by their gaolers to the shipping contractors, who took them across the Atlantic and sold the prisoners to plantation owners for the duration of their sentences.

The American revolt that began in the 1760s and turned into war in the 1770s was triggered by Britain's policy of taxing its colonial citizens even though they were allowed no say in the British Parliament – and at the same time that Britain was allowing the British East India Company tax breaks on tea being sold directly to America. On 16 December 1773 a number of Boston radicals dumped a large quantity of British-owned tea into Boston Harbor in what was to become known as the Boston Tea Party. Tough retaliatory measures by the British, including the closure of Boston Harbor, escalated the situation and, rather than isolating the Boston radicals, united many of the colonies in protest. The following year representatives of the colonies met in Philadelphia and resolved to boycott British trade and withhold taxes.

In 1775 the first shots of the war were fired in Massachusetts, and while the British managed to regain control of the area around Boston after what became known as the Battle of Bunker Hill, their win came at the cost of many of their troops.

The Americans now moved to establish the new Continental Army under General George Washington to bring many of the local militias into a coordinated fighting force. Over the next few years the fighting spread across all the colonies. In 1776 the British sent their biggest ever force across the Atlantic, and the colonies approved the Declaration of Independence. There was no way of going back.

The year 1777 was the last year of British ascendancy in the war. The following year the French, who had already been providing the colonists with support, joined the hostilities on the American side following the signing of an alliance between the French and Americans in Paris. For the next three years the armies fought a number of battles, until the Battle of Yorktown in Virginia in May 1781, when the British general Cornwallis surrendered and more than six thousand British troops were taken prisoner.

When news of Yorktown reached London, the Parliament moved to end the war, despite the opposition of King George III, who wanted a continued British military commitment until the insurrection was crushed. His prime minister, Lord North, duly continued the war but when faced with declining parliamentary support was forced to resign in 1783. (North would be replaced as prime minister by the 24-year-old William Pitt ('the Younger'), who would be the head of the government when the decision was made to establish a convict colony in Australia.)

The loss of the American colonies was a crushing blow to the prestige of the British Empire, and the peace treaty of Paris in 1783 only added to the British humiliation, with the first article of the agreement stating that 'His Britannic Majesty acknowledges the said United States'.

The loss of the United States also meant that Britain no longer had a convenient dumping ground for her surplus convicts. As the country had been unable to send convicts to America from the early days of the conflict, Parliament had passed the *Hulk Act* in 1777, which allowed for the confinement of the growing number of convicts on decommissioned British navy vessels on the Thames and other English rivers and ports. The *Hulk Act* was envisaged only as an interim measure until the American insurrection was quashed, but with the loss of the colonies the hulks would continue to be used as prisons in Britain until the middle of the nineteenth century.

By the late eighteenth century it was estimated that a hundred and fifteen thousand, or one in eight, people in London were living off crime in the city.[5] Horace Walpole complained that robbery in broad daylight had become so commonplace that 'one is forced to travel, even at noon, as if one was going into battle'.[6]

At the beginning of the 1700s criminal offences that attracted the death penalty had been limited to the most serious acts, such as murder and treason. By the end of the century more than one hundred additional crimes – almost all of them involving offences against property – had been made capital offences. Thirty-three had been added during the reign of King George II and a further sixty-three during the first decades of the rule of King George III.[7]

The new crimes that warranted execution included smuggling, selling a forged stamp, burglary, extortion, blackmail, larceny by servants, blackmailers who failed to surrender themselves, arson, wilful destruction of property, petty theft and the stealing of horses. Most of the new capital statutes were passed with very little discussion and 'were created . . . by a placid and uninterested Parliament. In nine cases out of ten there was no debate and no opposition.'[8]

So great was the increase in the number of capital offences that by 1800 Sir Samuel Riley was to observe that 'there is probably no other country in the world in which so many and so great a variety of human actions are punishable with loss of life than in England'.[9] However, despite the dramatic rise in the number of convicts sentenced to death, fewer were actually being executed. The judges in the courts of England were increasingly reluctant to send offenders to the gallows, and more and more death sentences were being commuted to transportation to America – even after such shipment had been suspended. It has been suggested that the judges deliberately 'went to invent technicalities in order to avoid infliction of the capital penalty', even though their actions were 'clearly outside the contemplations of the legislation'.[10]

As a consequence of this judicial leniency the proportion of those executed fell dramatically over the second half of the eighteenth century. In the 1750s about seventy per cent of those convicted were actually hanged, but by the time the First Fleet set sail barely a quarter of the condemned reached the gallows. By the end of the century the figure had dropped to less then twenty per cent.[11]

By the last quarter of the eighteenth century the gaols and prison hulks of England were overflowing, with their population increasing by more than a thousand a year. This was causing increasing public concern. Periodic riots by convicts spread alarm, and there was the ever-present fear that rampant diseases in the gaols would break out in the wider community.

There was also concern amongst some quarters for the prisoners themselves. Prison reformers were campaigning against the appalling conditions in the prisons and the hulks. Foremost among them was John Howard. Born in 1726 in Hackney in East London, Howard inherited considerable wealth in his 20s on the death of his successful merchant father. In 1773, when he was 47 years old, Howard was appointed high sheriff of Bedford and became shocked by the conditions he witnessed in the gaols.

In 1777, after studying prisons in England and other countries, he wrote a book titled *The State of Prisons in England and Wales: With Preliminary Observations, and an Account of Some Foreign Prisons and Hospitals*, which painted a devastating picture of the reality of prisons and brought into the open much of what had been out of sight and out of mind to genteel society. He also gave evidence to the House of Commons about convicts and the question of convict transportation.

Howard wrote that healthy men who entered the prison system were often soon reduced to illness and death. He said that disease was so rife that 'more prisoners were destroyed by it in gaols than were put to death by all the public executions in the Kingdom'.[12]

In some prisons, he said, there was no food allowance for the prisoners, and in others no fresh water. There was a shortage of fresh air and ventilation in most gaols, which were 'made poisonous to the more intense degree by the effusia of the sick'.[13]

Many of the prisons had no sewers, and in those that did, 'if not properly attended, they are, even to a visitant, offensive beyond expression'. Many had no bedding or straw and the prisoners were forced to sleep 'upon rags, others on bare floors'. He said that chaining prisoners in irons made walking and 'even lying down to sleep difficult and painful'.[14]

Howard was especially critical of the half of England's prisons that were privately run: 'In these the keepers protected by the proprietors and not so subject as other gaolers to the control of the magistrates are more apt to abuse the prisoners.'[15]

Howard called for the building of new, properly planned prisons that would have water pumps, baths, cooking facilities, an infirmary for the sick, clean air and ventilation, and workshops so the prisoners could be effectively employed. He also called for more effective regulation of the gaolers, including a ban on the sale of grog to the prisoners, and placed emphasis on hygiene and cleanliness: 'Every prisoner who comes to the gaol dirty, should be washed in the cold or warm bath and his clothes should be put in the oven . . . Every prisoner should be obliged to wash his hands and face before he comes for his daily allowance.'[16]

Largely as a result of the agitation of Howard and other prison reformers, legislation was passed in Parliament for the building of two new prisons, but funding was never made available and construction never began.

Parliament also passed legislation in 1777 for the rein-troduction of the overseas transportation of convicts, but the Bill did not prescribe to which countries the prisoners should be sent. With America closed it would be almost another decade before Botany Bay was selected, and in the meantime more and more convicts had to be crammed into the existing prisons and hulks in England.

The concept of transportation was not unique to the eighteenth century. Legislation had been introduced in Elizabethan England to banish certain criminals to lands 'beyond the seas',[17] but the practice had never taken on the dimension it had with regards to America or would later with the first and subsequent fleets to Australia.

Not everyone in Georgian society supported the idea of transportation. Many believed it was going too easy on the convicted criminals. Lord Ellenborough, who was later to become a member of parliament and chief justice, and who argued that capital punishment should be extended even further to include pickpockets, said he believed transportation was no more than 'a summer excursion, in an easy migration to a happy and better climate'.[18] However, to the convicts in England, transportation to Botany Bay was a frightening prospect, and Australia in the late eighteenth century might as well have been another planet.

At the time of the First Fleet Europeans knew little about the geography of the globe. The outline of the continents of the Americas and Africa was roughly known, but there was little knowledge of the hinterland or west of America or anything beyond a few of the coastal ports of Africa. Even less was known of Asia, and less again of the southern-hemisphere continents of Australasia and Antarctica.

The only concrete information the British had when they decided to establish a penal colony on the east coast of Australia was Captain James Cook's account of his voyage there eighteen years earlier, when the *Endeavour* spent barely a week in Botany Bay.

While Cook was the first to chart much of the east coast of what was then called New Holland, he was far from the first to discover Australia, as more than fifty European ships had seen or landed on the continent over the preceding two hundred years.

The earliest European visitors to the region had been the Dutch, Portuguese and Spanish. The Pacific Ocean had been named 'El Mar Pacifico' by the Portuguese navigator Ferdinand Magellan in the early sixteenth century, during his remarkable voyage from Portugal to Guam.

The first undisputed European sighting of Australia was in 1606, although there may have been some earlier discoveries. Around 1300 Marco Polo had made mention of the existence of a great southern continent but offered no first-hand knowledge of the place. Some archaeological evidence suggests that from 1500 a number of Portuguese, Dutch and Spanish ships may have touched on Australia's west and southern coasts, and it has been more recently claimed, by the author Gavin Menzies, that the Chinese explorer Zheng He charted much of the west coast in 1421.[19] There is also evidence of Asian ships regularly visiting the north of Australia from around 1600, including Indonesian traders who harvested the bêche-de-mer, or sea slugs, which were regarded as a delicacy and an aphrodisiac by many Chinese people.

In 1606 Dutch captain Willem Janszoon landed briefly on the west coast of the Gulf of Carpentaria in the *Duyfken*, wrongly assuming the land was part of Papua New Guinea. From 1616 a number of Dutch and other European ships reached the west coast of Australia. In 1642 Abel Tasman sailed below Tasmania, giving it the name Van Diemen's Land after the Dutch East Indies governor of Batavia, Anthony van Diemen. By 1644 – still more than a hundred years before Cook's first expedition – the Dutch were able to draw most of the coastline from

Cape York peninsula in the north of Australia around to the eastern end of the Great Australian Bight in the south, as well as the southern tip of Van Diemen's Land and parts of the coast of New Zealand.[20]

The first English ship to reach Australia was the *Cygnet*, a small trading vessel captained by William Dampier, who landed on the west coast in 1688, almost eighty years before Cook. Dampier was the first Englishman to provide what were to become many negative descriptions of the Australian Aboriginal people, whom he said were the 'miserablest people in the world', 'nasty people' and who 'differ little from brutes'.[21]

Even these incomplete reports and maps would not have been known by the uneducated convicts, of course. They would have had little knowledge of geography, and the worldly experience of most would have been confined to the area within walking distance of where they were born.

Far from seeing it as Lord Ellenborough's 'summer excursion', most of the convicts regarded transportation as the most severe punishment available next to death, one that was intended 'to purge, deter and to reform'.[22] They would be exchanging familiarity for hardship, hostility and the unknown. They would be saying goodbye to loved ones and friends and would have been aware there was little prospect of ever coming home.

2

THE BOTANY BAY
DECISION

*[T]here was a great plenty of fish . . . The grass was
long and luxuriant, and the eatable vegetables,
particularly a sort of wild spinage; the country was
well supplied with water; there was an abundance of
timber and fuel sufficient for any number of buildings,
which might be found necessary.*

The selection of the site on which to establish a convict
colony took many years, and Botany Bay was only chosen
as a last resort when all the other options had been
eliminated.

In 1779 the House of Commons established a committee
to find a workable solution to the escalating prisons
problem. The committee heard from a number of witnesses
who argued for the establishment of a convict colony in
various locations, including Gibraltar and sites along the
west African coast. It also heard from Duncan Campbell, a
contractor who had transported convicts to North America
but had recently 'declined contracting them upon the revolt
of the colonies of Virginia and Maryland'.[1]

The committee concluded that the current prison
arrangements in Britain were a failure:

In short, your committee must observe, that the whole
arrangement of the prisons, so far as they are

informed, is, at present, ill-suited, either in the economy of the state, or the morality of the people, and seems chiefly calculated for the safe custody of the persons confined, without due attention to their health, employment or reformation.[2]

The committee also recognised that it 'was not in the power of the executive Government at present to dispose of convicted felons in North America' and recommended that some other spot be found in 'any part of the globe that may be found expedient'.[3]

The most significant witness to appear before the committee was the famous botanist Joseph Banks, who was to be a major influence on the ultimate decision to send the First Fleet to Botany Bay. Banks' reputation had been cemented eight years beforehand when he had travelled as a 25-year-old to New Holland with Captain James Cook in the *Endeavour* and returned with hundreds of new species of plants.

When asked by the parliamentary committee where he thought was the best location for the establishment of a penal colony, Banks praised Botany Bay's fertile soil and plentiful water and food:

Joseph Banks Esq. being requested, in case it should be thought expedient to establish a Colony of convicted felons in any distant part of the Globe, from whence escape might be difficult, and where, from the fertility of the soil, they might be able to maintain themselves, after the fifth year, with little or no aid from the mother country, to give his opinion what place would be the most eligible for such settlement, informed your committee, that the place which appeared to him best adapted for such a purpose, was Botany Bay, on the coast of New Holland, in the Indian Ocean, which was about seven months voyage from England, that he apprehended there would be little possibility of opposition from the natives, as during his stay there in the year 1770, he saw very few and did not think there were above fifty in the neighbourhood, and had reason to believe the country was very thinly populated, those he saw were naked, treacherous, and armed with lances, but extremely cowardly, and constantly retired from our people when they made the least appearance and resistance. He was in the bay in the end of April and the beginning of May 1770, when the weather was mild and moderate, that the climate, he apprehended, was similar to Toulouse in the South of France having found the southern hemisphere colder than the northern, in such proportion that any given climate in the southern answered to the northern about ten degrees nearer the pole, the proportion of rich soil was small in comparison to the barren but sufficient to support a very large number of people; there were no tame animals, and he saw no wild ones during his stay of ten days, but he saw the dung of what were called kangaroos, which were about the size of middling sheep and difficult to catch; some of these animals he saw in another part of the bay, upon the same continent; there were no beasts of prey, and he did not doubt oxen and sheep, if carried there, would thrive and increase, there was a great plenty of fish, he took a large quantity by hauling the seine and struck several stingrays, a kind of skate, all very large, one weighed 336 lb. The grass was long and luxuriant, and the eatable vegetables, particularly a sort of wild spinage; the country was well supplied with water; there was an abundance of timber and fuel sufficient for any number of buildings, which might be found necessary.

Being asked, how a Colony of that nature could be subsisted in the beginning of their establishment, he answered, they must certainly be furnished, at landing with a full years allowance of victuals, rainment and drink, with all kinds of tools for labouring the earth and building houses; with black cattle, sheep, hogs, and poultry; with seeds of all kinds of European corn and pulse; with garden seeds; with arms and ammunition for defense, and they should likewise have small boats, nets and fishing tackle; all of which, except arms and ammunition, might be purchased at the Cape of Good Hope; and that afterwards, with a moderate portion of industry, they might undoubtedly, maintain themselves without any assistance from England.[4]

Banks was not the first person to argue for the establishment of a penal colony in the Pacific. Nearly a quarter of a century earlier the French writer and statesman Charles de Brosses had suggested that France settle a penal colony on the island of New Britain, Papua New Guinea, where felons could be purged from society. In an analogy with the prevailing medical practice of bloodletting, or leeching, he said, 'The political body, like the human body, has vicious humours which should be often evacuated.'[5]

The Englishman John Callander went on to say the same thing with regards to Britain in 1776. In his three-volume *Voyages to the Terra Australis* he said that Britain should found a colony on New Britain and explore the possibility of annexing New Holland, New Zealand and Tasmania.

When Banks was giving his evidence to the House of Commons committee, it was not yet known in London that Captain Cook had been killed. In February 1779 Cook had been searching for a passage linking the Pacific and Atlantic Oceans when he was murdered in Hawaii. Cook had provided his own assessment of Botany Bay when landing there with Banks back in 1770, and it was completely different from Banks' submission to the committee. Cook had said that the land was uncultivated and produced virtually nothing fit to eat.

At the time of their visit the aristocratic Banks had been at the height of his power and influence. Back in London he had the ear of the government, the Admiralty and the king. He was regularly consulted on a wide range of matters, including botany, earthquakes, sheep breeding and exploration, and was in the habit of corresponding with all the commanders of British exploration ships, whose captains regularly returned with more botanical samples for his analysis.

Banks was the only son of a wealthy landowner and was to maintain a lifelong interest in the family estates at Revesby Abbey in Lincolnshire. Both his father and his grandfather had been members of parliament. He had first travelled as a botanist to Newfoundland and Labrador in 1766 and was soon after elected as a member of the Royal Society.

When he had boarded Cook's *Endeavour* as a 'gentleman of fortune', he had taken aboard his own suite of eight staff, which included the noted naturalist Solander and two servants. Of Banks' party, only Banks, Solander and two tenants from his family estates survived the journey.

Banks became president of the Royal Society at the relatively young age of 35 and was heavily involved in the development of Kew Gardens. He became a trustee of the British Museum, a member of the Society of Antiquities and a member of many London clubs, including the Society of Dilettanti. In his later years he became a well-known spectacle in London, where he lived in New Burlington Street, overweight and crippled with gout, presiding over the Royal Society in a wheeled chair in full court dress, wearing the Order of the Bath.

Banks' glowing report to the committee is not only at odds with Cook's assessment but also strangely at odds with his own far less enthusiastic journal entries of the time. The *Endeavour* arrived in Botany Bay on 29 April 1770 and left on 6 May. Banks went ashore on five of those days with his colleague Solander and wrote a brief account in his daily journal. On the second day he was ashore, Banks wrote that the 'soil wherever we saw it consisted of either swamps or light sandy soil on which grew very few species of trees'. Four days later, on 4 May, he ventured a little further inland,

> where we went a good way into the country which in this place is very sandy and resembles something our Moors in England, as no trees grow upon it but every thing is covered with a thin brush of plants about as high as the knees.[6]

It is perhaps worth noting that Banks stood to gain from any settlement on the east coast of Australia. He had collected many botanical species when he had visited Botany Bay on the *Endeavour* and would benefit from any ships returning with more specimens. His influence would later result in British ships being modified to have sheds installed on their decks for the storage of botanical samples.[7]

Despite the committee's deliberations and Banks' recommendations, the decision on where to send the surplus convicts was deferred for many years. It seems that some of the British ruling elite were still hopeful that the American insurrection could be put down and the transport of convicts to the American colonies resumed. As late as 1783, before the formal surrender of the colonies, King George III was adamant that he would make no concessions to the Americans and remained of the view that 'unworthy' convicts would still be sent there: 'The Americans cannot expect nor ever will receive any favour from me, but permitting them to obtain men unworthy to remain in this island I shall certainly consent to.'[8]

That year the Botany Bay option was given further support by an American named James Matra, who had sailed with Banks and Cook on the voyage of 1768–71 and had consequently been to New South Wales. (New South Wales was given its name by Captain Cook. He never explained why he used the name in the journal he wrote on his way home in 1770, but it is believed that the land simply reminded him of South Wales.) On the voyage Matra had been a lowly seaman, and the only reference to him in Cook's log is a poor one, following Matra's involvement in a violent and drunken brawl.

Matra was an Italian American who had returned to England in 1781 from New York and wanted Britain to help those Americans who had remained loyal to the empire during the American War of Independence. In 1783 Matra submitted to the British Government 'A Proposal for Establishing a Settlement in NSW to Atone for the Loss of the American Colonies' and was able to meet and discuss the idea with a number of influential people, including Joseph Banks. Matra wrote of New South Wales:

> This country may afford an asylum to those unfortunate American loyalists to whom Great Britain is bound by every tie of honour and gratitude to protect and support, where they may repair their broken fortunes, and again enjoy their former domestic felicity.[9]

Even though the proposal to assist American loyalists was never actually embraced, many of the details of Matra's proposal were incorporated in the later British convict-settlement plan. Matra had suggested, for instance, that the settlement fleet stop at Cape Town to take on board plants and animals for the new colony – a stopover that the First Fleet did indeed make.

A striking feature of the Matra proposal that was also included in the official British plan for the convict colony was the suggestion that, to address the shortage of women, the settlers could send a ship across to nearby Pacific islands and simply take the women:

> When the landing is effected . . . the . . . ship may, if thought proper be dispatched to New Caledonia, Otahite, and other neighbouring islands to procure a few families there and as many women as may serve for the men left behind.[10]

Matra had managed to successfully lobby the support of Banks – whose own suggestions would also make it into the final plans – and included in his proposal the endorsement that 'Sir Joseph Banks highly approves of the settlement and is very ready to give his opinion of it; either to his Majesty's Ministry or others, whenever they may please require it'.[11]

After circulating his plan, Matra was able to gain an audience with the home secretary, Lord Sydney, who was to become a significant figure in the First Fleet story. Lord Sydney told Matra that the government was looking for a solution to the convict problem, so Matra amended his plan for an American colony to include convicts:

> When I conversed with Lord Sydney on this subject it was observed that New South Wales would be a very proper region for the reception of criminals condemned to transportation. I believe that it will be found that in this idea good policy and humanity are united.[12]

It is not clear whether Matra himself ever intended to be part of the new colony, but he was never to return to New South Wales. In 1786, while the First Fleet was being prepared, he managed to secure a minor British diplomatic posting to Morocco, where he would spend the rest of his life. He died in Tangier in 1806, aged 60.

Meanwhile the issue dragged on, with no decision from the government and the convict population still growing. In 1784 the House of Commons debated and passed a Bill titled *An Act for the Effectual Transportation of Felons and Other Offenders*, which stipulated the reintroduction of transportation but again did not mention any sites.

On 5 March 1785 a petition from the high sheriff and grand jury of the county of Wiltshire to the government typified the widespread concern about the overcrowded prisons and hulks:

> To his Majesties Secretaries of State.
>
> The country is overburdened with such a number of transports [hulks] which have been increasing for the last two assizes and is continuing to increase by the addition of many more sentenced to the same punishment we apprehend from the physicians employed for the purpose of inspecting the state of the gaols by the justices of the said county that there is a great danger of an epidemical distemper being the consequence of the close confinement of so many prisoners. We therefore humbly entreat that the [prisoners] may be removed from the said gaol with the utmost expedition.[13]

In April 1785 an increasingly frustrated House of Commons set up yet another committee to look at how its transportation Bill of the previous year might be given effect.[14] The committee heard how the hulks were failing to help address the convict problem and how being imprisoned on a hulk was more, rather than less, likely than standard imprisonment to corrupt newcomers and commit them to a life of crime. The usual destinations for transportation were again presented, including Africa, but these were rejected, largely because of evidence that the environments were too hostile.

Earlier in 1785 Attorney-General R. P. Auden had sent to his colleague Lord Sydney a detailed proposal for the transportation of convicts to Botany Bay. He had received the proposal from Sir George Young, an admiral in the navy, and added his own highly qualified recommendation:

> I profess myself totally ignorant of the probability of the success of such a scheme, but it appears to me, upon a cursory view of the subject, to be the most likely method of effectively disposing of convicts, the number of which requires the immediate interference of the government.[15]

It seemed that Auden wanted the problem solved in whichever manner was the quickest.

Young's plan emphasised the potential benefits of increased trade between countries in the Pacific and Indian Oceans and Britain, which at that time was consciously seeking to expand its empire in the face of its recent losses:

> Botany Bay, or its vicinity . . . with a fair open navigation . . . there is no doubt but that a lucrative trade would soon be opened . . . I think . . . that a territory so happily situated must be superior to all others for establishing a very extensive commerce, and of consequence greatly increase our shipping and number of seamen.[16]

The plan also took up the Matra idea of helping the displaced American loyalists to find a new place to live and argued it would be at less cost than any other option:

The American Loyalists would here find a fertile,
healthy soil, far preferable to their own, and well
worthy of their industry, where with a very small part
of the expense the crown must necessarily be at for
their support, they may be established now comfort-
ably and with a greater prospect of success than in
any other place hitherto pointed out for them.

It was Sir George Young who first excited the British with
the prospect of opening a new colony for the purpose of
growing New Zealand flax, which was of critical strategic
importance for making canvas and rope for the British
navy. Captain Cook had noted the value of the flax
during his explorations to the south seas some fifteen
years earlier, and Joseph Banks had brought back some
samples to England from the voyage. Sir George Young
believed it would be superior to what the British were
using:

The New Zealand flax-plant may be cultivated in
every part, and in any quantity, as our demands may
require. Its uses are more extensive than any vegetable
hitherto known, for in its gross state it far exceeds
anything of the kind for cordage and canvas, and
may be obtained at a much cheaper rate than those
material we at present get from Russia.

In these early years of the Industrial Revolution Young
also offered the tantalising prospect that the new
colony might provide the British Empire with rich
deposits of valuable minerals. His plan, too, suggested
that transportation to Botany Bay would cost less than
maintaining prison hulks in England and that Britain
would be permanently rid of the convicts because the
distance and expense made their return 'the most distant
probability':

> The very heavy expense the Government is annually
> put to for transporting and otherwise punishing the
> felons, together with the facility of their return, are
> evils long and much lamented. Here is an asylum open
> that will considerably reduce the first, and forever
> prevent the latter.[17]

By the year of Young's proposal, 1785, there was a public
clamouring for a decision on what to do with the rising
number of convicts, and there were fifty-six separate
requests and petitions from sheriffs, mayors, judges, town
clerks and gaolers calling for their removal.

In March 1786 the country was shaken when prisoners
on a hulk in Plymouth rioted and forty-four were shot,
eight of them fatally. At the same time the Lord Mayor of
London, Fraser, appealed to the government for something to be done about the overcrowded hulks.[18]

For months the government procrastinated while
'parliament, press, pamphlet and pulpit'[19] were all calling
for something to be done about the overcrowded prisons.
Rumours began circulating that Botany Bay would
emerge as the chosen solution.

In June the Cabinet considered a number of specific
sites for the resumption of transportation in Canada, the
West Indies and Africa, but again no decision was made.
Finally, two months later, in August 1786, Lord Sydney
advised the lords of the Treasury of the government's
decision.[20]

Lord Sydney, whose real name was Thomas
Townshend, was the home secretary but also the colonial
secretary in the government of William Pitt the Younger
for six years from 1783 to 1789. He was ultimately
responsible for the decision to establish a convict colony
in Australia and for the appointment of Arthur Phillip to
lead the expedition. Sydney was of aristocratic birth, the
Townshend family estate being Frognal House in Sidcup,

Kent. He began his political career in the House of
Commons and later moved to the House of Lords, before
becoming a viscount. There is considerable argument
about Sydney, who has been variously described as an
enlightened and progressive politician and a person who
'scarcely rose above mediocrity'.[21]

In his letter to the Treasury outlining the decision, the
main reasons he gave were the overcrowded prisons and
the fear of society being doubly threatened by escaped
convicts and the outbreak of disease. There was no
mention of creating a new colony that would benefit from
British trade or provide a refuge for American loyalists:

> The several gaols and places for the confinement of
> felons in this kingdom being in so crowded a state
> that the greatest danger is to be apprehended, not only
> from their escape, but for infectious distempers,
> which may hourly be expected to break out among
> them, his Majesty, desirous of preventing by every
> possible means the ill consequences which might
> happen from either of these causes, has been pleased
> to signify to me his royal commands that measures
> should immediately be pursued for sending out of this
> kingdom such of the convicts as are under sentence or
> order of transportation . . . His Majesty has thought
> it advisable to fix upon Botany Bay.[22]

In the end Botany Bay was a last resort, chosen because,
after years of deliberation and inquiry, the government
could come up with no better option.

Sydney's letter went on to instruct the Treasury 'to take
such measures' to provide the necessary shipping to
transport seven hundred and fifty convicts, 'together with
such provisions to last two years'.[23] The transport fleet
would take a route that would include stopping at the
Cape Verde Islands and the Cape of Good Hope, where it

would be authorised to pick up cattle and other live-stock for the convict settlement in New Holland. The expedition was to have all the necessary officers and assistants and would be accompanied by three companies of marines, who would stay in Botany Bay 'so long as it is found necessary'.

The decision was officially announced to the House of Commons in the king's Speech from the Throne in January 1787:

> A plan has been formed, by my direction, for the transporting a number of convicts, in order to remove any inconvenience which arose from the crowded state of the gaols in the different parts of the kingdom and you will I doubt not, take such further measures as may be necessary for this purpose.[24]

If Lord Sydney was responsible for policy, it was his deputy, Evan Nepean, who was to be responsible for the detailed implementation of the plan. Nepean was a 33-year-old undersecretary when the decision was made. He headed a branch of the Home Office that administered the British overseas colonies, and working on the details of the First Fleet was his first major appointment.

Nepean came from Saltash in Cornwall. He began his naval career working as a purser on a number of British ships along the American coast during the American War of Independence. In 1782 he became secretary to Lord Shuldham, a post-admiral in Plymouth, before being promoted a year later to work in London as Lord Sydney's undersecretary.

He was regarded as an excellent administrator and later became chief secretary for Ireland, a lord of the Admiralty and a member of parliament. He was made a baronet in 1802 and admitted to the Privy Council in 1804, was governor of Bombay from 1812 to 1819, and died in Dorset in 1822 after a short retirement. Arthur Phillip was later to name Nepean River, about fifty kilometres west of Sydney, in his honour.

At the time of the Botany Bay decision there was little rivalry between the European trading interests in the south Pacific, as the region had small populations and few exploitable natural resources. The British East India Company, which by now was emerging as the dominant trading influence in the Indian Ocean and north of Australia, expressed no interest in the venture, and commercial shippers, who may have been interested in the business of transportation, were more heavily involved in the much bigger slave trade.

Nor was there much reaction from the other European powers to the British decision, which was first reported in the British newspapers from September 1786. There was no hint that the other colonising powers of France, Spain, Holland and Portugal wanted to mount any counter initiative.

Britian's most obvious rival, France, showed little interest in the region until Napoleon sent Nicolas-Thomas Baudin in 1800 to explore New Holland and Tasmania – to which the British responded by establishing outposts at Fremantle and Perth on the west coast of Australia.

It has been argued that Britain had a strategic interest in controlling Australian waters, if not the land, but even this was subordinate to the imperative of doing something about the convict problem.

The Times came out in favour of the decision, arguing – erroneously as it turned out – that transportation was to cost less than the other schemes to deal with the growing number of convicts:

> There is one circumstance to be alleged in favour of the Botany Bay scheme in which it surpasses every

other mode for the punishment of felons which has hitherto been carried into execution. In every former scheme, whether of confinement and hard labour, ballast heaving on the Thames etc., etc., there was a constant and growing expense on the public, which could not be reduced so long as the punishment continued. In the present instant the consequence is quite reversed for after the second year it is to be presumed that the convicts will be in the habit of providing for themselves and the expense to the public will be extremely trifling.[25]

It had taken years of equivocation and procrastination, but now that the decision was made the British Civil Service and the Royal Navy began the intensive organisation required to carry it out. The biggest migration fleet up to that time left Portsmouth less than a year later.

3

ARTHUR PHILLIP

I cannot say the little knowledge I have of Captain
Phillip would have led me to select him for a service of
this complicated nature.

The man chosen to lead the expedition to Botany Bay and
become Britain's first governor to New South Wales was
Captain Arthur Phillip. When he was plucked from semi-
retirement at his Hampshire farm at nearly 50 years of
age, there was nothing particularly outstanding in his
career to recommend him, but he would prove to be a
good choice.

Arthur Phillip, like James Cook before him and Philip
Gidley King afterwards, was an example of how men
from modest backgrounds could still progress through the
ranks in the British navy in a way that was far less likely
at the time in the army, where class and connections were
totally dominant.

Phillip was born on 11 October 1738 in Bread Street in
the parish of All Hallows, London. His father, Jakob, had
come to England from Frankfurt to work as a language
teacher, and Phillip was said to have spoken a number of
languages, including German, passable Spanish, Portuguese
and English, which he is said to have pronounced with
a guttural German accent.[1] His mother was Elizabeth

Breach, who had been widowed before Phillip was born, having been married to Captain Herbert of the Royal Navy before she married Jakob.

When Jakob died, Phillip was admitted to the boys' naval school at Greenwich on 24 June 1751, at 12¾ years of age. The school had been established in the early eighteenth century for the sons of navy men who had died or been killed at sea, but it seems that Phillip's family connections helped to secure his placement. Not only had Captain Herbert been a Royal Navy man, but he had also been related to Lord Pembroke, who shared the family name of Herbert. Lord Pembroke was a prominent member of society and was to become a member of parliament and privy councillor, a major-general in the army and a Knight of the Garter. It is unlikely that Phillip would have been enrolled at Greenwich but for this patronage.[2]

After two and a half years, and having turned 15, young Phillip left the school to take the standard seven-year indenture, to Captain William Redhead on the merchant ship *Fortune*, which regularly sailed to Greenland and Europe. In 1755, however, after only two years, he was released from his apprenticeship (which, according to Phillip's biographer George Mackaness, was quite common)[3] and entered the navy shortly before the start of the Seven Years War to work as captain's servant on the *Buckingham*. Senior officers were permitted to take a number of servants with them on their ships, and being a captain's servant was the acceptable way for a young man like Phillip 'to learn the rudiments of his profession'.[4]

Later that same year he became an able seaman and a few months later, in early 1756, a yeoman-corporal before sailing from the West Indies to the Mediterranean, where he was involved in a battle with French ships off the island of Majorca on 20 May. Three of his colleagues were killed and another eight wounded in this battle. The commander of the British fleet, Vice-Admiral the Honourable John Byng, was accused of mismanaging the British effort, court-martialled, found guilty and shot.

Over the next few years young Phillip served on a number of different British warships, including the *Princess Louisa* and the *Ramillies*, before being transferred to the *Neptune*, where he was promoted to midshipman and was on his way to a career on the quarterdeck.

In 1759 he saw more action, this time on the *Aurora* in the battle of Quiberon Bay off the French coast near St Nazaire in the Bay of Biscay. More than twenty ships from each side were engaged, and the British won a famous naval victory.

In 1760 Phillip was promoted to master's mate and at 22 years old was steadily climbing the naval ladder and becoming involved in more battles. Later the same year he was on the *Stirling Castle* off Barbados during the bombardment of Port Royal, in which hundreds of people in the French port were killed or wounded.

In August 1762 the *Stirling Castle* was part of a British fleet of more than two hundred ships that successfully took Havana and 'completely destroyed the communication between Spain and her western Empire'[5] in what was to be a significant event in Spain's decline as a dominant European power. Before sailing back to England, Phillip transferred to one of the twelve captured Spanish ships in Havana harbour, the *Infante*, which was renamed *Infanta* and converted to a British navy vessel. Phillip must have impressed his superiors during the taking of Havana because he was promoted to the ship's fourth-lieutenant. On his return to London he was also given a handsome share of the prize money of more than £234 that had been taken from the Spanish.

By then the Seven Years War was drawing to a close, and Phillip's career was to enter more than a decade of comparative silence between April 1763 and January 1775.[6] A short time after being pensioned out of the navy on half-pay at 25, Phillip became a farmer near Lyndhurst in the New Forest, Hampshire, and married the widow of John Denison, who had been a successful merchant from King Street, Cheapside, in London. Margaret Charlotte Tybott had come from County Montgomery in North Wales, where her family had been fairly well-established farmers. She had also been well cared for in her late husband's will.

Not much is known about the marriage, but thirty years later the *London Observer* had the following to say:

> While on half pay [Phillip] married a widow lady, young and handsome, with a portion of £16,000. He became possessed of all of her fortune . . . [then] some circumstances occurred which induced Mr. Phillip to wish for a separation; he left his wife, restoring to her however, such part of her fortune as remained in his hands.[7]

The circumstances of Phillip's separation are not known, but over the next forty years there was an almost total absence of any reference in his reports and correspondence to his marriage or his wife. After he left the marriage, the only reference to Phillip in the navy records during this silent period states that he served on a fairly routine patrol on the *Egmont* for eight months between November 1770 and July 1771. Otherwise there is no known official reference to him until 1774, when he joined the Portuguese navy.

In 1773 hostilities had again broken out between Portugal and Spain, in what was to become known as the Third Colonia War (1773–77). Colonial rivalry between the two countries had been, according to the author McIntyre, 'simmering over three centuries, at times subsiding in treaties or royal marriages, at times whipping into flames of war'.[8] In the east the contest between the two countries centred on the Spice Islands, in what is current-day Indonesia, and in the west on the border between Spanish-controlled Argentina and Portuguese-controlled Brazil. By 1774 the Portuguese were moving to strengthen their tiny navy and looked to their long-time ally Britain for some experienced naval officers. Phillip sought and obtained permission from the British Admiralty to offer his services to the Portuguese, who immediately agreed to sign him up.

Phillip had as his referee Rear-Admiral Augustus John Healey, who said of Phillip, 'though only a lieutenant in the British service, he is thoroughly worthy of command'.[9] The deal was attractive to Phillip as the Portuguese agreed to appoint him captain and provide twice the rate of pay that they paid to local commanders.

The Portuguese minister to London, Senhor Luiz de Souza, advised Phillip of his appointment in January 1775, when he went to Portugal and boarded the *Nossa Senhora de Belem* as second captain. Shortly after he was transferred to the *Nossa Senhora de Pillar* and at last became commander of his own ship – twenty years after he had first put to sea and fourteen years after becoming a fourth-lieutenant. Over the next three and a half years Phillip would establish his reputation fighting with the Portuguese around the contested territories that separated Portuguese and Spanish colonies in South America.

While he was with the Portuguese navy, a story emerged about Phillip that helps explain his later deft handling of large numbers of convicts aboard the First Fleet. While transporting four hundred criminals from Lisbon to South America, an epidemic on board disabled so many of the crew that the ship could not be sailed. Phillip appealed to those convicts with sailing experience, saying that he would make representations on their behalf if they helped complete the journey. After safely reaching his destination, Phillip kept his side of the bargain, and the prisoners were subsequently given their freedom as well as land grants.[10]

Phillip was to serve as commander in the Portuguese navy for three and a half years before leaving in 1778 with high praise. He was particularly remembered for protecting the Portuguese port of Colonia on the River Plate, with only his ship, the *Pillar*, restraining a Spanish assault. For this the Portuguese viceroy, Marquis de Lavradio, commended him: 'This officer is most honourable and meritorious. When at Colonia, he, with only his own Frigate, made the Spaniards respect that fortress as they ought to.'[11]

Back in England in 1778 he managed to secure his first independent command of a British navy ship when he commanded the *Basilisk*, which was part of the English Channel fleet. However, his time on the *Basilisk* was brief, and within a year he was again paid off and again unemployed.

Back on his farm and largely idle Phillip wrote to Lord Sandwich appealing for work, saying he was prepared to serve 'in any part of the world whatsoever'. The approach was successful, and in 1780 he was appointed relief captain of a number of ships, including the *St Albans* and *Magnanime*, before being promoted to post-captain and transferred to the twenty-four-gun warship *Ariadne*, where he spent much of his time on routine patrols in the Baltic Sea.

It was on the *Ariadne* where Phillip met Philip Gidley King, who would become a loyal member of his court and a key player in the expedition to New South Wales. King was born in Launceston, Cornwall, where his father was a draper, although his grandfather had been a local attorney at law. At 13 years of age he had joined the navy as a captain's servant and served for five years

on the East India run. For the next three years he served
in American waters as a midshipman on the *Liverpool*,
where he was eventually commissioned as lieutenant. In
1780, now 22 years old, he served under Phillip on the
Ariadne before going across to the sixty-four-gun
Europe when Phillip was given command of the larger
ship in 1782. Under Phillip's command the *Europe*
sailed to India via the Cape of Good Hope and to South
America. The *Europe* would be the last posting for
Phillip, and he again retired on half-pay in 1784 before
being appointed to head the expedition to New South
Wales in 1786.

Lieutenant Edward Spain, who also sailed on the
Europe, said that Phillip allowed four women to be
brought aboard at Port Praya in the Cape Verde Islands,
but only because 'one [of them] he had a sneaky kindness
for and had he given permission to her alone the reason
would have been obvious to the officers and the ships
company'.[12]

Phillip arrived back at Spithead on 22 April 1784 and
was yet again laid off from further service. After this date
we know little about what he did until he was appointed
governor of New South Wales two years later, except that
he took leave for about a year to visit the south of
France.

The circumstances of his appointment to head the
convict expedition to New South Wales are somewhat
mysterious. While he certainly was not appointed from a
position of obscurity, there was nothing in his career that
suggested he stood out as the most suitable candidate for
the post.

The announcement did not please the first lord of the
Admiralty, Lord Howe. He made it clear in a letter to
Lord Sydney that even though Phillip was a navy man, he
was not the choice of the Admiralty:

> I cannot say the little knowledge I have of Captain Phillip would have led me to select him for a service of this complicated nature. But as you are satisfied of his ability . . . I conclude he will be taken under your direction.[13]

Lord Sydney responded by saying 'presumably he was appointed on his merits as he appears to have no private influence with his superiors'.[14]

But could this really have been the case? There is some indication that Sir George Rose, the undersecretary of the Treasury, was the minister responsible for making the decision. Rose's estates were at Cuffnels near Lyndhurst, so he was a near neighbour of Phillip, who was then a gentleman farmer in the same district. Later, in New South Wales, Phillip would name the rich farming land he found twenty-five kilometres west of Sydney 'Rose Hill' in honour of Sir George. Evan Nepean, Lord Sydney's deputy, may also have had some say in the appointment. Nepean knew Phillip well from his earlier career, when Phillip had been attached to the Portuguese navy and Nepean responsible for spies and intelligence. Perhaps Phillip did have a certain amount of influence with the right people after all.

We are fortunate that Phillip's personal vision for the colony of New South Wales survives. A short time after his appointment, while he was working in London in a little office in the Admiralty on the preparation of the fleet before its departure from Portsmouth, Phillip outlined his thoughts for the voyage and the settlement. They were recorded in his own handwriting on small sheets of paper and, although undated, are thought to have been written in January or February 1787.[15] Many of the things he wrote about were later included in the detailed instructions he received from the government on 2 April 1787, which suggests that Phillip helped shape the design of his role of governor.

Phillip wrote that he wanted to arrive in New South Wales some months ahead of the convicts to prepare the settlement:

> By arriving at the settlement two or three months before the transports many and very great advantages would be gained. Huts would be ready to receive the convicts who are sick . . . Huts would be ready for the women; the stores would be properly lodg'd and defended from the convicts . . . The cattle and stock would be likewise properly secured . . .[16]

Phillip planned to pick up the last of his supplies at the Cape of Good Hope but did not want any food or grog loaded onto the ships carrying convicts, where it might be stolen. He also said that, during the voyage, he wanted to regularly inspect the convict transport ships, 'to see they are kept clean and receive the allowance ordered by the government'.[17]

Phillip was well aware that the confinement of large numbers of convicts below decks and in overcrowded conditions would create a health hazard and required special care. He also saw the need for the protection of female convicts:

> The women in general I should suppose possess neither virtue nor honesty . . . But there may be some . . . who still retain some degree of virtue, and these should be permitted to keep together, and strict orders to the Master of the transport should be given that they are not abused and insulted by the ship's company, which is said to have been the case too often when they were sent to America.[18]

Phillip planned to create good relations with the local
Aboriginal people and to civilise them, but he also wanted
to prevent any involvement of the convicts with them:
'The convicts must have none, for if they have, the arms
of the natives will be very formidable in their hands, the
women abused, and the natives disgusted'.[19]

In compliance with the British Government's plan for
the new settlement Phillip proposed to send ships to the
Pacific islands to bring women to New South Wales to
address the gender imbalance.[20]

Curiously, Phillip did not believe the convicts should be
allowed to be part of the new colony, even at the end of
their sentences:

> As I would not wish convicts to lay the foundations of
> an empire, I think they should ever remain separated
> from the garrison, and other settlers that may come
> from Europe, and not be allowed to mix with them
> even after the seven or fourteen years for which they
> may be transported may be expired.[21]

However, what he did not know then – and would only
be told after being in the new colony for more than two
years – was that the British Government very much saw
the convicts' passage as one way and was counting on
them remaining in the new colony for good.

Phillip was also awake to the risks of the convicts
escaping from the colony and wrote about how security
was to be maintained by limiting boats coming ashore:

> Ships may arrive at Botany Bay in future. On account
> of the convicts, the order of the port for no boats
> landing but in particular places, coming on shore
> and returning to the ships at stated hours, must be
> strictly enforced.

With regard to punishing the convicts Phillip's vision was surprisingly tolerant, or naive, when he suggested that he thought it possible to avoid imposing the death penalty: '[D]eath, I should think, will never be necessary – in fact I doubt if the fear of death ever prevented a man of no principle from committing a bad action'.[22]

Phillip felt there were only two crimes that warranted the death penalty – murder and sodomy – even though he must have been aware of the widespread homosexuality among seamen, who were often away at sea for years at a time with few or no encounters with women.

> For either of these crimes I would wish to confine the criminal till an opportunity offered of delivering him as a prisoner to the natives of New Zealand, and let them eat him. The dread of this will operate much stronger than the threat of death.

Phillip may not have had the high profile that would have made him an attractive choice for governor of the new colony, but he was an experienced farmer, and very few others who made up the First Fleet settlers had any background in working on the land. Wisely Phillip set as a high priority the building up of farm-animal numbers in Botany Bay. He knew he would only be able to carry a limited number of animals on the little ships to the new settlement and it would therefore be important to maximise the breeding not only of the government-owned stock but also of the privately owned animals brought with officers:

> As the getting a large quantity of stock together will be my first great object, till that is obtained the garrison should, as in Gibraltar, not be allowed to kill any animal without first reporting his stock, and receiving permission.

When the First Fleet eventually reached Australia, much of what Phillip had envisioned was to be achieved, but he was to encounter problems he had not foreseen. He had no real way of knowing the full extent of the struggle they would experience while trying to build the new colony. Nor did he have any inkling of the crisis they would face in the first years of settlement, caused by the shortage of food.

4

PREPARATION FOR THE VOYAGE

*[W]e beg leave to propose that the wives of the [two
hundred and forty-seven] marines going to Botany
Bay, not exceeding ten to each company, which will
not in the whole amount to more than forty women,
may be allowed to embark with them.*

The fleet was to take more than fourteen hundred people
– including seven hundred and fifty convicts, several
hundred soldiers and officers, some wives and children
and the ships' crews – to the new colony on the other side
of the world.

The organisation for the venture, which would take
nine months, included the commissioning of eleven ships,
the appointment of the officials to lead the expedition and
the loading of supplies sufficient for the long voyage and
for two years' subsistence after arriving.

The first move came from Lord Sydney, who wrote to
the lords of the Treasury on 18 August 1786 asking that
the necessary arrangements be made for the transport of
the convicts:

My Lords,
I am . . . commanded to signify to your Lordships his
Majesty's pleasure that you do forthwith take such

measures as may be necessary for providing a proper number of vessels for the conveyance of seven hundred and fifty convicts to Botany Bay, together with such provisions, necessaries and implements for agriculture as may be necessary for their use after their arrival.[1]

At the same time Lord Sydney communicated the king's decree that marines be recruited 'not only to enforce due subordination and obedience but for the defense of the settlement against incursion by the natives'. He continued:

His majesty has been pleased to direct that one hundred and sixty private marines, with a suitable number of officers and non commissioned officers, shall proceed in the ship of war and the tender to the new settlement, where it is intended they shall be disembarked for the purposes before mentioned.[2]

Two weeks later Lord Sydney wrote to the Admiralty with a specific request for the organising of the ships necessary for the transportation fleet:

My Lords,
The King having been pleased to signify his Royal Commands that seven hundred and fifty of the convicts now in this kingdom under sentence of transportation should be sent to Botany Bay, on the coast of New South Wales, in the latitude of thirty-three degrees south, at which place it is intended that the said convicts should form a settlement, and that the Lords of the Treasury should forthwith provide a sufficient number of vessels for their conveyance thither together with provisions and other supplies for their subsistence, as well as tools to enable them to erect habitations, and also implements for agriculture . . .[3]

During the voyage out the marines were to be spread out on the different ships to maintain order among convicts. Once they reached New South Wales, they were to serve for a term of three years, after which they could either return to England or settle as farmers in the new colony.

The full requirements for this venture were contained in a 'Heads of a Plan', which was drawn up in Lord Sydney's office, probably by his deputy Evan Nepean, and sent from Whitehall to both the Treasury and the Admiralty. By this stage there was no pretence that the venture had any higher ambition than disposing of the convicts and no mention of the settlement otherwise contributing to the good of the British Empire.

The plan outlined the route the fleet would take to New South Wales and the seeds and plants and animals that should be collected on the way for the settlement. The navy commander of the fleet would be authorised to spend whatever was necessary at the Cape of Good Hope 'to obtain cattle and hogs, as well as seed grain, all of which must be procured for the new settlers, with a view to their future subsistence'.[4] It was hoped that by the time the First Fleet had consumed all of the food it had itself imported, the new colony would be producing much of its own requirements.

Also in the Heads of a Plan were minute details of the tools that would be needed for the clearing of vegetation and the creation of the new settlement. This included three hundred chisels, a hundred and seventy-five hand saws and hammers ('one for every four men'), a hundred and forty drawing knives and augers (large drills), a hundred wood planes, broad axes and adzes (an arched axe with the blade at right angles to the handle), fifty pickaxes, forty cross-cut saws, frame saws and wheelbarrows, thirty grindstones, twelve ploughs and ten forges. Among the other supplies to be taken on the ships were two thousand spikes, a thousand squares of glass, two hundred pairs of hinges, one hundred locks, ten barrels of nails and a large number of fish hooks.

It was envisaged that the settlers would build their own homes when they arrived in New South Wales. For the initial period financial provision was made for five hundred tents for the convicts and a hundred and sixty for the marines.[5] A special two-storey tent was to be provided to Arthur Phillip as his temporary residence.

The plan calculated the necessary clothing for each male convict to be two jackets, four pairs of woollen drawers, one hat, three shirts, four pairs of worsted stockings, three frocks, three trousers and three pairs of shoes. The budgeted cost for outfitting each convict was two pounds, nineteen shillings and sixpence.[6] The plan did not elaborate on the items of clothing for the women, other than to say 'the expence of clothing female convicts may be computed to amount to like sum'.[7] However, when the fleet eventually sailed from Portsmouth nine months later, it left without enough clothing for the women.

The plan also suggested – as the Matra proposal had a few years earlier – a simple solution to the anticipated shortage of women in the new colony: a ship should be sent to the nearby Pacific islands to collect some. This proposed large-scale removal of women to another country was wholly a pragmatic measure, as it was felt that otherwise 'it would be impossible to preserve the settlement from gross irregularities and disorders'.[8]

In a later instruction it was made clear that the women could not be abducted:

> [W]henever [the ship] shall touch on any of the islands
> in those seas . . . you are . . . to instruct [your] com-
> manders to take on board any of the women who may
> be disposed to accompany them to the said settlement.
> You will, however, take especial care that the officers

who may happen to be employed upon the service
do not, upon any account, exercise any compulsive
measures, or make use of fallacious pretences, for
bringing away any of the said women from the places
of their present residence.[9]

As well as cultivating flax in the new colony, as had been
proposed by Sir George Young of the Admiralty, the
settlers were to consider going to New Zealand for timber
that could be used for the masts of ships.[10]

Phillip's initial written instructions, issued by King
George in London and presented to him when he was
formally commissioned as governor at the Court of
St James on 12 October 1786, were very brief:

George the Third Etc., to our trusted and well loved
Captain Arthur Phillip, greeting:
We, reposing especial trust and confidence in your
loyalty, courage and experience in military affairs, do,
by these presents, constitute and appoint you to be
Governor of our territory called New South Wales . . .
You are therefore carefully and diligently to discharge
the duty of Governor in and over our said territory by
doing and performing all and all manner of things
thereunto belonging . . . and you are to observe and
follow such orders and directions from time to time as
you shall receive from us . . .[11]

He was not to receive his detailed instructions until he
was about to leave Portsmouth with the fleet the
following year, only weeks before his departure.

At the time he was given his formal commission, Phillip
was also ordered to colonise a vast territory roughly the
size of Europe, stretching some three thousand kilometres
from north to south from the very top of Cape York on
the east coast of Australia to the south of Tasmania. From

east to west the claimed territory was also some three thousand kilometres, from 135 E, which is roughly a vertical line down the middle of Australia, to the east coast and beyond, taking in 'all islands adjacent in the Pacific Ocean'.

Britain's claim to such a large part of the world was based on a convention that had emerged in the seventeenth and eighteenth centuries whereby European powers accepted that the nation to first discover and navigate an area had first claim to own and occupy it – and Cook had been the first to navigate the east coast of Australia and claim it for Britain. The Dutch, Portuguese and Spanish had for hundreds of years effectively colonised lands they had discovered and developed these outposts into strategically located trading ports in the new world and the south seas. The Dutch had been the first to regularly sail to the west coast of New Holland but had made no attempt to establish a settlement or claim the land.

A major challenge in the implementation of the plan was the organising of sufficient shipping to transport almost fifteen hundred people. The Admiralty responded quickly to the request and within six weeks of the official order, in October 1786, was able to confirm that the first two ships would be available within another two weeks. One was a small warship, the *Sirius*, which was to become the flagship of the First Fleet, and the second was an even smaller support vessel, the *Supply*:

> We immediately ordered the *Sirius*, one of his Majesty's ships of the sixth rate,[12] with a proper vessel for a tender, to be fitted for this new service; and that the ship will be ready to receive men by the end of the month.[13]

The *Sirius* and the tender *Supply* were the only Royal Navy vessels of the prospective eleven. The other nine were contracted from private owners. Six were designated for the transport of the convicts and three were for carrying supplies.

The British Government paid ten shillings per ton per month for each of the privately contracted ships. The charges would apply until the ships returned to Deptford, except for the three that would be released from government service when they unloaded in New South Wales before going on to China to pick up a cargo of tea for the British East India Company.

By today's standards the ships were tiny. The largest was only a hundred and thirty-two feet, or less than forty metres, long and a little over thirty feet (nine metres) wide. The smallest was only seventy feet (twenty-one metres) long and barely twenty feet (six metres) wide.

To look at, all of them were fairly similar. They were all blunt nosed and round bodied with three masts, except for the supply ship the *Friendship* and the navy ship the *Supply*, both of which had only two masts. The flagship of the fleet, the *Sirius*, had been built in 1780 as the *Berwick* for the East India trade but, as Lieutenant Philip Gidley King recorded, it was badly burnt in a fire before being bought, rebuilt and renamed by the navy in 1786:

> She was built on the river [Thames] for an east country [East India Company] and in loading her she took fire and was burnt to the wales.[14] The Government wanted a roomy vessel to carry stores abroad, in 1781 purchased her bottom and she was rebuilt with such stuff as, during the war, could be found. She went two voyages to the West Indies, as the *Berwick*, store ship; and without any repairs she was reported, when the present expedition was thought of, as fit for the voyage to New Holland. She was then renamed the *Sirius*, so called from a bright star in ye southern constellation of the Great Dog.[15]

The *Sirius* was in no way a glamour flagship. Although the largest of the fleet, it sailed badly and slowly, and it leaked. It was later dismissed by Lieutenant Philip Gidley King, who sailed on it, as the 'refuse of the yard'.[16]

The *Sirius* was to carry a hundred and sixty passengers, with Arthur Phillip as its captain. Before leaving England it was fitted with extra guns, as it was intended that they could be taken ashore in the new settlement if fortifications were needed.

Prior to the journey John Hunter, who would become a significant figure in the new colony and later serve as governor of New South Wales, had been working for Phillip helping to prepare the flagship and was on the lookout for an appointment. He explained in his journal how it came about:

> I had some reason, during the equipment of these ships, to think that I might be employed upon this service in some way or other, and as Captain Phillip was appointed Governor of the new settlement, and of course had much business to transact in London, I frequently visited the *Sirius* and frequently received his directions in anything that related to filling her ... On the 9th of December [1786] the ship being ready to fall down the river, we slipped the moorings and sailed down to Long Reach where we took in the guns and the ordnance stores. On the 15th, I was informed by a letter from Mr Stevens, Secretary to the Admiralty, that there was a commission signed for me in that office, and desiring I would come to town and pick it up.[17]

Hunter had initially been impressed with the *Sirius*, which he described as 'exceedingly well calculated for the service'. He was commissioned as 'Second captain of His Majesty's ship *Sirius* with the rank of Post Captain, and with the power to command her in the absence of her Principal Captain',[18] which meant that while Phillip had overall command of the fleet, Hunter was effectively in command of the flagship. Hunter would consequently be paid the full captain's pay and permitted to take with him four servants on the ship.

Born in Edinburgh, the son of a shipmaster, Hunter joined the navy as a captain's servant before becoming a seaman and then midshipman. He passed his exams to become lieutenant in 1760 but, as a man without a fortune, his rise was long and slow and he was not given his first commission for another twenty years. Hunter was 50 years old when he sailed on the *Sirius*.

Other officers who sailed on the *Sirius* and who would play significant roles in the First Fleet story included Lieutenants William Bradley and William Dawes, and the ship's surgeon, George Worgan, who took his piano aboard with him.

The second navy vessel, the *Supply*, was the fastest ship in the fleet. Weighing only a hundred and seventy tons – about a third of the weight of the *Sirius* – it was to carry fifty people and a limited amount of supplies and was skippered by Lieutenant Henry Ball. With the advantage of speed came the disadvantage of capacity. As Lieutenant Philip Gidley King was to complain, 'Her size is much too small for a long voyage which added to her not being able to carry any quantity of her provisions and her sailing very ill renders her a very improper vessel for this service.'[19]

The government set in train a process to hire the rest of the fleet from private contractors. While each of the nine chartered ships was to have its own captain, or master, they were to come under the charge of Lieutenant John Shortland, the navy agent, who in turn reported to Arthur Phillip.

On 14 September 1786 *The Times* ran the story that the 'Government is now about settling a colony in New

Holland in the Indian seas and the commissioners for the
navy are now advertising for 1500 tons of transport'.[20]
Advertisements for the hire of ships were placed on public
notice boards and in the newspapers.

Within a month the government confirmed it had an
acceptable bid for the supply of shipping from William
Richards, a London shipping broker. Richards was born
in 1735, the son of a tailor, and by the mid-1780s had
become a wealthy shipbroker, having made most of his
money organising shipping to the American colonies. He
advised the government that he was able to provide the
ships for the transportation of the convicts at a cheap
rate, because he had done a deal with the British East
India Company for some of them to sail on to China after
dropping off the convicts and their supplies in New South
Wales. All were contract merchantmen, in that they had
been built and operated as commercial cargo ships and
would require conversion for the carriage of the convicts.

The Admiralty had a great deal of experience in contracting ships for the movement of troops overseas and
was meticulous with the details of the contract. It was
stipulated that the ships should be adequately ventilated
and regularly cleaned out and fumigated. The prisoners
were to be supplied with clothing, bedding and adequate
rations, and were to be given the opportunity of exercise
on deck when the ships were safely at sea.

After all the arrangements were made, the responsibility for ensuring the contract was complied with during the
voyage rested with the navy agent, which was extremely
difficult because the agent could only be on one of the
ships at a time and was unable to supervise the daily
management of all the others while on the open sea.

The First Fleet's agent, John Shortland, was also responsible for supervising the conversion of the contract ships
to carry convicts, which involved securing the prisoners'
accommodation behind a bulkhead below decks and

building a security wall across the middle of the ship above
the deck. Separate accommodation was required on those
ships that carried both male and female convicts so there
could be 'no communication whatsoever with each other',
in the words of Sir Charles Middleton, comptroller of the
Admiralty.[21] Following the conversions Shortland was to
assemble the prisoners from the hulks and gaols and load
them onto the transport ships in London, Portsmouth and
Plymouth.

Shortland was 48 years old when he became the navy
agent for the convict transports. He had joined the navy
as a 15-year-old midshipman and served in Newfoundland, the West Indies and Gibraltar. He had then spent a
fairly undistinguished twenty-five years with the navy
transport service supervising the conveyance of troops –
largely to and from the American colonies. Shortland's
appointment was criticised by the Admiralty, who felt
that a better choice could have been made had they been
consulted, but Arthur Phillip was to be impressed by
Shortland and argue that his hard work contributed to the
success of the First Fleet voyage.

The Shortland family would become prominent in the
early history of Australia. Two of Shortland's sons also
travelled with the First Fleet: 18-year-old John sailed as
master's mate on the flagship *Sirius* and 16-year-old
Thomas George sailed as the second mate on the
Alexander. Son John would stay on in the colony for
several years after his father returned to England, before
going back himself with Captain John Hunter in 1791.
He returned in 1795 with the now governor Hunter and
would later explore and give the latter's name to the
Hunter River, which is about a hundred and fifty
kilometres north of Sydney.

John Shortland senior was to command some of the
transports of the First Fleet on their ill-fated return to
England after unloading the settlers and their provisions

in New South Wales. When he finally reached England, he was promoted to captain but never promoted again and retired as a naval officer at 57 years old at Whitby in Yorkshire.

Having a navy agent on the First Fleet with overall responsibility for the transport of convicts was a new arrangement. Until the American War of Independence the transportation of convicts had been the total responsibility of the private shipping contractors. Shortly before the Admiralty had been ordered to arrange the ships of the First Fleet, two contractors, Turnbull and Macaulay, had put a proposal to the British Government that they manage the entire venture, but their offer was not accepted. The government felt that the establishment of a new colony at the other end of the earth should not be left in the hands of those whose only interest lay in getting their cargo to its destination and unloading it on arrival.

Initially there were to be five ships for transporting the convicts: the *Alexander*, the *Charlotte*, the *Scarborough*, the *Friendship* and the *Lady Penrhyn*. Later it was realised that another ship was needed, and the *Prince of Wales* was added. The three ships commissioned to carry the required two years' worth of supplies were the *Golden Grove*, the *Fishburn* and the *Borrowdale*.

The largest of the transport ships in the fleet, the four-hundred-and-fifty-ton *Alexander*, measured a hundred and fourteen feet (thirty-five metres) long and thirty-one feet (nine and three-quarter metres) wide. According to the official navy report it was to leave Portsmouth carrying almost two hundred male convicts, thirty-seven marines and one wife of a marine, plus the ship's crew.[22] For a ship of this size, the crew would have numbered nearly a hundred, compared with that of the smallest ship, the *Supply*, which would have numbered only around thirty.

The transport *Scarborough* was the next largest, at a hundred and eleven feet (thirty-four metres) long and thirty feet (nine metres) wide and weighing four hundred and eighteen tons. It was to carry two hundred and ten male convicts, thirty-four marines and the ship's crew.

The transport *Charlotte* was a hundred and five feet (thirty-two metres) long and a little over twenty-eight feet (eight and a half metres) wide. It was to carry eighty-eight male and twenty female convicts with two of their children, forty-four marines, six wives and a child, plus the ship's crew.

The transports *Lady Penrhyn* and the *Prince of Wales* were almost identical in size, at a hundred and three feet (thirty-one metres) long and a little over twenty-nine feet (nine metres) wide. Both ships carried women convicts. The *Lady Penrhyn* was to carry a hundred and two women convicts with five children, six marines and the ship's crew. The *Prince of Wales* carried almost all of the families of the marines. In addition to the ship's crew, it boarded thirty-one marines, sixteen wives and six children, a hundred women convicts and one of their children.

The *Friendship* was the smallest of the transports, weighing only two hundred and seventy-eight tons. At barely seventy-five feet (twenty-three metres) long, it would carry forty-four marines, three of their wives and five children, in addition to its crew. It would also take eighty-eight convict men, twenty-four convict women and three of their children.

The private supply ships the *Fishburn* and the *Golden Grove* were both a hundred and three feet (thirty-one metres) long and twenty-nine feet (nine metres) wide. The *Fishburn* also carried twenty-eight passengers in addition to its crew and the *Golden Grove* twenty-two passengers, including the Reverend Richard Johnson, his wife and their servant. The *Borrowdale* was seventy-five feet (twenty-three metres) long and carried twenty-four passengers and its crew.

Ever mindful of money the Treasury was keen to make

sure that the contracted ships were used for the transport of the First Fleet for as short a period as possible, so as to keep the hire costs to the government at a minimum. George Rose, the undersecretary of the Treasury, wrote to Phillip Stephens, the undersecretary of the Admiralty, to say they wanted the ships released from Botany Bay as soon as possible to carry out their tea run to China:

> I am commanded by their Lordships to desire that you will move the Lords of the Admiralty to direct the captain of the Kings ship . . . to take care that no unnecessary delay happens on the passage to Botany Bay, or on their departure from thence, and that he uses his best endeavours to enable the ships under his command to reach China by the 1st January, 1788.[23]

The last months of 1786 saw the filling of a number of other key positions, some of which would be successful, others not. It was not difficult to attract competent officers to the project. Many saw these expeditions as an opportunity for career advancement and even fame. In the decades leading up to the colonisation of Australia, the navy had been involved in a number of non-military voyages of scientific discovery that had captured the public imagination and made their participants famous. Also the recruits for Botany Bay were well aware that a number of those who had been on the early expeditions had successfully published handsome illustrated journals of their travels, which had been snapped up by an enthusiastic public. Sure enough, a number of the officers with the First Fleet would hurry to publish their journals – some before they had themselves returned to England.

Whether or not those on board the First Fleet ships expected fame, many became well-known figures and were to be instrumental, in one way or another, in the early days of the colony.

Major Robert Ross was appointed as the commander of the marines. He was initially assigned to sail on the *Sirius* but later in the voyage transferred to the *Scarborough* for the rest of the journey. He would prove to be a constant problem for Phillip and for many of the others he dealt with in the new colony.

Reverend Richard Johnson, sailing on the *Golden Grove*, would become the hardworking chaplain in the new settlement, having been given the role at the age of 34. Distressed by what he regarded as the depravity of the convicts, Johnson went to a lot of trouble to take with him plenty of material with which to help straighten their twisted souls. With the help of the Society for the Promoting of Christian Knowledge he loaded aboard the First Fleet four thousand two hundred books, including a hundred Bibles, a hundred Books of Common Prayer, four hundred testaments, five hundred psalters and two hundred Church catechisms. In addition he took a large number of pamphlets on moral guidance, including a hundred and ten copies of *Exhortations to Chastity*, a hundred copies of *Dissuasions from Stealing*, two hundred copies of *Exercises Against Lying* and fifty copies of *Caution to Swearers.* No doubt Johnson wanted the convicts to benefit from all this, but only a tiny proportion of the new settlers – mainly the officers – could actually read.

Johnson belonged, of course, to the Church of England. Despite the fact that around three hundred of the convicts on the First Fleet were Catholics, no priest was planned for them. Thomas Walshe, a Catholic priest, wrote to Lord Sydney saying that the Catholic convicts had an 'earnest desire some Catholic clergyman may go with them', but despite saying he 'would be so happy as to be permitted to go' without pay or any support from the government, the offer was not accepted.[24]

Phillip's two most valued officers, Captain John Hunter and Lieutenant Philip Gidley King, were to prove loyal supporters of their chief and would both eventually become governor of the colony.

David Collins, sailing on the *Sirius*, had been appointed the colony's judge advocate. He would have the major responsibility of administering justice in the new colony and would become a valuable supporter of Phillip. Collins would also keep one of the most extensive journals of the settlers, covering the many years he spent in Britain's new colony.

John White was 30 years old when he accepted the appointment as chief surgeon with the First Fleet, having been in the navy for ten years and served as a surgeon on ships in the West Indies and India. As the senior medical officer he would have a great deal to do with the remarkably good health record of the convicts on the voyage to New South Wales. In the new colony he worked in the most difficult circumstances, operating in a small tent hospital and treating outbreaks of scurvy, smallpox and the hundreds of diseased and dying convicts who arrived on the ill-fated Second and Third Fleets. He returned to England after five years, pleading ill health, and later resigned rather than go back to New South Wales.

A number of other surgeons were appointed under John White. They were spread around the transports for the voyage out. The job of a surgeon in the convict service was far from attractive. It was demanding, the conditions appalling and the pay poor. With more appealing opportunities elsewhere the general standard of surgeons on convict ships was low. The work generally attracted novices fresh from the lecture room, the mediocre or the 'embittered failures'.[25]

William Redfern, who later ran the Colonial Medical Establishment, said that many of the surgeons were 'ill qualified to take charge of two hundred to three

hundred men about to take a long voyage through various
climates and under particularly distressing circumstances'
and that many were all too 'devoted to inebriety'.[26]

Among the surgeons was William Balmain, who sailed
on the *Alexander* and would later in Sydney fight a duel
with his boss, John White. The surgeon appointed to the
women's convict ship the *Lady Penrhyn* was John
Turnpenny Altree, who took ill and was taken off the ship
in Tenerife. He was replaced by Arthur Bowes Smyth,
who would be another to keep a journal covering the
voyage and his time in New South Wales.

Along with the appointment of personnel, during these last
months of preparation the exact amount of food to be
consumed on the voyage was calculated. The marines were
to have the same rations as the seamen: seven pounds of
bread a week, four pounds of beef, two pounds of pork,
two pints of peas, three pints of oatmeal, six ounces of
butter, three-quarters of a pound of cheese, half a pint of
vinegar and three and a half pints of rum.[27] The convicts
were to be given about two-thirds those quantities and
were denied grog, except when it was prescribed by the
surgeon for the sick.

Phillip was involved with almost every detail of the
fleet's planning. With only one month to pass before its
departure, he wrote to Undersecretary Nepean asking
about the number of caps for the convicts, supplies for the
wives of marines, whether the judge advocate could bring
along his servant and whether enough port wine could be
loaded for the officers.[28]

The navy agreed that some of the marines sent out to
maintain order and defend the colony could take their
wives and children but stipulated that the number of
wives be limited to forty, so as to minimise the need for
provisions on the voyage out and in the new settlement:

As it is usual when any regiments are sent upon service to his Majesty's colonies or plantations to allow them to take with them a certain number of women, we beg leave to propose that the wives of the marines going to Botany Bay, not exceeding ten to each company, which will not in the whole amount to more than forty women, may be allowed to embark with them.[29]

There would be two hundred and forty-seven marines and marine officers leaving Portsmouth, and many were to feel aggrieved at having to leave their families behind.

Among the other key appointments to the venture was Baron Augustus Theodore Henry Alt, who would be the colony's surveyor-general. At 56 years of age Alt may have been the oldest official to sail with the First Fleet. He was born in London, the son of Heinrich Alt, a German, and his English wife, Jeanetta. He began service in the British army as a 23-year-old ensign in 1755 and served in France and Germany, fighting in the siege of Gibraltar in 1779. Alt would be one of a number of officers to marry a convict and have children with her. In Sydney he would marry Ann George, a 'shoe binder'. She had been convicted and sentenced to seven years' transportation as a 22-year-old in the Old Bailey in 1785 for stealing three shillings from a man whom her accomplice, Eleanor McCabe, had picked up in a pub. Henry Alt and Ann George would have two children together: Lucy was born in 1790 and a son, Henry George, was born in 1799. Ann died in 1814 in Parramatta, west of Sydney, and her husband died the following February.

The planning of the First Fleet was, for its time, a colossal undertaking that involved the most impressive devotion to detail down to the required number of fish hooks, nails and door hinges that would be loaded on the ships and taken to help build the New South Wales settlement. Little attention, however, appears to have been given to the suitability of the convicts selected for the voyage. Many were too old or too ill, and a number of them would die while they were locked on the transports at Portsmouth waiting for the fleet to sail. It seemed that the welfare of convicts was a matter of the lowest priority.

5

THE CONVICTS

COURT TO PRISONER: How old are you?
PRISONER: Going on nine.
COURT: What business were you bred up in?
PRISONER: None, sometimes chimney sweeps.
COURT: Have you any father and mother?
PRISONER: Dead.
COURT: How long ago?
PRISONER: I don't know.

The convicts loaded onto the transports of the First Fleet were not chosen with any regard for their fitness for the long voyage or for their ability to contribute to the building of a new colony once they reached Botany Bay. Remarkably, it also appears that no consideration was given to how much of their sentences the convicts had left to serve when they were put on the fleet. More than forty per cent had been convicted either in 1784 or before,[1] and since most were committed to seven years' transportation, several hundred would have served more than half of their sentences when they arrived in New South Wales in 1788. This was to prove a major headache for Governor Arthur Phillip, who sailed with no convict records and had no way of confirming whether prisoners who claimed they had completed their sentences were telling the truth.

Many had been condemned to be hanged for stealing food or items of clothing, but their death sentences were commuted to transportation. Only those too frail to walk were excluded from consideration, and fourteen pregnant women convicts were boarded who would give birth during the voyage. Many were old or ill when delivered from the hulks and prisons to the transports, and a number were to die before the fleet left Portsmouth.

Almost sixty per cent of the First Fleet's convicts had been sentenced for stealing food or other goods of relatively low value. Thirteen per cent were guilty of burglary or breaking and entering, and a further fifteen per cent had been convicted of highway robbery, robbery with violence or grand larceny. The remainder were found guilty of living off fencing, swindling, forgery or some other offence.[2]

A large number of the convicts had been destined for transportation to America or Africa and had served some years of their sentence in English prisons or on prison hulks before being sent to Botany Bay. For example, 43-year-old Thomas Eccles had been sentenced in Guildford in Surrey in March 1782 to be hanged for stealing bacon and bread but 'reprieved for service in Africa for life'.[3] Eccles was in prison for five years before being transported to Botany Bay on the *Scarborough*.

Twenty-one-year-old Mary Braund (who would later become better known as Mary Bryant when she escaped from New South Wales) had been found guilty of assaulting and robbing Agnes Lakeman of a silk bonnet and other goods. In 1786 in the Exeter court in Devon she was condemned 'To be hanged. Reprieved. Transported seven years.'[4] She sailed on the *Charlotte* to Botany Bay.

Twenty-two-year-old Edward Pugh was convicted in 1784 in the Gloucester court for stealing a great-coat and

'Ordered to be transported to America for seven years.'[5] He sailed to Botany Bay on the *Friendship*.

A captain of the marines on the First Fleet, Watkin Tench, who was also responsible for censoring the convicts' letters to their families while the fleet was waiting to sail from Portsmouth, said that fear among the convicts was a constant theme:

> The number and content of [the letters] varied according to the disposition of the writers but whose constant language was an apprehension of the impracticality of returning home, the dread of the sickly passage and the fearful prospect of a distant and barbarous country.[6]

A number of the convicts, such as Thomas Limpus, had already been sent in chains to Africa and America before being sent aboard the First Fleet. On 8 October 1782, almost five years before the First Fleet sailed, 15-year-old Limpus had been sentenced in Westminster Court to seven years' transportation 'to some of his Majesty's plantations in Africa' for stealing a 'cambrick handkerchief valued at 10 shillings'.[7]

Limpus had been 'chained two and two together' with about forty other prisoners below the decks of the slave trader *Den Keyser* and sent to St Louis, in current-day Senegal, on the west African coast. With him were two other prisoners who would also find themselves on the First Fleet, John Ruglass and Samuel Woodham.

Ruglass and Woodham had been originally convicted together at the Old Bailey in 1781 for highway robbery, having held up, with three others, William Wilson and stolen from him a silver shirt buckle, a handkerchief and some money, with a total value of one pound and four shillings.

All three – Limpus, Ruglass and Woodham – would manage to get back to England. Limpus was later to tell the Old Bailey that, on arrival in Africa, he and other convicts were left to survive as best they could on an island off the coast. Limpus said that they were given no provisions and that, after getting work with the local governor, he had managed to find his way onto a ship working his passage back to England:

> On the 3rd of last December, I was landed on the island of Goree, with nineteen more, the soldiers were drawn up in a circle on the parade, the Lieutenant of the island ordered us all into the middle of it, and told us we were all free men, and that we were to do the best we could, for he had no victuals, there was a ship lay in the bay, I went on shore several times and did work for the governor, I remained there till the time I came home, which was last Saturday was three weeks.[8]

Ruglass was to give a similar explanation to the court in London. The British governor Lacey, he claimed, had 'sent them off and would not give them any victuals'.[9]

So, within a year of being sentenced to seven years' transportation, Limpus and the others had managed to find their separate ways home. Within three weeks Limpus was recognised as a convicted criminal, re-apprehended and brought before the Old Bailey, charged with 'returning from transportation' before the end of his term.

Limpus was this time condemned to be hanged, but the sentence was commuted to transportation to America – even though by that time there were virtually no convict ships still going there. In April 1784 Thomas Limpus was one of a hundred and seventy-nine convicts, including twenty women, who sailed from England on the *Mercury*, which would be one of the last convict ships to make an attempt to sell prison labour to the Americans.

However, the convicts on the *Mercury* mutinied when the ship was sailing along the English Channel off the coast of Devon. Most if not all the prisoners were recaptured, either while still at sea attempting to reach the shore or having already reached land, and many were to sail on the First Fleet.

The average age of the First Fleet's convicts was around 27. Nearly fifty per cent were under 25 and only five per cent were older than 45.[10] The oldest male was believed to be Joseph Owen, who was in his early 60s; the youngest was John Hudson, who was nine years old when he was convicted and sentenced to transportation. The youngest female was 13-year-old Elizabeth Hayward, a clog-maker who had stolen a linen dress and a silk bonnet. The oldest woman was Dorothy Handland, who was believed to be 82 years old when she sailed with the First Fleet. Dorothy had been convicted at the Old Bailey in February 1786 for perjuring herself in an earlier trial and sentenced to seven years' transportation.[11] She hanged herself from a gum tree in Sydney Cove in 1789.

John Hudson's case is as good an illustration as any that the British judicial system took no account of the age of offenders. He was brought before Justice Hall at the Old Bailey two weeks before Christmas in 1783 and sentenced to seven years' transportation. He had been found guilty of 'feloniously breaking into'[12] the house of William Holsworth at one o'clock in the morning the previous October and stealing a linen shirt, five silk stockings, a pistol and two aprons, which had a combined value of one pound and two shillings. He was not convicted on the charge of burglary.

In evidence the court was told that the boy had entered the house by breaking a windowpane, leaving 'marks of toes, as if someone had slided down the window in the inside of the shutters'. When asked by the court if they were large or small toes, the witness Holsworth replied, 'They were small toes . . . I took the impressions of the foot and of the toes that were on the table upon a piece of paper as minutely as I could.'[13]

Hudson had also been seen by a woman, Sarah Baynes, as he was trying to wash himself clean of soot in a boarding-house washtub in East Smithfield. Nearby she saw the stolen silk stockings and aprons. Also in evidence John Smith told the court that he recognised Hudson as the boy who came and tried to sell him some of the stolen goods the week after the robbery:

> I am a pawnbroker. On the 17th of October, the boy at the bar brought this shirt to pledge about seven in the morning. He said it belonged to his father. I asked who had sent him. He said his mother. I stopped him.

Only John Hudson didn't have a father, or a mother, as the proceedings of the Old Bailey record.

> COURT TO PRISONER: How old are you?
> PRISONER: Going on nine.
> COURT: What business were you bred up in?
> PRISONER: None, sometimes chimney sweeps.
> COURT: Have you any father and mother?
> PRISONER: Dead.
> COURT: How long ago?
> PRISONER: I don't know.

Hudson was one of thousands of abandoned or orphaned children left poor and destitute trying to survive in the recesses of urban England. Many died young of malnutrition, cold, exhaustion, neglect, cruelty and a range of ugly infections and diseases.

It is not known how Hudson survived before he was sent to prison, except the account he gives of working as a chimney sweep. Chimney sweeping required children who were small enough to crawl up the insides of chimney flutes as narrow as ten inches (twenty-four centimetres) to clean away thickened soot. The job was extremely unhealthy and dangerous, and there was a large death rate among the children due to falling down chimneys, asphyxiation, smoke inhalation or lung cancer.

Hudson was initially sent to Newgate in London and survived several months of the prison's 'depravity, profanity, wretchedness and degradation',[14] probably because the conditions in the gaol were little different than those he had been used to at large.

For many of the convicts, young or old, life in prison in England was no worse, and in some respects better, than trying to survive on the outside. John Nicol, who was to sail as a steward on the all-women convict transport the *Lady Juliana* in the Second Fleet, said that many of the convicts were hardened and indifferent to prison life and enjoyed the guarantee of food and somewhere to sleep:

> I witnessed many moving scenes and many of the most hardened indifference. Numbers of them would not take their liberty as a boon; they were thankful of their present situation. Many of these from country jails had been allowed to leave it to assist in getting the harvest, and voluntarily returned. When I enquired their reason, they answered, 'How much more preferable is our present situation to what it has been since we commenced our vicious habits? We have good victuals and a warm bed. We are not ill treated, or at the mercy of every drunken ruffian, as we were before. When we rose in the morning, we knew not where we would lay our heads in the

evening, or if we would break our fast in the course of the day.[15]

Hudson's inclusion in the First Fleet was the second attempt to transport him. Three years before being put on board the *Friendship* in Portsmouth with ninety other convicts bound for Botany Bay, he too had been sent from London on the *Mercury* in April 1784 bound for America when the convicts mutinied and took the ship.

Hudson and another boy, 13-year-old James Grace, were in one of the *Mercury*'s two small boats off Torquay when they were recaptured. The two boys and a number of convict mutineers were able to escape the death penalty because they were technically still at sea when they were apprehended – nothing to do with Hudson and Grace being juveniles.

Young James Grace would also join John Hudson on the First Fleet to Botany Bay. He had been found guilty of theft at the Old Bailey only a month after Hudson, in January 1784, when he was charged with stealing ten yards of silk and some silk stockings and sentenced to seven years' transportation.[16] During his trial a 15-year-old servant boy, George Windsor, told the court that he saw the defendant in Oxford Street, London, with his hand through a broken glass window taking out the silk goods. In his defence Grace said that, while he took the stockings, the window was already broken, which resulted in his being found guilty of burglary but not of breaking and entering.

After their recapture both Grace and the now ten-year-old Hudson were tried for 'returning from transportation' before their term had expired, convicted, sentenced again to transportation and sent to Exeter prison in Devon and then to the *Dunkirk*, a de-masted former warship that had been converted to a prison hulk in Plymouth harbour. There they waited to see where fate would deposit them next.

6

PORTSMOUTH

A corpse sew'd up in a hammock floated alongside our
ship. The cabin, lately occupied by the third mate
Jenkinson, who died of a putrid fever the night before
I came on board, and was buried at Ryde, was fresh
painted and fumigated for me to sleep in.

The preparation for the First Fleet's departure from
Portsmouth was characterised by chaos, disease, promiscuity and death. It would take nine months to prepare and
load the two navy ships, six convict transports and three
supply ships with fifteen hundred people and two years'
provisions and equipment.

While the convicts dreaded the thought of being
banished and transported, it was reported in the press at
the time that the government received 'upward of a
thousand applications' from others wanting to join the
expedition.[1] The applicants included various military
officers who saw the venture as good for their career
prospects and 'upwards of fifty women, wives of
convicts', who had travelled to Portsmouth hoping to be
allowed to go with their husbands, only to be referred
back to their 'respective church parishes'.[2] According to
another press report a number of women applied directly
to the Treasury in London to go with their convict men

but, after being referred to Evan Nepean, 'the petitioners were dismissed'.[3] In late 1786 *The Times* reported that there 'are now about three hundred felons under sentence of transportation in Newgate, most of whom are to be sent with the transports to Botany Bay'.[4]

The first convicts began to be loaded onto the transports in Portsmouth towards the end of 1786. From October the order was given 'for the men to work double tides' to speed up the loading of the ships.[5] Many of the first prisoners to be loaded were to spend more than a year on their ships before being landed at Port Jackson in late January 1788. At the beginning of their ordeal it was winter in England, and they were locked up in the lower decks of the transport ships where it was cold, dark and damp.

The arrival of hundreds of these convicts at Portsmouth, with many of their cronies and families turning up on shore, caused panic among the locals, many of whom closed and locked their businesses until the fleet left. The press was to report a wave of violent crime as 'gangs of thieves and robbers' descended on Portsmouth from London:

> The town and neighbourhood [is] infested with numerous gangs of thieves and robbers, and that scarce a night passes in which some persons are not robbed or some houses broken open. The villains are supposed to have belonged formerly to the hulks at Woolwich and to have come down to see their former friends and companions.[6]

In early 1787 hundreds more convicts were rowed down the Thames from the hulks and from Newgate prison and loaded at Woolwich on the convict transport ships the *Alexander* and the *Lady Penrhyn*. These were then sailed down to Portsmouth with the two navy ships the *Sirius* and the *Supply* to meet up with the rest of the fleet in a journey that was to take several weeks.[7]

Not all the prisoners were transported directly to Portsmouth by ship, however. More than two hundred were first brought from London overland to Plymouth, chained together on carts and escorted 'under proper guard'.[8] There they were loaded aboard the *Charlotte* and the *Friendship*, which were in Plymouth harbour, along with two hundred and thirty-nine male and fifty-one female convicts who were already being held in Plymouth on the *Dunkirk* prison hulk, before being sailed around to Portsmouth to join the rest of the fleet.

In the first days the cautious masters of the transports kept the prisoners, including the women on the *Lady Penrhyn*, in chains below decks, exchanging one type of metal shackle for another. Sixteen male convicts on the *Alexander* and a woman on the *Lady Penrhyn* were to die before the fleet departed Portsmouth. In fact more convicts were to die before the fleet left England and on the first leg of the journey to Botany Bay than during the many months of the rest of the voyage.

The fleet would not sail until May, and there was already concern about the outbreak of disease among the convicts on the transports. Arthur Phillip successfully sought permission from Nepean for the transports to be moved several miles out to sea into Spithead. There the convicts could, for part of the day, be allowed out of their cramped quarters up onto the deck, where they could get some fresh air.

> You will, sir, permit me to observe that it will be very difficult to prevent the most fatal sickness amongst men so closely confined; that on board that ship which is to receive two hundred and ten convicts there is not a space left for them to move in sufficiently large for forty men to be in motion at the same time, nor is it

safe to permit any number of men to be on deck while
the ship remains so near the land. On this consideration, I hope you will order the *Alexander* and *Lady
Penrhyn* to join his Majesty's ship *Sirius* immediately,
and proceed to Spithead, where more liberty may be
allowed the convicts than can be done with safety in
the river.[9]

The chief surgeon of the fleet, John White, had first gone
to Plymouth from London on 7 March 1787, two months
before the fleet eventually departed. He carried with him
various dispatches from the secretary of state and the
Admiralty authorising the loading of convicts for transportation.[10] He had travelled overland for two days in
'the most incessant rain I ever remember', to be greeted by
gale-force winds at Plymouth that delayed the loading of
the convicts from the *Dunkirk* hulk onto the *Charlotte*
and *Friendship*. The ships were then to sail round to
Portsmouth with the convicts 'placed in the different
apartments allotted for them'.[11]

When White arrived at Portsmouth, he recommended
to Phillip that the *Alexander* be temporarily evacuated so
the ship could be fumigated. Phillip communicated
White's advice to the government: 'The surgeon states the
situation of the convicts to be such that I am under
the necessity of requesting . . . ordering lighters from
Portsmouth yard to the *Alexander*, to receive the convicts
while the ship is cleaned and smoked.'[12]

Based on advice he received from White in Portsmouth,
Arthur Phillip was also to complain that the convicts were
being sent there in a state wholly unsuitable for being
aboard ship and at sea:

> The situation in which the magistrates sent the
> women on board the *Lady Penrhyn* stamps them with
> infamy – tho' almost naked, and so very filthy, that

nothing but clothing them could have prevented them from perishing, and which could not be done in time to prevent a fever, which is still on that ship.[13]

On White's prompting, Phillip was to propose a series of measures to improve the health of the convicts, including washing and dressing new arrivals in clean clothes before loading them onto the transports, allowing the sick a little wine and supplying all of them with some fresh meat while they were in Portsmouth Harbour.

It was not only the convicts who were sick and dying. By early 1787 a number of the marines had arrived at Portsmouth to be assigned to the different transport ships to oversee the convicts. The marine commander Major Robert Ross had also arrived and complained that conditions on the *Alexander* and the other ships in Portsmouth Harbour were so bad that his men were falling ill and dying. Many had been assigned quarters in lower decks 'under where the seamen are berthed' and where they were 'excluded from all air'. He complained of this in a letter to Stephens, the secretary of the navy:

> I have to request you will please to inform their Lordships that the sickness that has, and still does prevail among the marine detachment embarked upon the *Alexander*, transport, gives me a great degree of concern. Since the time of their first embarkation no less than one sergeant, one drummer, and fourteen privates have been sent sick on shore from her, some of whom, I am informed, are since dead.[14]

Ross had also written to Nepean to complain about the food rations his marines were receiving:

> I likewise beg to observe to you that the contractors for the victualling the marines have not put any flour

on board the transports for their use, and of course,
as they are the only people deprived of that necessary
article, which I believe was never intended to be the
case, may I request that you will use your endeavours
to get the mistake rectified, as you know that the
preservation of their health is of the utmost consequence on the present occasion.[15]

Ross was a larger-than-life character who would become
unpopular with other officers and a thorn in the side of
Governor Arthur Phillip when the fleet reached New
South Wales. He jealously guarded his command over the
marines and was difficult to handle.

At 47 Ross was one of the oldest officials on the First
Fleet, along with Arthur Phillip and Captain John Hunter.
It is widely believed that he was born in Scotland,
although details of his family are not clear. He joined the
marines as a 16-year-old second-lieutenant, which
suggests that he came from an established family or was
at least well connected.

In his early career with the marines he served in the
Seven Years War against the French in north America for
nearly four years and was involved in the siege of French-
held Louisbourg in Nova Scotia in 1758 and the capture
of Quebec the following year. He appears to have been
well regarded and was promoted to first-lieutenant in
1759, captain in 1773 and brevet-major in 1783. He also
fought in the American War of Independence and was
involved in the pyrrhic victory at the battle of Bunker Hill
in Massachusetts in 1775, when the British incurred more
than two hundred dead and eight hundred wounded to
achieve victory. On his way home to England on the
Ardent he was captured by the French but subsequently
returned as part of an exchange of prisoners. From 1781
he served in the Mediterranean and the West Indies until
he was appointed lieutenant-governor to Arthur Phillip.

Ross sailed to New South Wales and took with him his eight-year-old son, whom he signed up to the marines and later, in Sydney, attempted to have commissioned as an officer.[16]

Also arriving at Portsmouth were the twelve surgeons whom the 'Government had appointed at the public expense to go to Botany Bay'.[17] Arthur Bowes Smyth, the 37-year-old assistant-surgeon who replaced the ill John Turnpenny Altree, described the appalling squalor that confronted him when he went aboard the women's convict ship the *Lady Penrhyn* in March to take up his cabin:

> A corpse sew'd up in a hammock floated alongside our ship. The cabin, lately occupied by the third mate Jenkinson, who died of a putrid fever the night before I came on board, and was buried at Ryde, was fresh painted and fumigated for me to sleep in.[18]

While waiting for the fleet to sail, Bowes Smyth was able to go for long walks on the mainland and the Isle of Wight, an escape not available to the convicts being held mostly below deck on the transports. Back on the ship Bowes Smyth recorded how many of the women convicts who had never been on a ship before 'were very sick with the motion of the ship' out in Spithead.[19]

Bowes Smyth was born in Tolleshunt D'Arcy in Essex, the seventh son of a surgeon, and as a youth would follow in his father's footsteps, working locally as a surgeon, before signing up with the First Fleet.

The officers had many weeks to kill waiting for the fleet to sail, but marine captain Watkin Tench found good uses for the time:

> Unpleasant as a state of inactivity and delay for many weeks appeared to us, it was not without its

advantages; for by means of it we were able to establish regulations among the convicts, and to adopt such a system of defence, as left us with little to apprehend our own security, in case a spirit of madness and desperation had hurried them on to attempt our destruction . . . An opportunity was taken, immediately on their being embarked, to convince them, in the most pointed terms, that any attempt on their side, either to contest the command, or to force their escape, should be punished with instant death; orders to this effect were given to the sentinels in their presence.[20]

The ships' officers and the marine officers were from a totally different world from the ordinary seamen and the marine privates and would enjoy a very different experience of the voyage to the rest. They were also given the added incentive of a year's pay in advance before leaving England.[21]

The officers were far better accommodated on the ships than anyone else, even if by today's standards their quarters were tiny. Usually they shared a cabin, which was typically five feet by seven feet (one and a half by two metres) and large enough only for two bunks and a little storage space.

Some of the more senior officers had their own cabin and were also able to take servants with them, which produced the expected envy from those who were not. This sentiment was echoed by the surgeon John White, who had not yet left for Plymouth when he learned that the chaplain Richard Johnson had been given approval to take his servant. Sitting in the Hungerford Coffee House on The Strand, he wrote directly to Evan Nepean to plead his own case:

Sir,
Finding that the Revd. Mr. Johnson is to be allowed the privilege of taking with him to Botany Bay a

servant, I hope it will not be deemed unreasonable or improper if I solicit a like indulgence. Being . . . without a servant, my situation must be truly uncomfortable . . . you . . . must know and admit the inconveniences I shall be subject to, not only on the passage, but after landing without one . . . I have apply'd to Captain Phillip, who has no objection.[22]

While at sea, the officers ate and drank better than anyone else. The captain could mess with other officers or eat alone and would sometimes keep his own table or invite other officers to join him to be served by his own servants. The other officers would be served their meals at a dining table in a wardroom and would drink port and other wines. Their diet would be more varied and regularly supplemented by the slaughter of a chicken, a pig or some other animal on board, and the officers were usually far less likely to contract scurvy than the ordinary sailors.

The marines and seamen would be lucky to have a bench on which to sit while they ate and were fed a ration based on salted meat, dried peas, rice and 'hardtack' bread. The meat was either pork or beef that had been dried and salted and stored in barrels. The notorious hardtack bread, which was the basis of the seafarer's diet for several hundred years, was made from wheat or barley and was baked brick hard and devoid of moisture, like a biscuit. Normal bread would only be edible for about a week if stored in cool and dry conditions and even less if it was damp or hot. Hardtack bread could last practically indefinitely but was less palatable, very hard to chew and often infested with weevils. The men would also have some of the fruit or vegetables that had been loaded aboard at the last port of call, until they ran out, and were entitled to a daily grog ration that was invariably half a pint of foul-tasting rum.

The officers' clothes also differentiated them from everyone else on the ships, their uniforms being colourful and absurdly impractical. The dress coat was full skirted with very deep cuffs and had much in common with the formal suits of the mid-eighteenth century, except that instead of silk or velvet it was made of hard-wearing wool that would have been extremely hot in the tropics. The outfit's one practicality was that it dramatically distanced those who gave the orders from those who carried them out.

There were several hundred sailors on the First Fleet, although no exact number was ever recorded – they were all expected to return with their ships to England and were not part of the calculation of those who would form the colony in New South Wales.

Most of the sailors were merchantmen who were contracted to work on the privately owned convict-transport ships. The rest were Royal Navy seamen who had volunteered, or had previously been pressed into service in wartime. Signing up enough sailors for the navy ships was not difficult because, as Lieutenant Philip Gidley King noted, 'a great number of seamen were at this time out of employ and the dockyard was constantly crowded with them'.[23]

Among those who signed up to sail on the flagship *Sirius* was the 25-year-old American Jacob Nagle. Nagle was born in 1762 in Pennsylvania into a German Presbyterian Reformist family that had migrated to America around 1750. In 1777, at 15 years old, he joined his father in the American War of Independence in fighting against the British. Nagle recalls seeing General George Washington, who 'came riding up to the Colonel Procter with his life guards with him and enquired how we came on' in September that year during the Battle of Brandywine.[24]

After three years with the armies of George Washington the young Jacob Nagle joined the American navy and later transferred to the privateers, which were the privately owned American ships that were encouraged to sink and pirate any ships in British colours. In November 1781 he was captured by the ships HMS *Royal Oak* and HMS *La Nymphe* and pressed into service in the Royal Navy with sixteen other American sailors. He was later to be rescued from the island of St Kitts by the French, who were American allies, but subsequently recaptured by the British. It was here in the Caribbean that his involvement on the American side of the war ended and a twenty-year career with the British Navy began.

With the announcement of the end of the War of Independence in April 1783 plans were made for the English to return home. The Royal Navy ship *Prudent* arrived in Portsmouth with Nagle aboard several months later. After being paid off, Nagle tried to get home to America and, with a fellow crew member, took a stagecoach to London. Things there, however, did not go according to plan:

> By this time London was full of sailors. The men of war being all paid off, and the American ships were gone full of passengers from London and no possibility of getting work, or a ship, and what few did get work for a shilling a day.
>
> Our money getting short, we begin to look out for a ship of any kind. The ship *Sippio*, man of war, was then shipping men for different stations laying in the river abreast Woolwich. We went down and shipped on board . . . We sailed for Spithead.[25]

Nagle was to transfer to the HMS *Ganges* in Portsmouth, on which he would sail for the next three and a half years, largely transporting British soldiers to different ports before jumping at the opportunity of joining the First Fleet:

I was now near four years on the *Ganges* and often applied to the captain for my discharge, but could not get it, when the *Sirius*, twenty-eight-gun freighter came round the Downs to Spithead commanded by Captain Hunter and Governor Phillip bound for Botany Bay with a fleet of eleven sail of transports, the *Supply* brig as a tender, full of men and women convicts and soldiers, with provisions and stores. The Governor having the privilege of taking any men that turned out from the men of war, there was a great number turned out, but the captain took his pick, all young men that were called seamen. A hundred and sixty in number, no boys and no women allowed. Seven of us volunteered out of the *Ganges* . . . I was put into the Governor's barge.[26]

He was lucky enough to be assigned to Phillip's boat crew and over the next few years would spend a lot of time close to Phillip and other officers. He said that he kept a journal at the time but it was lost, possibly with the sinking of the *Sirius* off Norfolk Island a few years later. Nagle returned to England in 1792 and eventually went back to America, where, years later, around 1822, he wrote his memoirs, *The Nagle Journal*. Despite being barely able to write 'behind the façade of misspelling, meaningless commas and semi colons, questionable capitalizations and never ending sentences',[27] it is a fascinating eyewitness account of the settlement of Australia.

Most of the sailors aboard the First Fleet had more normal lives. They and the customs and practices they followed were very typical of their times. Most eighteenth-century seamen would have first gone to sea as boys, commonly between the ages of ten and 12, beginning work both on deck and on the rigging, where nimbleness was required. By the age of about 16 most had matured and become able to work aloft, reef sails, knot and splice ropes and steer the ship. At the same time their bodies took on the characteristic broad-shouldered, barrel-chested physique – the result of heavy hauling and lifting and often being bent double over the yards – while the constant roll of the ship gave them a 'peculiar rolling gait'.[28]

At sea the sailors would normally be divided into watches, usually two, which shared the work, and into messes of eight to ten individuals for catering. Each mess was a self-assembled group of like-minded men, usually with the same skills and rank. They shared the domestic chores of preparing food, collecting cooked dishes and washing up. These small groups formed the core of shipboard life and were the basis of effective teamwork, working together in key areas, perhaps in the rigging or as a gun crew.

They had no personal space on the ship and would sleep, usually in hammocks, in a common area below decks that had little space for private effects and no provision for washing or relieving themselves, which was always done up on deck.

Most sailors worked at sea for a decade or two before settling down and working on shore or in coastal seafaring. Some remained at sea for as long as they were physically able, often moving into more skilled work as a master, responsible for the navigation of the ship.

The clothes worn by the ordinary sailors aboard ship were completely practical. At work they wore long trousers that could be rolled up, short-waisted jackets that kept the body warm and, in colder weather, heavy knitted pullovers. These clothes were either supplied by the ship or made from raw materials that the men purchased on board. Most worked barefoot, for extra grip on the ropes while aloft.

By the time of the First Fleet, at the end of the eighteenth century, many of the sailors would have been tattooed. The tattoo had become popular with European seamen after they were introduced to it by Polynesian societies in the south Pacific. It is widely believed that the practice was first taken up by the seamen of Cook's voyages from 1768 to 1770. A number of the crew thought a tattoo would be the perfect souvenir to bring back from their exotic experience. It is said that Joseph Banks had his discreetly applied to his buttocks, while the majority of sailors were more interested in having theirs on display.

Discipline aboard ship in the eighteenth century was enforced with fairly brutal beatings. There was little point imprisoning men on the ships, so offenders were typically flogged then forced to return to work as soon as they were physically able. The whip was usually a cat-o'-nine-tails, which had nine leather strands, each with metal studs that would tear the flesh from the back of the person being punished. The rest of the crew were assembled on deck and forced to witness the punishment as 'the theatre of example', with marines drawn up with loaded muskets between sailors and officers.[29] Sometimes the punishment would be suspended on the advice of the surgeon if the person being flogged became unconscious or was thought to be at risk of dying while tied to the flogging board.

The two hundred and fifty marines who were to maintain order during the voyage of the First Fleet and provide security for the settlement once they reached Botany Bay were largely from a similar lower class background to the convicts and seamen and were similarly poor and uneducated. They were also disciplined severely – in fact they were flogged more frequently for breaches of rules than were the convicts, which was to become one of a number of sources of resentment when the marines reached New South Wales.

The marines were a big influence on the shaping of early Australia. In the absence of free settlers in the first years of the new colony many of the marines – and particularly marine officers – would become its principal farmers and merchants. Within a few years they monopolised most of the economic activity in New South Wales. Most of the marines were single when they signed up with the First Fleet, but this did not mean, as we have seen, that all of those who were married were permitted to take their wives and children with them. Ralph Clark was just one of the marines who were devastated at having to leave their families behind:

> May the 13th, 1787. Five o'clock in the morning. The *Sirius* made the signal for the whole fleet to get under way. O gracious God send that we may put in at Plymouth or Torquay on our way down the channel that I may see our dear and affectionate Alicia and our sweet son before I leave them for this long absence. O Almighty God hear my prayer and grant me this request.[30]

Twenty-seven-year-old Clark was from a humble background in Edinburgh, where his father had been a gentleman's servant. Ralph had joined the marines as a 17-year-old and volunteered for the expedition to Botany Bay because he was ambitious for promotion. Three years before the departure of the fleet Clark had married Betsy Alicia Trevan from Devon, and their son, Ralph Stuart, was born the following year. Clark was to keep a highly personal and intimate diary in which he mourns the separation from his 'beloved Betsy' and 'my sweet boy'.

When he reached New South Wales, he was promoted to acting lieutenant on the death of the marine captain O'Shea. After two years he was sent to the settlement on Norfolk Island with the marine commander Major Robert

Ross and other marines. While he was in Sydney, he lived for a while with a convict woman, who bore him a son.

Clark was to return home to England in June 1792 with most of the other marines who had sailed with the First Fleet. Tragically, within two years, Clark, his wife and his son would all die. Early in 1794 his wife died after giving birth to a stillborn daughter. In June Clark died of yellow fever on a naval ship in the West Indies, and his son, who was a young midshipman on the same ship, died of the same disease ten days later.

While the loading of the fleet stretched on from January through to May, Phillip returned to London and did not join the fleet again until days before it set sail. While in London, he was regularly appraised of preparations in Portsmouth. In April he was to complain that a hundred and nine female convicts had been loaded onto the *Lady Penrhyn* when there should have been only a hundred and two.[31]

It was one of many occasions when Phillip was to show his frustration with the organisation of the venture. At one stage he protested that the amount of ammunition ordered for the marines' muskets was 'very insufficient', and earlier he had demanded to know why the advance wages to which the staff were entitled had not been paid, because they were 'much distressed' and needed the money to fit themselves out for the voyage.[32]

In March 1787 an exasperated Phillip wrote to Lord Sydney to warn him that many marines and convicts would die because of inadequate provisions being made for the journey:

> I fear, my Lord, that it may be said hereafter the officer who took charge of the expedition should have known that it was more than probable he lost half the garrison and convicts, crowded and victualised in such a manner for so long a voyage.[33]

Over the next weeks there was further correspondence between Phillip and the government before Lord Sydney replied directly to Phillip at the end of April, only a few weeks before the fleet departed. Sydney reassured Phillip 'that any supplies which it may be necessary to provide for the maintenance during the voyage will be obtained and paid for'. He added that should the fleet find itself short of supplies, it would have the authority to purchase what it needed at ports 'where the convoy may touch' during the voyage.[34]

By staying and working in London, Arthur Phillip was able to liaise directly with Evan Nepean, who, as the deputy to Lord Sydney in the Home Office, was the most important single figure in the organisation of the venture. Nepean was a key figure not only in organising the First Fleet but also in the administration of the new colony in New South Wales in its early years, and was a useful ally for Phillip.

As the day of their departure drew nearer, many of the crew and the convicts said their goodbyes, wrote their wills and otherwise put their affairs in order. Major Robert Ross, who had been an active soldier for more than twenty-nine years, wrote to Evan Nepean pleading for his wife and children to be taken care of if he did not survive the venture:

> You know my daily pay to be the whole of the fortune I am possessed of . . . My only view in mentioning the situation in which cruel necessity compels Mrs Ross and my young family is, that in case of any accident should deprive them of their all, in depriving them of me, you will then permit me to hope that your friendly assistance and interest shall be employ'd in endeavouring to procure for the widow and fatherless some compensation from the public . . . Could I but be assured that Mrs Ross and the little ones would have

your friendship to plead their cause in support of their claim, my oppress'd mind would then be reliev'd in some measure from a weighty load of the care and anxiety.[35]

When Phillip returned to Portsmouth a week before the fleet was to leave, all of his colleagues were already aboard, including the colony's judge, David Collins, who was to sail with Phillip on the *Sirius*.

The 31-year-old Collins was born in Ireland and came from a fairly well-established family. His grandfather, Abel Roper, had written the first edition of *Collins' Peerage* in 1709 and his father was a marine officer who attained the rank of major-general. In 1770 young David joined his father's division as a 14-year-old ensign and became a second-lieutenant a year later. In 1775 he was fighting the Americans in the War of Independence and, like Major Robert Ross, was at the battle of Bunker Hill. The following year he was stationed at Halifax, Nova Scotia, and, now 20 years old and a full lieutenant, married Maria Stuart, the daughter of a British officer. In 1781, back in England with the rank of captain, he joined the *Courageux* in the Channel squadron. In 1783 he was retired on half-pay.

Like a number of his fellow officers Collins volunteered most probably because he was bored with being retired on the half-pay that had come with peacetime. It is also believed that his father encouraged him to seek the job as judge advocate even though he had no formal legal training.

Unlike those officials who would take their wives with them, David Collins left his wife in England. He would not return for another ten years, and when he did he found his wife ill. However, Maria recovered sufficiently to help her husband publish his journal in England in 1802, and two years later Collins left his wife again to take up the position of lieutenant-governor in New South Wales, with the responsibility of establishing a new settlement in Port Phillip Bay, near present-day Melbourne. Collins found the new site deficient in water and timber and successfully applied to move his entire settlement to Hobart Town on the Derwent River in Tasmania.

He was never to see Maria again. He had one child with her, a daughter who died in infancy, but fathered four other children in Sydney and in Hobart. Like many of his fellow officers Collins was to live with convict women. In Sydney he lived with Nancy Yates and had a son and daughter with her. She had sailed as a 19-year-old on the *Lady Penrhyn* in the First Fleet after being convicted in the York court in 1785 for stealing printed cotton worth five pounds. She had been sentenced to be hanged but reprieved and transported for seven years. Later, in Hobart, Collins lived with 16-year-old Margaret Eddington, the daughter of a convict couple, and had two children with her in 1808 and 1809.

Collins died suddenly in Hobart in March 1810, three weeks after his 54th birthday. According to Maria her husband died insolvent, leaving her with only thirty-six pounds a year, the pension of a captain's widow. She repeatedly appealed to the Colonial Office, and she was eventually granted an allowance of one hundred and twenty pounds a year, retrospective to January 1812, in consideration of her husband's services in superintending the commencement of the settlement at Hobart Town. She died in Plymouth on 13 April 1830.

Back in Portsmouth at the end of April 1787 the fleet was ready to sail, but first it had to confront a series of last-minute problems. With less than a week to go the marines discovered they would not be issued with a grog ration once they arrived at the new settlement. In a protest note to their officers they argued that the grog

would be 'requisite for the preservation of life' in the new
colony:

> We, the marines embarked on board the *Scarborough*,
> who have voluntarily entered on a dangerous expedi-
> tion replete with numerous difficulties . . . now conceive
> ourselves sorely aggrieved by finding the intentions of
> the Government to make no allowance of spiritous
> liquor or wine after our arrival at the intended colony
> of New South Wales.[36]

Arthur Phillip had tried to warn the government the
previous December that there would be 'much discontent'
in the garrison if the marines were denied a grog ration.[37]
On 8 May, with the matter still unresolved, Phillip wrote
again to Nepean, pleading the marines' case and repeating
his warning that trouble would inevitably result if they
were denied the grog:

> They all in general expected the usual allowance of
> wine or spirits . . . They have no market to go to, and
> I fear much discontent amongst the garrison. I wish
> such an allowance could be granted them; indeed
> I fear very disagreeable consequences if they have not
> the same allowance of spirits in the garrison as the
> marines and seamen are allowed on board the *Sirius*
> and they certainly were told they should be victualled
> in the same manner.[38]

Phillip sent his letter not knowing that the government
had relented and that a letter of permission written by
Lord Sydney three days beforehand was on its way. It was
too late to procure the grog and load it in England before
the fleet left, so Phillip was given approval to spend up
to £200 buying the drink in either Tenerife or Rio de
Janeiro.[39]

On Thursday 10 May Phillip's orders to set sail were defied by the sailors:

> The wind this morning coming round from the southeast, I made the signal and got under weigh, but the seamen on several of the transports refused to get their ships under sail . . . unless they were paid what wages were then due.[40]

Judge David Collins revealed the reason in his journal:

> On the Thursday following [Phillip] made the signal to prepare for sailing. But here a demur arose among the sailors on board the transports, who refused to proceed to sea unless they should be paid their wages up to the time of their departure alleging . . . they were in want of many articles necessary for so long a voyage.[41]

The officers of the fleet held different views about the strike. Phillip saw the seamen on the transports as the contractors' responsibility and was impatient to sail. Collins thought the demands of the men 'appeared reasonable',[42] and Lieutenant Philip Gidley King, second in command on the *Sirius*, was also sympathetic:

> I think the seamen had a little reason on their side . . . They had been in the employ upwards of seven months, during which time they have received no pay except their river pay and one month's advance.[43]

John White was less charitable and recorded that he thought the men were drunk and that the trouble arose 'more from intoxication than from nautical causes'.[44]

The contractors would not pay the sailors, and the strike ended when Phillip ordered that those men not prepared to sail be put ashore and replaced with a number of naval seamen who were on the *Hyaena*. This Royal Navy ship had been ordered to escort the fleet for the first hundred leagues (about five hundred kilometres) of its voyage, out through the English Channel and into the Atlantic Ocean.

The fleet was almost delayed again by the late delivery of bread by the contractors, but Phillip hastened its loading when he 'ordered it to be sent on board' on the night of Friday 11 May.[45]

Finally, on the night of Saturday 12 May, Phillip ordered that the fleet should prepare to leave early the next morning. At three o'clock on Sunday morning all the ships were ready. At four the signal was given from the *Sirius*, and by six the whole fleet was under sail.

The total number of people in transit on these ships was now almost fifteen hundred, although accounts of the exact number are wide-ranging. Phillip's own return gives a total of seven hundred and seventy-eight convicts and thirteen children. There is no complete record of the number of ships' crew, which would likely have totalled over four hundred and would have included the navy officers who were to stay in New South Wales, as well as all of those who returned on the transports after the convicts and supplies were unloaded in the new colony. Phillip's biographer Mackaness says there were two hundred and ten naval seamen, two hundred and thirty-three merchant seamen and a total of two hundred and fifty-two officials – marines and marine officers – giving a grand total of one thousand four hundred and eighty-six.[46]

The First Fleet, heavily laden with passengers, supplies and equipment, was finally on its way.

7

THE VOYAGE

*I never met with a parcle of more discontent fellows in
my life. They only want more provisions to give it to
the damned whores the convict women of whom they
are very fond since they broke through the bulk head
and had connections with them.*

The First Fleet's initial progress was as faltering as its
departure had been, as the sailors discovered that
the ships were difficult to sail. The American seaman
Jacob Nagle, aboard the *Sirius*, complained that the ship
was 'so deep with stores, and having large buttocks, we
could scarcely steer her until we got better acquainted
with her'.[1]

As the fleet passed the Isle of Wight, Watkin Tench went
below deck to register the mood of the convicts:

By ten o'clock we had got clear of the Isle of White,
at which time, having little pleasure in conversing
with my own thoughts, I strolled down among the
convicts, to observe their sentiments at this juncture.
A very few excepted, their countenances indicated a
high degree of satisfaction, though in some the pang
of being severed, perhaps forever, from their native
land could not be wholly suppressed.[2]

By noon on the first day they passed the Needles, on the west of the Isle of Wight, heading to the port of Santa Cruz on Tenerife in the Spanish-controlled Canary Islands. This first leg of their journey would entail more than three weeks of sailing, covering almost two thousand kilometres to their southerly destination off the coast of north Africa.

For the first three days of the run down the English Channel there was a rising swell and rain and 'great sea sickness', particularly among the convicts who had never been to sea before. On the second day they could see the Devon coast and on the third many boats off Falmouth harbour. They also saw many fishing boats out on the sea, and one, according to Arthur Bowes Smyth on the *Lady Penrhyn*, 'came alongside and all the hands in her were very drunk'. Later in the day they passed the lighthouse at Eddystone and the Lizard peninsula on the Cornish coast, which for many of the fleet would be the last they would ever see of England.

This was the first time that all of the ships comprising the First Fleet had sailed together, so they had little idea of their comparable sailing ability. Shortly after starting the journey the officers 'had the mortification' to discover that two of the convict transport ships, the *Lady Penrhyn* and the *Charlotte*, sailed 'exceedingly bad', and the *Charlotte* fell so far behind that at the beginning it had to be towed by the navy escort, the *Hyaena*.[3] These differences in speed and sailing ability were to create difficulties later on in the voyage and would cause Arthur Phillip to eventually split the fleet, taking the faster ships ahead and leaving the slower ones behind to follow as best they could.

The first serious accident occurred after three days at sea. A marine corporal, Baker, lost his balance in the rough seas and accidentally fired off his musket. John White, who was on the *Sirius* at the time, witnessed the incident:

Extraordinary as this incident may appear it is no less true . . . On laying the musquet down which he had just taken out of the arms chest Corporal Baker was wounded by it in the inner ankle of the right foot. The bones after being a good deal shattered, turned the ball, which taking another direction, had still force enough left to go through a harness-cask full of beef, at some distance, and after that to kill two geese that were on the other side of it.[4]

After a week, and when the ships were well out to sea, Phillip ordered 'to release from their irons' those convicts who were still fettered but sufficiently well behaved. Captain Tench recorded that the disposition of the convicts immediately improved, and Captain Hunter also noted that the additional freedom of the criminals would better their health as they could now 'wash and keep themselves clean'.[5]

The following day the navy agent John Shortland began to visit each of the transports to collect information about the convicts' 'trades and occupations' for Arthur Phillip, who was already planning the building of the settlement in New South Wales.[6]

Towards the end of the first week, as the convoy was still battling its way in heavy rain westward along the English Channel, the sailors on the contracted convict transport ship the *Friendship* went on strike, demanding an increase in their meat ration from one and a half pounds to two pounds a day. Lieutenant John Shortland came aboard from the *Sirius* and told the sailors there was not enough meat carried on the ships to increase the daily ration, but he did promise them an increase in their pay.

It seems that the sailors wanted the extra food not for themselves but to pay the convict women for sex. While a prison wall had been built below decks in England to keep the convicts separated from the crew, the sailors had

already broken through a hole in the barrier on the
Friendship to reach the women. Ralph Clark kept a
detailed diary of the voyage and was not impressed:

> I never met with a parcle of more discontent fellows
> in my life. They only want more provisions to give it
> to the damned whores the convict women of whom
> they are very fond since they broke through the bulk
> head and had connections with them.[7]

Having cleared the English Channel, the convoy turned
southwards into the Atlantic Ocean, and the *Hyaena*,
which had escorted the fleet for the first week, turned
back towards Portsmouth.

The *Hyaena* left the convoy some two hundred
kilometres west of the Scilly Isles, as the seas were getting
higher heading into the notoriously rough Bay of Biscay.
The conditions made it difficult for Phillip to find out
what was happening on the other ships before he wrote
and sent his first report back with the returning *Hyaena*.[8]
He consequently sealed his letters unaware that on the
Scarborough the captain was thwarting what he believed
was a planned mutiny by the convicts. When Phillip
learned of the planned uprising, he hastily penned a note,
which he managed to get to the *Hyaena* before it was too
far away:

> Since I sealed my letters I have received a report from
> the officers on board the *Scarborough* respecting the
> convicts, who it is said, have formed a scheme for
> taking possession of the ship. I have ordered the ring-
> leaders on board the *Sirius* . . . I have no time to enter
> into particulars.[9]

The planned mutiny had apparently been plotted by two
convicts on the *Scarborough*, Phillip Farrell and Thomas

Griffiths. Before they could organise the support of other convicts, though, they were betrayed to the ship's officers. According to Captain Hunter's journal the men had planned to free other convicts, take control of the ship and quietly sail away from the rest of the fleet at night.[10] Such a plan was feasible as both of the plotters were experienced sailors. Before being convicted and sentenced to seven years' transportation at the Old Bailey for stealing a one-shilling handkerchief, Phillip Farrell had been boatswain's mate on the navy ship HMS *Goliath*. Thomas Griffiths had been the master of a French privateer during the American War of Independence before being convicted of stealing cloth at a value of two pounds, also at the Old Bailey, and sentenced to seven years' transportation in 1784.

Once the plot was uncovered, the two men were rowed over to the *Sirius*, flogged, put in irons and then sent to another of the transports, the *Prince of Wales*. The traitor who revealed their plan before it could be carried out was transferred to another of the convict ships for his own safety.

Despite the high drama at the time Phillip was to say in a letter sent three weeks later from Tenerife that he did not think there was too serious a threat to the security of the *Scarborough*:

> In my letters by the *Hyaena* I mentioned the apprehen-
> sions the officers on board the *Scarborough* were under,
> and though I did not then think they had reason to be
> seriously alarmed. As some of the convicts had behaved
> very ill, two of the supposed ringleaders were ordered
> on board the *Sirius*, punished, then sent on board the
> *Prince of Wales*, where they still remain.[11]

About halfway to Tenerife the officers and men were to witness an incident that would give them a valuable insight into Arthur Phillip's thinking about the future of the New

South Wales settlement. It occurred when the duty officer
on the *Sirius*, Sergeant Maxwell, ordered the flogging of
two seamen who were not on deck during their watch.
Jacob Nagle described the incident in his journal:

> The Governor ordered every officer on board the ship
> to appear in the cabin, even the boatswain's mate and
> told them all if he [k]new any officer to strike a man on
> board, he would break him immediately he said, those
> men are all we have to depend upon, and if we abuse
> those men that we have to trust to the convicts will rise
> and massacre us all. Those men are our support and if
> they are ill treated they will all be dead before the
> voyage is half out and who is to bring us back again?[12]

When the fleet reached the Canary Islands – or the
Madeira Isles, as they were then known to the English –
on 2 June, a further eight convicts had died, in addition to
those who had died before the fleet left Portsmouth. Five
of the eight had died on the *Alexander*. One of the dead
was Ishmael Colman, of whom John White recorded the
following: 'worn out by lowness of spirits and debility,
brought on by long and close confinement, [Colman]
resigned his breath without a pang'.[13]

By now a total of twenty-one convicts had been lost on
the *Alexander*, the unhealthiest ship in the fleet, to fever,
pneumonia and dysentery, which included the sixteen
convicts who had died on the ship while waiting to sail.
However, the rate of fatalities on all ships began to fall
after Tenerife, and John White was to observe that the
convicts were generally in better health than before
the fleet first set sail.[14]

At the time of the English fleet's arrival in Tenerife the
Canary Islands had been under Spanish control for three
hundred years, since becoming part of the Spanish Empire
in the late fifteenth century. While Spain's influence as a

world seafaring power had for a long time been on the
wane, the port of Santa Cruz remained strategically
important to Atlantic shipping.

On arrival at the port the English fleet was met by the
Spanish authorities, who inquired about its business. The
next morning, as protocol dictated, Arthur Phillip sent his
loyal deputy Lieutenant King to wait on the local Spanish
governor, Marquis Branciforte, while everyone else stayed
on the ships. When King attended the governor to
announce the arrival of Phillip and the English fleet,
he apologised for the *Sirius*'s not saluting the fort in the
customary way because there were too many stores
packed on the deck of the flagship to allow it to fire its
guns. As Hunter wrote in his journal, the next morning
they received

> a very polite reply from the governor, signifying his
> sincere wishes that the island might be capable of
> supplying us with such articles as we were in want of,
> and his assurances that every refreshment the place
> afforded we should certainly have.[15]

The following day Governor Branciforte agreed to receive
Phillip, who attended the palace with ten of his officer
colleagues. It was Monday 4 June, when the English
would normally have been celebrating the king's birthday,
but the business of the fleet put paid to the normal celebrations, leading the marine commander Major Robert
Ross to complain that insufficient respect was shown to
the British monarch.

The meeting with the Spanish governor went well, and
John White, who attended the audience, gave the
following account of him in his journal:

> He is rather above the middle size but cannot boast
> of much embonpoint; his countenance is animated; his

deportment easy and graceful; and both his appearance
and manners perfectly correspond with the idea univer-
sally entertained of the dignity of a grandee of Spain.
This accomplished nobleman, as I have been informed,
is not a Spaniard by birth, but a Sicilian; and descended
from some of the princes of that island.[16]

Two days later Arthur Phillip and his party were treated
to a lavish dinner at the governor's palace, where the
extravagance amazed the English, who were accustomed
to more restrained entertainment.[17] King was to say, 'We
were received and entertained with the liberality and
elegance for which the Spaniards are so much distinguished.'[18] The desserts made a particular impression on
Watkin Tench, who was also at the dinner:

> The profusion of ices which appeared in the dessert
> I found surprising considering that we were enjoying
> them under a sun nearly vertical. But it seems the
> caverns of the Peak very far below the summit afford
> at all seasons ice in abundance.[19]

During the week the fleet was able to acquire some, but
not all, of the supplies it needed. Tenerife's economy
depended on being able to sell its fresh produce to the
ships that called in on the next legs of their journeys.
However, the English fleet was of an exceptional size and
it is unlikely that the port had ever before been challenged
to provide for so many people at once. The timing was
also unfortunate, as the English arrived before much of
the food they needed was ready for harvest. The
vegetables that could be procured were, according to
White, 'rather scanty, little besides onions being to be got;
and still less of fruit, it being too early in the season'.[20]

Stocking up on fresh food, particularly fruit, was a
vital protection against scurvy, and the fleet was able to

take on board large quantities of figs and mulberries, which were then in season. This was accompanied by a temporary improvement to the standard of all rations. The marines were each given a daily ration of a pint of wine, instead of spirits, and a pound of fresh beef, rather than salted meat. They also received a pound of fresh bread and some fresh vegetables. The convicts were not given wine but received three-quarters of a pound of fresh meat and a pound of fresh bread or rice, as well as some fresh fruit and vegetables. The fleet also took aboard some wine but was to stock up further when reaching its next port of call, Rio de Janeiro.

While the English had no choice but to purchase fresh meat from the Spanish colony, they baulked at the high price of local bread, so instead they drew on their own supply of dried hardtack biscuits.[21]

While in Tenerife, a number of officers took the opportunity to do some sightseeing. Captain Hunter of the *Sirius* describes how expatriate English merchants took him and a number of colleagues on a trip to the island's old capital, Laguna, some four miles' walk to the north side of Tenerife.[22] On another day they went to the Catholic festival of Corpus Christi, where they witnessed a colourful procession followed by solemn worship. This prompted an indignant comment from the Anglican Richard Johnson that it was all 'superstition and idolatry'.[23]

When the officers went ashore to see the celebrations, all of the English sailors were kept on board their ships for fear that their usual drunken behaviour might disrupt the event and offend the locals.

Jacob Nagle described in his journal an incident that occurred later during their stay. After rowing Governor Phillip ashore, he and other crew members went to a local inn and he had his pocket picked. It seems that Phillip had unexpectedly returned to his boat to be rowed back out to the *Sirius* and the other oarsmen made a run to get back on time, leaving Nagle to pay for the wine. Nagle said his purse suddenly disappeared as he was paying the bill and that the innkeeper then strip-searched an old woman beggar who was standing nearby and found his purse behind her neck. He was impressed by the 'dexterous hand in whipping it out of my pocket' and was relieved to have his money back. He was even more relieved that the 'Governor excused my not being at the boat' when he had wanted to be taken back to the ship.[24]

The fleet had intended staying in Tenerife only a few days but needed to stay a week because of how long it was taking to load fresh water onto the ships for the next leg of the journey. Captain Hunter noted that the water pipe to the port only allowed two small boats to fill their casks at the same time, which made supplying water to all eleven ships very protracted.

On the night before the fleet was finally to leave, a convict on board the *Alexander*, John Powers, escaped. He managed to get up on deck, lower himself over the side into a small boat and row away. Powers first rowed over to a Dutch East Indiaman anchored in the harbour but his offer to sign up as a member of the crew was rejected. He then rowed to a nearby beach, where he intended to hide until the fleet left Tenerife. The next morning a search party of marines set out in search of him, as Hunter recorded in his journal:

> A little westward of the town they discovered the boat
> beating on the rocks and rowing in to pick her up they
> discovered the fellow concealing himself in the cliff of
> a rock, not having been able to get up the precipice.
> The officer presented a musket at him and threatened
> if he did not come down and get into the boat he
> would shoot him. The fellow complied rather than
> run the hazard of being shot and was taken on board,

punished and put in irons until we got to sea, when he
was liberated in the same manner as the rest.[25]

On 10 June the fleet left Santa Cruz and headed south for
the Cape Verde Islands off the west coast of Africa –
about fifteen hundred kilometres' sailing – where they
planned to stop briefly for more fresh water and whatever
fresh food could be purchased before heading across the
Atlantic to Rio de Janeiro. Captain Hunter said that the
main reason for wanting to stop at Port Praya Bay was to
stock up on a fresh supply of vegetables, having not been
able to procure them in Tenerife. The fleet reached Port
Praya on the island of St Tiago on 19 June and had
already dropped anchor when Phillip had misgivings
and abandoned the stopover. Phillip said in a letter to
Evan Nepean:

> I should have stopped for twenty-four hours at Port
> Praya but when off that port light airs of wind and
> a strong current making it probable some of the
> ships might not get in, I did not think it prudent to
> attempt it.[26]

He decided to head on with the supplies they already had,
even though it would inevitably lead to water restrictions
before they reached Rio de Janeiro.

Over the next few weeks the fleet headed further south
and occasionally passed other ships, including a
Portuguese trader that fell in with the convoy for a week,
a ship from the coast of Guinea bound for the West Indies
and an English ship bound for the Falkland Islands.[27] The
high temperatures, humidity and heavy tropical rain
would have distressed and confused the convicts, who
would have been ignorant of geography and climate, and
the threat to the health of those on the *Charlotte* became
a particular concern to Surgeon John White:

The weather became exceedingly dark, warm, and
close, with heavy rain, a temperature of the atmosphere
very common on approaching the equator, and very
much to be dreaded, as the health is greatly endangered
thereby. Every attention was therefore paid to the
people on board the *Charlotte*, and every exertion used
to keep her clean and wholesome between decks. My
first care was to keep the men, as far as was consistent
with the regular discharge of their duty, out of the rain;
and I never suffered the convicts to come upon deck
when it rained, as they had neither linen nor clothing
sufficient to make themselves dry and comfortable after
getting wet: a line of conduct which cannot be too
strictly observed, and enforced, in those latitudes.[28]

Another hazard of these latitudes struck aboard the
Prince of Wales, which suffered a plague of bugs.
Lieutenant Ralph Clark recorded that his colleague
Lieutenant William Faddy had to kill over a hundred of
the insects in his small sleeping area before he was able
to get any sleep.[29]

As they sailed over the equator and into the southern
hemisphere, the ships' crews celebrated the 'crossing of
the line'. In a traditional ceremony that paid homage
to the god of the sea, Neptune, those sailors who were
crossing the equator for the first time were compelled to
be ritually ducked in water, lathered with tar, greased and
shaved.

At night the heat and humidity became insufferable,
and it was decided to remove the hatches above the
convict quarters to allow in some air. This was not
without its consequences, however, as White recorded
with distaste:

In the evening it became calm, with distant peals of
thunder, and the most vivid flashes of lightning I ever

remember. The weather was now so immoderately hot that the female convicts, perfectly overcome by it, frequently fainted away; and these faintings generally terminated in fits. And yet, notwithstanding the enervating effects of the atmospheric heat, and the inconveniences they suffered from it, so predominant was the warmth of their constitutions, or the depravity of their hearts, that the hatches over the place where they were confined could not be suffered to lay off, during the night, without a promiscuous intercourse immediately taking place between them and the seamen and marines.[30]

The living conditions for the convicts at sea were appalling. Many had already spent years in cramped, overcrowded prisons and hulks in Britain and would now spend eight months locked up in even more congested quarters in the bowels of the transports. While the ships' officers and crews had opportunities to escape the ships and go ashore when the fleet was in port, the convicts were kept on board, and for much of this time they were locked up below deck.

Because of the risk to security there were no portholes in the convicts' quarters, and the risk of fire meant the banning of candles below decks, which meant the convicts were always in the dark as well as lacking any fresh air. Rats, parasites, bedbugs, lice, fleas and cockroaches thrived on all the ships. Their bilges (the lowest part of the ship, into which all of its excess liquids tend to drain) became foul and the smell overwhelming to the convicts who were locked below decks. The convicts' exercise area in the open air at the front of the ships was only a few metres long, because all of the transports had a high wooden security wall with large metal spikes installed across the deck next to the mainmast to keep the prisoners well away from the quarterdeck and the rear of the ship.

On the way to Rio de Janeiro the number of convicts who fell ill jumped dramatically. Reports of a large number of sick convicts on the transport *Alexander* brought John White across from the *Sirius* to investigate, upon which he found the following:

> The illness complained of was wholly occasioned by the bilge water which had by some means or other risen to so great a height that the panels of the cabin and the buttons on the clothes of the officers were turned nearly black by the noxious effluvia. When the hatches were taken off the stench was so powerful that it was scarcely possible to stand over them.[31]

White complained to Phillip, who, in turn, ordered the master of the *Alexander*, Duncan Sinclair, to pump out and regularly replace the bilge water. After this measure the surgeon recorded that the health of the convicts improved.

The filth of the lower decks was made worse by the lack of regard of some of the convicts for hygienic behaviour. At one point in the tropics Margaret Hall on the *Friendship* was put in irons for 'shitting between decks' rather than off the poop deck, as was required.

There is no surviving convict's account of the experience below decks on the First Fleet, but on a later convict ship the Irish political prisoner John Boyle O'Reilly was to write of the conditions:

> When the ship was becalmed in the tropics the suffering of the imprisoned wretches in the steaming and crowded hold was piteous to see. They were so packed that free movement was impossible. The best thing to do was to sit each on his or her berth, and suffer in patience. The air was stifling and oppressive. There was no draught through the barred hatches.

The deck above them was blazing hot. The pitch dropped from the beams and burned their flesh as it fell. There was only one word spoken or thought – one yearning idea in every mind – water, cool water to slake the parching thirst. Two pints of water a day were served out to each convict – a quart of half putrid and blood warm liquid. It was a woeful sight to see the thirsty souls devour this allowance as soon as their hot hands seized the vessel. Day in and day out, the terrible calm held the ship, and the consuming heat sapped the lives of the pent up convicts. Hideous incidents filled the days and nights as the convict ship sailed southward with her burden of disease and death.[32]

The appalling conditions of the prisoners did nothing, however, to halt the prostitution and promiscuity involving the convict women and the crews. White describes the behaviour of the women as being 'so uncontrollable that neither shame (but of this they had long lost sight) nor the fear of punishment could deter them from making their way through the bulkheads to the apartments assigned to the seamen'.[33]

Ralph Clark was equally damning in his judgement of the convict women's sexual conduct on the voyage: 'I never could have thought there were so many abandoned wenches in England. They are ten thousand times worse than the men convicts and I am afraid that we will have a great deal more trouble with them.'[34]

Such was Clark's disgust that he looked forward to 21-year-old Sarah McCormick's illness giving those who had fornicated with her their just deserts:

[T]he doctor has been oblige[d] to bleed her twice today and says that she will not live the night out – She is now quite speechless I am apt to think

(God forgive) if it is not so, that she is eating up with
the p[ox] . . . She is one of them that went through the
bulk head to the seamen – I hope she has given them
some thing to remember her.[35]

Clark's low opinion of the convict women and his
repeated declaration of love for his wife in his daily
journal entries did not prevent him from striking up a
relationship with 17-year-old Mary Branham, a convict
on the *Lady Penrhyn* who would become his mistress in
the new colony and mother his child. And this was after
recording in his diary before reaching the Cape of Good
Hope:

Two of the convict women that went through the
bulkhead to the seamen . . . have informed the doctor
that they are with child . . . I hope the commodore
will make the two seamen that are the fathers of
the children marry them and make them stay in
Botany Bay.[36]

Mary Branham was only 13 years old in 1784 when she
was sentenced in the Old Bailey to transportation for
seven years for stealing two petticoats, some clothing
and some cloth that was worth a little more than two
pounds.[37]

Clearly neither of the main punishments – flogging and
chaining below decks for prolonged periods of time – was
an effective deterrent. Under Arthur Phillip's influence
discipline aboard ships was more lenient than severe – a
policy that was not always enthusiastically endorsed by
the governor's colleagues. Captain John Hunter, although
a loyal deputy to Phillip, believed that the flogging of
convicts Farrell and Griffiths for only twenty-four strokes
and then releasing them from their chains shortly afterwards was too lenient a punishment for their planned

mutiny on the *Scarborough*: 'This indulgence had no doubt left it more in the power of those who might be disposed to exert their ingenuity in so daring an attempt to carry their plan into execution with a greater probability of success.'[38]

When convicts became ill on the ships, there was not a great deal that could be done for them, and in most cases they were left until they got better or died. The best that most of them could hope for was a medicinal measure of rum. Unfortunately this almost always came hand in hand with the other common remedy of the time: bleeding. Draining blood from the patient was a widely used treatment for convict and non-convict patients alike. While the practice is now highly discredited and believed to have taken more lives than it saved, by the time of the First Fleet it had become a standard treatment for almost every ailment.

The reasoning behind bleeding goes back to the fifth century BC, when ancient Greeks believed that many diseases were caused by an excess of 'humours' in the blood. Every surgeon on the First Fleet carried a range of instruments designed to puncture the flesh of the patient and suck out various quantities of blood.

Convict deaths were an accepted part of the journey, and when anyone died there would usually be a burial at sea, which involved a simple funeral ceremony, the reading of prayers and the sliding of the deceased's body, weighted and wrapped in cloth, over the side of the ship.

Most individual convict deaths were not worthy of any special mention, but there were a number of records involving the death of small children. Ralph Clark was moved to record how a small child of a convict died in the middle of the night and was buried at sea the next morning:

> The doctor was called up to see one of the convict
> womens children which was very ill and had been

almost ever since it had been on board. It departs
at two o'clock this morning, poor thing. It is much
better out of this world than in it . . . At half after
nine committed the body of Thomas Mason to the
deep. Henry Lovall, one of the convicts read prayers
over it.[39]

One of the convicts was lost when he fell overboard
on the *Alexander* and drowned. He had apparently fallen
into the seas in a high wind. The *Alexander* quickly
lowered a boat and the *Supply* doubled back to aid the
search, but there was a squall and a high swell and
he couldn't be found. Also, on the *Prince of Wales*, the
convict Jane Bonner fell and crushed her spine and died
six days later.[40]

The crossing of the Atlantic Ocean from Tenerife to Rio
de Janeiro with less fresh water and fresh supplies than
they had planned took almost two months. As a
precaution the water ration was cut to three pints per day
for everyone a month after the fleet left Santa Cruz (which,
although difficult for those on the First Fleet to adjust to,
was still more than those on the Second Fleet would
receive). The decision was made after Phillip called all the
masters of the fleet's ships to the *Sirius* to assess how much
water was left and how much was being used. With the
new ration came the stipulation that the water could only
be used for personal consumption, and washing and
laundry had to be done with seawater.

Two weeks after the imposition of water restrictions,
and with a strong south-westerly wind pushing the fleet
along at good speed, Phillip agreed to lift the water ration
from three pints to two quarts per day.

By the end of July, only about eight hundred kilometres
and a week's sailing away from Rio de Janeiro, many of
the ships began to run short of food, and the last goose
was killed and eaten by the officers on the *Lady Penrhyn*.

The ships' crews supplemented their diet with the flying fish that landed on the decks of the ships, along with fish that they caught more conventionally.

Throughout this long leg of the voyage Phillip continued to have difficulty keeping the fleet together, given the differences in sailing speed of the different vessels. The fastest was the *Supply*, which not only helped the *Alexander* in its search for the man overboard but also spent much of the time turning to escort the slower ships. The slowest continued to be the *Lady Penrhyn*, which constantly struggled to keep up with the others. Eventually the *Supply*, which was again sailing ahead of the rest of the fleet, signalled it had sighted land on 2 August.

Before the fleet reached Rio de Janeiro, the wind died away, and it would take another four days to reach the harbour. In these conditions it passed a number of ships from a variety of countries, including a ship from Guinea with slaves who were 'of a strong and robust appearance' and formed 'an extensive article of commerce'.[41]

Rio de Janeiro, or St Sebastian as it was then more commonly named, was a vital part of the Portuguese network of strategically positioned ports that linked up its trading empire, which dated back to the early sixteenth century. At the time of the First Fleet's arrival Rio was a thriving port, even though the Portuguese Empire, like the Spanish, had been in decline for more than a hundred years, while Britain was only beginning to build hers.

Portugal possessed the earliest and the longest-lived modern European empire, spanning nearly six hundred years from the early fifteenth to the twentieth century. The Portuguese explorer Bartholomew Diaz rounded the Cape of Good Hope in 1488, and a decade later Vasco da Gama reached India. In 1500 Pedro Alvares Cabral landed in South America, which would lead to the establishment of Brazil. Throughout the 1500s Portugal established a network of ports from Lisbon to Japan, including Goa in south-west India, Mozambique and Angola in Africa, Malacca in southern Malaya, Macao in China, Ormus in the Persian Gulf and Nagasaki in Japan.

Rio de Janeiro, with an estimated population of forty thousand,[42] was rich in its own right and exported gold, sugar, rice and rum. Its fine harbour, strategically placed on the east coast of South America, was on the trade-wind route to not only the Americas but also Asia.

Arthur Phillip later explained why he favoured the apparently odd route of travelling to the southern tip of Africa via South America:

> It may appear perhaps, on a slight consideration, rather extraordinary, that vessels bound to the Cape of Good Hope should find it expedient to touch at a harbour of South America. To run across the Atlantic, and take as part of their course, that coast the very existence of which was unknown to the first navigators of these seas, seems a very circuitous method of performing the voyage. A little examination will remove this apparent difficulty. The calms so frequent on the African side, are of themselves a sufficient cause to induce a navigator to keep a very westerly course: and even the islands at which it is so often convenient to touch will carry him within a few degrees of the South American coast.[43]

Indeed, when the First Fleet eventually reached the Cape of Good Hope, it would encounter an American ship in Table Bay bound for India that had taken longer to sail directly from the Canary Islands than it had taken in sailing via Rio de Janeiro.

On arrival in Rio de Janeiro it was again Lieutenant Philip Gidley King who was sent ahead into the port to announce to the Portuguese governor the arrival of the fleet. All eleven ships sailed into Rio in relatively good shape, considering they had been travelling for three months and had last taken aboard fresh food and water two months earlier in Tenerife. However, by the time the fleet was anchored in the harbour between twenty and thirty convicts had come down with the expedition's first outbreak of scurvy.[44]

By the eighteenth century disease – and, most prominently, scurvy – was the largest killer of seafarers, responsible for about fifty per cent of all deaths at sea. (Accidents, largely involving falling from the rigging onto the deck or into the sea, accounted for about thirty per cent; shipwrecks, fire and explosions accounted for about ten per cent; and the remainder were due to fighting enemies at sea.)

It would take the European seafaring powers almost two hundred and fifty years from the first voyages of discovery in the early fifteenth century to find for themselves the simple remedy to this terrible disease, which caused livid spots to appear all over the body, bleeding from every orifice, the loss of teeth, depression and death. Until the mid-eighteenth century long sea journeys had come at great human cost, and phenomenally high levels of fatalities were accepted as inevitable until it was learned that the disease could be largely avoided with a regular intake of fresh food, particularly fruit and vegetables (although, of course, there was no understanding back then of the reason for this: their vitamin C content). By the time of his great voyages of exploration in the 1760s and 1770s Captain James Cook had successfully controlled the disease, and nearly twenty years later the lessons were well known to Captain Phillip and the surgeons of the First Fleet.

The arrival of the ships in port allowed the scorbutic convicts to be treated with a fresh-food diet, while the others were in a condition that delighted the fleet's officers. Captain John Hunter was to boast that the

general health of the fifteen hundred confined to the small
ships of the fleet was probably better than to be found in
any English town with a similar population.[45]

Arthur Phillip was to report back to England from Rio
de Janeiro that the good health of the convicts was also
due to the policy of getting them out regularly onto the
decks both during the day and at night.[46]

During their stay in the port John White would
regularly row around the different transports in the
harbour to check the condition of the convicts, while the
fleet chaplain Reverend Richard Johnson attended to
their spiritual needs by going around to conduct church
services on the decks of the ships on Sundays.

The stopover also allowed repairs to the ships, particularly to the *Sirius*, which was found to be leaking badly.
As Phillip was to report to the Admiralty from Rio de
Janeiro in a letter that would be carried on the next ship
leaving for England, both the top, or spar, deck and the
gun deck of the ship were leaking badly and the seams
between the decking needed to be refilled, or 'caulked'.[47]

The English were especially welcomed in Rio de
Janeiro on this occasion as Arthur Phillip was well known
and highly regarded by the Portuguese due to his service
in the Portuguese navy during the war with Spain.[48] He
had also formed a friendship with the governor, Don Luis
de Varconcellos, having met him on an earlier visit to Rio
de Janeiro in 1783 when Phillip had arrived on the sixty-
four-gun Royal Navy ship *Europe*.

While guests of the Portuguese, Phillip and his officers
were extended every courtesy – which on occasion was
taken to excessive lengths. Whenever Arthur Phillip was
ashore, he was attended by palace guards, who would
parade at the wharf steps and escort him and his party
around the city. Jacob Nagle, one of the rowers on
Phillip's barge, recorded Phillip's embarrassment at this:

> The Governor often landed in different parts of the
> town, round about the skirts, because he did not wish
> to trouble the guards, but land where we would, we
> could see the soldiers running to wherever we landed
> and parade under an arrest for him.[49]

As part of their hospitality the Portuguese permitted the
English to pitch a tent on the little island of Enchandos,
about two kilometres further up the river from the
anchored fleet, to use as Phillip's land office while they
were in port. They also allowed Lieutenant William
Dawes, an astronomer, to unload his scientific equipment
and use the island for experiments, which included
measuring and calculating the time.

The 25-year-old Dawes was a lieutenant in the
marines, but his great passion was science and astronomy,
and he was to make a big contribution to New South
Wales as a surveyor and in planning the layout of the new
settlement. He was later to fall out with Governor Arthur
Phillip, whom he believed did not support scientific
discovery.

Dawes had joined the marines as a 17-year-old second-
lieutenant on 2 September 1779, and in September 1781
as a 19-year-old was wounded in action against the
French off Chesapeake Bay during the American War of
Independence. When he volunteered for service with the
First Fleet to New South Wales, he was known as a
competent astronomer, and on the recommendation of
the astronomer royal, Reverend Dr Nevil Maskelyne, he
was supplied with instruments and books for an observatory by the Board of Longitude. Dawes was asked
especially to watch for a comet expected to be seen in the
southern hemisphere in 1788.

The convicts were held on the ships, locked below
decks in the sweltering heat, but the crew were able to
enjoy some shore leave. A number of them were to record

their visits and the exotic birds, butterflies, insects and other wildlife they saw, as well as the colourful markets and coffee houses where 'they had coffee in great plenty, sweetmeats and a great variety of rich cakes'.[50]

The marines spent most of their time on the ships but were permitted occasional shore leave if they acquired a special pass. While in Rio harbour, a number of them were punished for sexual relations with the convict women. Cornelius Connell, a private in the marines, was given a hundred lashes after he was caught having sex with some female convicts, and Thomas Jones was caught trying to bribe one of the sentries to let him get below decks and among the women. Two other privates, John Jones and James Riley, were charged with similar offences but acquitted for want of evidence.[51]

The English officers were again struck by the colour and the splendour of the Roman Catholic church services. Being from Protestant backgrounds, they were accustomed to more subdued worship, in grey churches with little decoration or pomp. A number of them witnessed the celebration of the Feast of the Assumption and were amazed at what they saw, including the *Lady Penrhyn* surgeon Bowes Smyth:

> The church was decorated in a most superb manner, there was a band of music playing in the church yard . . . The ladies who appeared publicly at the windows and in the procession were elegantly dressed [resembling] actresses at a puppet show in Bartholomew Fair . . . At night there was a grand display of fireworks off the top of one of the churches.[52]

John White described the well-dressed citizens and how the churches were decorated with flowers and 'most brilliantly illuminated'. The 'multitudes' paraded, prayed, sang hymns and bought coloured beads from hawkers, and the throng 'jostled' to gain admission to the churches to fall on their knees and 'pray with fervour'.[53] But he was shocked at the number of well-dressed women in the crowd who were 'unattended' and who, after dark, would 'bestow their favours' on strangers as well as acquaintances.

He also described how the well-to-do were carried about the city. In earlier times they had been conveyed in 'elegant cotton hammocks' adroitly made by the native Indians, but they had been replaced by a fashion for sedan chairs: not as good as those in London but able to be carried 'at a great rate . . . borne on the shoulders of two slaves'.[54]

Bowes Smyth noted how he and many of the English officers in Rio had lost their fitness, such that previously easily accomplished physical exertions now took their toll: 'Being very much fatigued with my long walk yesterday I remained on board all this day: nor is it to be wondered at that I should be a good deal tired having been without any exercise for nine weeks.'[55]

While the officers only recorded the more reputable pursuits, Jacob Nagle was to later write more honestly about the typical behaviour of sailors, when he was attacked after picking up a prostitute in a local bar. Nagle and his companion were granted shore leave and had a sergeant for protection who did not want to walk the city streets but wanted to sit 'in the punch houses all day'. After Nagle left the tavern with a woman he had picked up for the night, a man followed and was about to attack him with a sword, when luckily a soldier arrived on the scene in the nick of time:

> One evening two of us got in to a grog shop . . . and
> a very handsome young woman being there who was
> very familiar with me and asked me home with her.
> I accepted the offer and had walked one square, arm

in arm . . . up came a Portuguese with a great cloak
on and pushed me away from her . . . He drew back
and drew his sword and was raising his sword over
his head to make a cut at my head. At that instant a
soldier turned the corner . . . drew his sword and
guarded the blow he was going to make [at me].
Another soldier . . . abused him and threatened to cut
him down for meddling with me, but the fellow
begged their pardons and said I had taken his wife
from him. The soldiers sent him and her about their
business and told me she was a poota, which is a
whore. I thought I was well off to be clear of them.[56]

Criminal ingenuity also continued at every opportunity.
When the fleet came in to any port, little bumboats would
pull alongside and sell food and other wares to the crew.
In Rio de Janeiro some convicts were buying food from
them using counterfeit money. The coins had been very
well constructed by Thomas Barrett on the transport
Charlotte, with the help of other convicts. They were
coined from old buckles, buttons from the marines and
pewter spoons during the long voyage from Tenerife. John
White recorded that the fake currency was almost good
enough to be passed off as the real thing:

> The impression, milling, character, in a word, the
> whole was so perfectly executed that had the metal
> been a little better fraud, I am convinced, would have
> passed undetected . . . The adroitness . . . gave me a
> high opinion of their ingenuity, cunning, caution and
> address; and I could not help wishing that these
> qualities had been employed to more laudable
> purposes.[57]

Thomas Barrett had already been twice condemned to
execution and twice committed to transportation.[58] He

would eventually be the first convict to be hanged in New South Wales.

The fleet stayed almost a month in Rio, where its officers were able to purchase plenty of fresh food, particularly oranges, to supply to all the crew and convicts. The oranges were so abundant that it was possible for everyone to be fed several each day. Captain Hunter said that there were so many oranges in season that some of the boats passing the transports would throw 'a shower of oranges' onto the decks.[59] John White wrote, 'the commissary supplied the troops and convicts with rice (in lieu of bread), with fresh beef, vegetables, and oranges, which soon removed every symptom of the scurvy prevalent among them.'[60]

Before leaving, the fleet also loaded many plants and seeds for planting in Botany Bay, including coffee, cocoa, cotton, banana, orange, lemon, guava, tamarind, prickly pear and eugina or pomme rose, 'a plant bearing fruit in shape like an apple and having the flavour and odour of a rose'.[61] However, the biggest purchase while the fleet was in Rio was a hundred and fifteen pipes (sixty-five thousand litres) of rum for the remainder of the voyage and for the first three years of the new settlement, which no doubt would have been a great relief to the marines, who had earlier feared there would be no rum ration in the new colony.

The local rum was produced from aquadente, a by-product of sugar cane. Such a huge surge in demand sent the local retail price of rum soaring by more than twenty-five per cent and forced the fleet to offset its costs by buying only half the planned amount of the spirit for medicinal purposes.[62]

The large intake of grog required the reorganisation of the cargo of the entire fleet: 'It has been necessary that the store ships might receive the spirits to move part of the provisions from them to the transports.'[63]

As things turned out, the rum was of poor quality and was to attract criticism when the settlers reached Sydney and had to drink it. Robert Ross was to say that 'in taste and smell [it] is extremely offensive', adding that his marines drank it only out of 'absolute necessity'.[64]

The fleet was also able to purchase some of the vital stores that had been missing when it left Portsmouth, including cloth for the women convicts' clothing and musket balls.

A few days before departing Rio de Janeiro, Jane Scott, the wife of marine sergeant James Scott, gave birth to a baby daughter after a twenty-seven-hour labour on the *Prince of Wales*. Baby Elizabeth Scott was to be one of the nine girls and twelve boys born on the ships of the First Fleet. She was more fortunate than the fourteen children born to the convict women, who would have been wrapped in torn-up adult clothing as there were no provisions made for convict babies when the ships were prepared in Portsmouth. This was in spite of the fact that many of the women were obviously pregnant before the ships set sail. The first child born to a convict was the daughter of Isabella Lawson, born less than three weeks out from Portsmouth on 31 May.

Sergeant Scott, meanwhile, had little formal education but managed to keep a diary of the voyage and his three-year stay in Sydney. He and his wife were to have another child in the new colony, a son named William, who was born three years later on 4 June 1790.[65] Scott and his little family left New South Wales to return home to England in October 1791 and arrived back at Portsmouth eight months later, in June 1792.

Arthur Phillip was able to do a little spying before the fleet recommenced its journey, and he sent back to England information he had acquired about the Spanish military defence of Montevideo. The English were still technically at war with Spain at the time and had contemplated invading the Spanish port, which was some thousand kilometres to the south of Rio de Janeiro. In a letter sent secretly to the British Government before leaving the city, Phillip provided details of the two thousand two hundred Spanish soldiers that defended the north and south sides of the River Plate in the city of Montevideo, which was a larger force than previously thought.[66] The stopover in Rio de Janeiro had been valuable in a wide array of ways.

8

LEAVING CIVILISATION

*It was natural to indulge at this moment a melancholy
reflection which obtruded itself upon the mind. The
land behind us was the abode of civilized people; that
before was the residence of savages. When, if ever, we
might again enjoy the commerce of the world, was
doubtful and uncertain ... All communication with
families and friends now cut off, [we were] leaving the
world behind us, to enter a state unknown.*

On 1 September, after almost a month in the port and, as
White recorded, 'having now procured everything at Rio
de Janeiro that we stood in need of, and thoroughly
recovered and refreshed our people', the fleet was ready
to continue its journey.[1]

Phillip was to spend the next two days writing lengthy
reports to Lord Sydney and his deputy Evan Nepean,
which would be sent back on the next ship leaving Rio for
London. It would be the last opportunity for Phillip to
communicate with England until the fleet reached the
Cape of Good Hope on the southern tip of Africa, which
was more than six weeks away.

A number of officers who were unable to continue on
with the fleet were left behind to be put on the next
available ship back to England. They included Micah

Morton, the master of the *Sirius*, who had been badly injured when unmooring the ship in Santa Cruz harbour two months earlier. Two midshipmen were also sent home; one had been injured and the other was suffering from 'a venereal complaint which being long neglected is not likely to be cured at sea'.[2] They were put on a British whaling ship that had called into Rio to repair leaks.

On 4 September the fleet weighed anchor. As the convoy left to sail back across the Atlantic on the prevailing westerly wind to the Cape of Good Hope, the Portuguese on shore fired off a twenty-one-gun salute, which was answered by the *Sirius*. Such a salute was 'a very high and uncommon compliment', and an indication of the good relationship between the visiting English and the resident Portuguese.[3]

Four days after leaving Rio de Janeiro the convict Mary Bryant gave birth to a baby daughter and named her after the transport ship she was carried in, the *Charlotte*. Little Charlotte would later die of a fever in a small boat off the African coast following a daring and spectacular escape attempt by her mother and a number of other convicts.

The winds picked up and the fleet made good progress thanks to a solid south-westerly. However, the high seas made many of the passengers seasick and battered the *Lady Penrhyn*, which was leaning so far with the wind that the sea ran into the portholes. By the middle of September the ships were finally moving into cooler latitudes.[4]

On 19 September another convict was lost overboard, this time from the *Charlotte*, as White described:

> William Brown a very well behaved convict, in bringing some clothing from the bowsprit end where he hung them out to dry, fell overboard. As soon as

the alarm was given that a man was overboard, the
ship was instantly hove to, and a boat hoisted out, but
to no purpose. Lieutenant Ball of the *Supply*, a most
active officer, knowing . . . that some accident must
have happened bore down; but, notwithstanding
every excursion, the poor fellow sank before either the
Supply or our boat could reach him. The people on
the forecastle, who saw him fall, say that the ship
went directly over him, which . . . must make it
impossible for him to keep on the surface long enough
to be taken up.[5]

Towards the end of September the weather turned nasty
and the fleet spent a week battling against a gale.
Lieutenant Ralph Clark, aboard the *Friendship*, said the
sea was so rough that those marines sleeping with the
convict women were washed out of their beds.[6]

The *Sirius* was also labouring in the conditions and on
inspection was found to have a number of serious
problems below the waterline. Lieutenant Philip Gidley
King complained that the ship should not have passed its
inspection in England:

For these days past and a rolling sea, the ship has
laboured very much . . . A discovery has also been
made which tends to prove . . . the extreme negligence
of the Dock Yard officers in not giving the *Sirius* the
inspection they certainly ought to have done . . . On
inspection we found that not only were the top
timbers rotten but also many of the futtocks were in
the same condition.[7]

Only a month after the fleet left Rio de Janeiro, the stores
of fresh food were once again exhausted, and rations
consisted largely of salted meat. The officers were
sometimes able to break the monotony of their diet; on

one occasion a sheep was killed on the *Lady Penrhyn* and shared with the officers on the *Alexander*.[8]

On 6 October, a week before the fleet was due to arrive at the Cape of Good Hope, there was another attempted mutiny, this time on the convict transport the *Alexander*. The uprising was organised by the same John Powers who had escaped and been recaptured when the fleet was in Tenerife four months earlier. With the help of the seamen on the ship, Powers and a number of other convicts were armed with iron bars. They planned to take control of the ship by overpowering the marines shortly before they arrived at the Cape of Good Hope.

Before the mutineers could rise up, they were betrayed to the master of the *Alexander*, Duncan Sinclair, who alerted his marines, strengthened the watch and locked all the convicts below decks. Powers was removed to the *Sirius*, where he was chained to the deck. The four seamen accused of assisting the insurgents were flogged and replaced by seamen from the *Sirius*, and the convict who had betrayed the plot was moved for his own protection to the *Scarborough*.[9]

The arrival at the Cape took longer than expected as the fleet was being blown away from the port. 'The wind is driving us farther to the southward than we want to go,' complained Lieutenant Ralph Clark.[10] To bring the fleet back on course, Phillip ordered all the ships to stay close to the flagship *Sirius*.

Finally, at daylight on Saturday 13 October the fleet sighted Lyons Head 'five leagues away' and with a fresh breeze soon saw the Cape of Good Hope ahead. By nightfall the fleet was anchored in Table Bay, where there were already more than twenty American, French, Danish, Portuguese, Dutch and English ships lying at anchor.[11]

The first European to discover the Cape of Good Hope, the Portuguese explorer Bartholomew Diaz, sailed around the southern point of Africa in 1586. Diaz had originally called it the Cape of Storms, but the name was later changed by the Portuguese King John II to the Cape of Good Hope. Table Mountain was given its name by another Portuguese, Antonio da Saldania, some seventeen years later.

The Cape was not regularly used until 1652, when Jan van Riebeeck was sent by the Dutch East India Company to establish a halfway station to provide fresh water, vegetables and meat for its trading ships travelling to and from the East Indies.

At that time the Dutch were a major European trading power, with a network of ports at New Amsterdam (now New York), Suriname and Guyana in South America and Antilles in the Caribbean. The Dutch East India Company's biggest trading area was the Dutch East Indies, which covered a large area of current-day Indonesia, Malaysia and West Papua New Guinea.

In the early nineteenth century Cape Town came under British control, but at the time the First Fleet arrived at the end of 1787, the port was there very much to serve Dutch maritime interests first and those of the British and other nations second. Arthur Phillip and his fleet were to find the hospitality in Cape Town very different from the treatment they had received in the Portuguese-controlled port of Rio de Janeiro and the Spanish port of Tenerife.

The fleet stayed in the Cape for longer than it had planned. It had formally asked the Dutch governor for supplies and had to wait more than a week for a reply.[12] While the crews and passengers waited, they had to make do with their own limited diet of ship's rations, supplemented by a small amount of fresh rations provided by the Dutch port authority.

Lieutenant Philip Gidley King was once again the first sent ashore, this time to purchase food for the last long leg of the voyage to New South Wales. He hoped to buy eighty thousand pounds of flour, sixty bushels of wheat and eight hundred bushels of barley. However, he returned to say that the governor had told him that the colony was itself short of food and none could be spared for the English.

The day after the fleet's arrival, Sunday 14 October, it was officially allowed to enter the port and Phillip, together with a number of officers, presented himself to Governor Van de Graf. A polite exchange led to more discussions about buying food. The governor told Phillip that they could purchase livestock and wine, but that there was a shortage of grain following recent disappointing harvests.

In the following days Phillip took lodgings on shore and began to talk to local traders:

> As I found on inquiry that the last years crops had been very good, I requested by letter to the Governor and Council permission to purchase what provisions were wanted for the *Sirius* and *Supply*, as likewise corn for seed, and what was necessary for the livestock intended to be embarked at this place.[13]

To add to their troubles the harbour provided little shelter for the ships, which led Phillip to complain:

> This bay cannot be properly called a port, being by no means a station of security, it is exposed by all the violence of the winds, which set into it from the sea; and is far from sufficiently secured from those which blow from the land. The gusts, which descend from the summit of Table Mountain, are sufficient to force ships from their anchors . . . The storms from the sea are still more formidable; so much so that ships have frequently been driven by them from their anchorage and wrecked at the head of the Bay.[14]

Phillip's fellow officers were equally unimpressed and compared the Cape unfavourably to the exotic Rio de Janeiro. Bowes Smyth wrote that even the appearance of the shoreline was unappealing:

> There are many gallows and other implements of punishment erected along the shore and in front of the town. There were also wheels for breaking felons upon, several of which were at this time occupied by the mangled bodies of the unhappy wretches who suffered upon them: their right hands were cut off and fixed by a large nail to the side of the wheel, the wheel itself elevated upon a post about nine or ten feet high, upon which the body lies to perish.[15]

The city boasted a Calvinist church and a Lutheran church, and the impressive Dutch governor's house with its adjacent parklands reminded some of the English visitors of St James' Park in London. John White noted that the gardens were overlooked by a hospital, which was generally 'pretty full' when ships arrived after a long voyage.[16]

While the fleet waited in the harbour, many of the convicts and marines fell seriously ill with a putrid fever. White reported that the disease was worst on the *Charlotte*, where thirty were ill and a number expected to die.[17]

After a few days limited fresh food rations, including soft bread, beef, mutton and greens, started to arrive and were rowed out to the ships. All of the officers who could be spared were allowed on shore leave, where they could take lodgings and buy 'the comforts and refreshments to be enjoyed on land for the last and longest stage of their voyage'.[18]

Surgeon White made a number of typically stern observations about the women in the Cape:

The habits and customs of the women of this place are extremely contrasted to those of the inhabitants of Rio de Janeiro. Among the latter a great deal of reserve and modesty is apparent between the sexes in public. Those who are disposed to say tender and civil things to a lady must do it by stealth, or breathe their soft sighs through the latticework of a window, or the grates of a convent. But at the Cape, if you wish to be a favourite with the fair, as the custom is, you must in your own defence (if I may use the expression) *grapple* the lady, and paw her in a manner that does not partake in the least of gentleness. Such a rough and uncouth conduct, together with a kiss ravished now and then in the most public manner and situations, is not only pleasing to the fair one, but even to her parents, if present; and is considered by all parties as an act of the greatest gallantry and gaiety. In fact, the Dutch ladies here, from a peculiar gay turn, admit of liberties that may be thought reprehensible in England; but perhaps as seldom overstep the bounds of virtue as the women of other countries.[19]

White was also unimpressed with the local Dutch military:

The Cape militia differ from the English in not receiving pay or wearing regimentals. In fact they should rather be called volunteers, who turn out for the protection of their own property, and are not subject to strict military discipline. Most of them wore blue coats, with white metal buttons, awkwardly long, and in the cut and shape of which uniformity had not been attended to. Neither was it visible in the other parts of their dress or accoutrements; some wore powder, others none, so that, upon the whole, they made a very unmilitary appearance. The officers are chosen annually from among themselves. Some of these, indeed, I observed to be very well dressed. Neglect, non-attendance, and every other breach of their military rules, is punished by fine or forfeiture, and not corporally. At this burlesque on the profession of a soldier, I could not help observing that many of them had either got intoxicated that morning or were not recovered from their overnight's debauch.[20]

The long wait for approval to purchase and load the supplies, with the convicts mostly locked below decks and most of the crew kept on board ship, began to grate on everyone's nerves. The convicts fought with each other and the marines were regularly drunk and disorderly.

On 20 October a brawl between marines erupted aboard the *Scarborough*. Thomas Bullimore, one of those involved, would be murdered by other marines shortly after arriving in Sydney.

Two days later a marine was flogged for stealing and fighting on the *Alexander* and another for insubordination on the *Charlotte*. The troubles did not end there. The second mate of the *Friendship*, Patrick Vallance, fell overboard while drunk: 'He had gone to the head to ease himself . . . [and] . . . although three men jumped overboard after him they could not save him, for soon after he sank and has not been seen since.'[21]

Although October is the second month of spring in the southern hemisphere, the weather was cold for much of the stay in Table Bay. High winds and rough seas threw the ships around, and for several days no supplies could be taken out to them as it was too dangerous to row to and from the shore. It was so rough that a boat belonging to the supply ship the *Borrowdale* came adrift and was blown out of the harbour towards Penguin Island. Another boat belonging to a Dutch East India ship anchored in the bay was overturned and two of its crew members drowned.

Finally, after eight days, Phillip received the letter he had been waiting for from the Dutch governor, approving the purchase and loading of supplies that would allow the fleet to be on its way once again.

The fleet immediately began to load up in earnest. All were aware that they needed to take with them everything they would need for survival in the new colony. Daniel Southwell, a midshipman on the *Sirius*, wrote home:

> It was a time of constant bustle as this being the last port we must take every advantage of it, for the leaving behind of many articles that are requisite and necessary would beyond here, be irreparable: and this therefore now keeps us constantly employed in getting the ships supplied with water and all the species of provision that are proper.[22]

During the next few weeks the fleet took on a large quantity of rice, wheat, barley and Indian corn, and a variety of seeds and plants, which included 'fig trees, bamboo, Spanish reed, sugar cane, vines of various sorts, quince, apple, pear, strawberry and oak, myrtle'.[23]

The loading of water and other supplies was a major task for ships coming in to port, but at least the facilities here were better designed than those at Tenerife and Rio de Janeiro. At the eastern end of the harbour there was a long wooden pier that had a number of cranes and water pipes running along it so that a number of scoots, or small boats, could load water at the same time.[24]

While still in Table Bay, the ships' carpenters constructed wooden stalls on the already congested decks of the *Sirius* and the transports, and more than five hundred animals were brought aboard, including cows, bulls, pigs, horses, ducks, chickens, sheep, goats and geese. The sight led one of the surgeons on the *Sirius*, George Worgan, to write to his brother in England, noting that each ship now looked like a 'Noah's Ark'.[25]

The animals were considered of the highest priority, and the women and some of the men convicts on the *Friendship* were moved to other ships to make way for thirty-five sheep. The decks of all the ships were now crowded with penned animals, whose urine and faeces would seep through the deck and onto the convicts below.

As much as the fleet could possibly carry was loaded aboard. On the decks of the *Sirius* alone were six cows with calf, two bulls and a number of sheep, goats, pigs and chickens.

In addition to the stock for the settlement a number of officers took what livestock they could on board – intended not only for the remainder of the passage but also for their private farms when they reached New South Wales.

The ships also needed to be loaded with a large amount of fresh feed to keep the animals alive for the next two months. Unfortunately there was only a limited amount of space on the ships, and the hay feed would run out before the fleet reached Botany Bay, with many of the animals becoming emaciated and dying.

Finally, on 13 November, 'with all people clear of scurvy',[26] according to White, the fleet left the Cape. There was great relief at finally getting away from what had been too long a stay at a decidedly unpleasant port. Yet, as David Collins was to observe, the relief was mixed with anxiety, sadness and fear. Many felt as they headed away from the Cape that they were leaving behind all connections with the civilised world:

> It was natural to indulge at this moment a melancholy reflection which obtruded itself upon the mind. The land behind us was the abode of civilized people; that before was the residence of savages. When, if ever, we

> might again enjoy the commerce of the world, was
> doubtful and uncertain. . . . All communication with
> families and friends now cut off, [we were] leaving the
> world behind us, to enter a state unknown.[27]

The long haul to the east coast of Australia across the
Great Southern Ocean would take more than two months
and prove to be the most difficult leg yet. For the first five
days after leaving the Cape the fleet made virtually no
progress, as the ships were running into a fierce headwind. Even this early Phillip was concerned that with the
delay they would run out of fresh water before reaching
Botany Bay and decided to put everyone back onto the
reduced allowance of three pints of water per day.[28]

Soon the livestock started to die. On 16 November
Lieutenant Ralph Clark noted that chickens were dying
on the *Lady Penrhyn* from disease every day; and then the
Borrowdale came alongside and reported it too was
losing a lot of chickens and other livestock.[29]

In the middle of November there was an epidemic of
dysentery, first among the convicts and then spreading to
the marines, prevailing with 'violence and obstinacy' until
Christmas.[30] No medication seemed to work, and the
disease was only eventually eradicated by 'unremitting
attention to cleanliness'. Despite the large number who
were brought down with the dysentery over a six-week
period, only one died, a marine private named Daniel
Creswell, who experienced the 'most acute agonizing
pain' ever seen by the chief surgeon John White.

During the middle of the night on 24 November one of
the seamen on the *Prince of Wales* fell from the topsail
yard into the sea. It was so dark, and the ship was
travelling so fast, that any attempt to rescue him seemed
futile, and no search was launched.[31]

Only two weeks after leaving the Cape, Phillip decided
to split the fleet and take the fastest ships ahead. His plan

was to explore the coast of New South Wales around Botany Bay and decide on the best site for the new settlement before the others arrived.

While the decision to split the fleet may have come as a surprise to his fellow officers, Phillip had planned it before leaving England, hoping to begin on the work of establishing the settlement.

He may have suspected that Botany Bay might be a less than ideal site for settlement and that he would need a bit of time to explore other possible sites. Banks' journals would have been available to Phillip, the navy and the government, so Phillip may well have read his earlier, more negative comments concerning the bay as well as the fulsome recommendation he gave to the parliamentary committee.

Over the next two days Phillip and some of his officers transferred from the flagship *Sirius* to the smaller, faster *Supply* and ordered that the three fastest transports, the *Alexander*, the *Scarborough* and the *Friendship*, leave the rest of the fleet and sail ahead with him. Expecting to reach New South Wales a few weeks earlier than the slower ships, he also took with him some convicts with gardening and carpentry skills who could help prepare the colony for the arrival of the others. Lieutenant Clark noted:

> Lieutenant Ball of the *Supply* came on board with orders from the commander and Major Ross and took away two convicts Thomas Yardsley, a gardener and Will Haynes, a cabinetmaker . . . The commodore means to take *Scarborough* and *Alexander* with him also and that is the reason that he is taking all the gardeners and carpenters that are in the fleet in the *Supply*, to have some houses and some ground turned over against the arrival at Botany Bay.[32]

According to Philip Gidley King, who was to transfer from the *Sirius* to sail ahead with the governor on the *Supply*, Phillip hoped to arrive sufficiently far ahead of the bulk of the fleet to be able to explore more than two hundred kilometres of coastline north of Botany Bay:

> The governor flatters himself that he shall arrive at the place of our destination (Botany Bay) a fortnight before the transports, in which time he will be able to make his observations on the place whether it is a proper spot for the settlement or not and in the later case he will then have time to examine Port Stephens before the arrival of the transports on the coast.[33]

Before leaving England, Phillip had been given permission to consider sites in New South Wales other than Botany Bay. He had written to Evan Nepean the previous March while still in London asking if he was allowed 'to make the settlement in such port as I may find the most convenient and the best answer to the intentions of the Government'.[34] The government wrote back to Phillip saying 'there can be no objection to you establishing any part of the Territory'.[35] However, Phillip was reminded that he was required to release the transport ships in the fleet back to the contractor as soon as possible after arriving in New South Wales. This meant he would have to decide the location of the new colony before the bulk of the convoy arrived at its destination, rather than after.

A week before the fleet had left Portsmouth, Lord Sydney had told the Admiralty that Phillip had been given the authorisation to split the fleet:

> I am commanded to signify to your Lordships the Kings pleasure that you do authorize Captain Phillip upon his leaving the Cape of Good Hope to proceed if he thinks fit, to the said coast of New South Wales

in the *Supply* tender, leaving the convoy to be escorted
by the *Sirius*.[36]

King recorded that the three fast transports sailing with
Phillip would be in the care of Lieutenant John Shortland,
the navy-appointed agent for the transports.

Meanwhile, the bulk of the fleet was left under
the charge of John Hunter, the captain of the *Sirius*. The
other six ships that formed the second convoy included
the three slowest convict transports, the *Lady Penrhyn*,
the *Charlotte*, and the *Prince of Wales*, and the three
supply ships, the *Golden Grove*, the *Borrowdale* and the
Fishburn.

Tons of fresh water was transferred in little boats from
the *Alexander* and the *Scarborough* to the slower
transports, as it was anticipated they would be at sea
longer and would be in greater need of supplies.

It was to be another week before the winds that had
prevented the fleet from making any significant progress
finally changed and swung around behind them from the
north-west. King recorded that they were now being
swept along in 'very strong gales and a great sea'.[37] The
wind was so strong that it tore off the *Prince of Wales*'
topsail, or main topgallant yard, causing another sailor,
Yorgan Yorgannes, to be washed overboard and lost.

The *Supply* and the faster transports had taken a
different route, but they too were to encounter rough
sailing. John Easty, a sailor on the *Scarborough*, described
it as 'the heaviest sea as ever I saw'.[38]

Throughout December the four ships of the advance
party sailed further into the Great Southern Ocean. On
the *Supply* Lieutenant Philip Gidley King recorded the
discomfort of all aboard:

Had very strong gales of wind from the south west to
the north west with a very heavy sea running which

keeps this vessel almost constantly under water and renders the situation of everyone on board her, truly uncomfortable.[39]

Life for the convicts in these conditions was even more difficult. The high winds and rough seas meant they were forced to stay cramped, wet and cold below decks. The hatches were battened down for most of this leg of the journey, and they would have had very little opportunity of seeing any daylight.

As Christmas approached, the wind abated before picking up again, leading King to observe that 'the cold is in the extreme here as in England at this time of year, although it is the height of summer here'.[40]

On 3 January the *Supply*'s crew and officers saw land, which they knew to be Van Diemen's Land (Tasmania). As the four ships from the advance fleet turned around the south-eastern tip of Tasmania and headed north, they were confronted with difficult conditions. The journey of more than a thousand kilometres up the coast to Botany Bay would take them another two weeks, struggling in the face of northerly winds and an adverse current, before they were able to reach Botany Bay. Meanwhile, the *Alexander*, the *Scarborough* and the *Friendship*, which had fallen behind weeks before, caught up and arrived in the Bay a day after the *Sirius*.

If the first division of the fleet had found the going from the Cape of Good Hope to Botany Bay rough, the bigger, slower, second division also had its problems.

Immediately after the *Supply* and the three fastest transports had sailed ahead, Captain Hunter made his first big, independent decision. He ordered the seven ships under his command to change course to a more southerly route:

> I was at this time of [the] opinion that we had kept in
> too northerly a parallel to ensure strong and lasting
> westerly winds, which determined me, as soon as
> Captain Phillip had left the fleet, to steer to the
> southward and keep in a higher latitude.[41]

The decision would subject the ships under his command
to the most dangerous sailing since they left England, but
Hunter was correct. The new route proved faster, and
they would arrive in Botany Bay seven weeks later and
only a day after the last of the faster transports.

In mid-December and roughly halfway from the Cape
to Botany Bay they passed Kerguelen Island, which they
found to be 'remarkably cold . . . although it was the height
of summer'. Hunter was happy with their progress:

> We had at present every prospect of excellent passage
> to Van Dieman's land for although the wind
> sometimes shifted to the north east it seldom
> continued for more than a few hours before backing
> around again to the south west or north west.[42]

A few days before Christmas scurvy broke out among the
convicts, first on the *Prince of Wales* and then the *Charlotte*.
In the absence of fresh food, which was now close to being
exhausted, the cases were treated with essence of malt and
some wine, the only effective anti-scorbutic available.[43]

On Christmas Day the seamen worked normally and
the officers tried to celebrate. On the *Prince of Wales*
Sergeant Scott of the marines recorded that they ate beef,
pork with apple sauce, plum pudding and drank four
bottles of rum, which was the 'best we veterans could
afford'.[44] Judge David Collins on the *Sirius* said they tried
to celebrate Christmas dinner in the traditional English
way but noted that the weather was too rough to allow
any real enjoyment.

By the end of December the seas were 'mountains high'. On the *Lady Penrhyn* the water was ankle-deep on the quarterdeck, women convicts were washed out of their berths and the water had to be bailed out from below decks in buckets. On New Year's Day, according to Arthur Bowes Smyth, the sea poured through a hatchway and washed away the bedding from his cabin:

> Just as we had dined, a most tremendous sea broke in at the weather scuttle of the great cabin and ran with a great stream all across the cabin, and as the door of my cabin not to be quite closed shut the water half filled it; the sheets and the blankets being all on a flow. The water ran from the quarterdeck nearly into the great cabin, and struck against the main and missen chains with such force as at first alarmed us all greatly, but particularly me, as I believed ship was drove in pieces. No sleep this night.[45]

Newton Fowell also described the high winds and threatening seas that persisted into the New Year, in a letter to his father: 'This Year began with very bad tempestuous weather, it blew much harder than any wind we have had since our leaving England.'[46]

As the weather worsened, the fleet was forced to reduce the sail and slow down. The rolling of the ships in the rough seas was particularly difficult for the animals that had been penned on the decks. They were now in a very poor state, having had little grazing food for the seven weeks since they left the Cape. On the *Fishburn* and the *Golden Grove* about three-quarters of the chickens on board had died, which led a number of the crew to suspect they had been diseased in the Cape of Good Hope before they left. Captain John Hunter described the plight of the cattle, horses and sheep carried on ships that were not designed for such cargo:

The rolling and labouring of our ship exceedingly
distressed the cattle, which were now in a very weak
state, and the great quantities of water which we
shipped during the gale, very much aggravated their
distress. The poor animals were frequently thrown
with much violence off their legs and exceedingly
bruised by their falls.[47]

It was not until the end of the first week of January that
the bulk of the fleet passed around the bottom of
Tasmania and began the journey northwards up the coast
of New South Wales to Botany Bay. Captain Hunter had
intended to stop and collect grass for the livestock, but he
decided it would be too hazardous to land on the rocky
coastline and pressed on to Botany Bay. That night,
believing Van Diemen's Land was part of the same coast
as their destination of Botany Bay, the officers on the
Lady Penrhyn toasted 'two bumpers of claret'; one to the
success of the voyage and the other to safe anchorage in
Botany Bay.[48]

White recorded that they saw an unexpected sight
as they sailed along the coast of Tasmania: 'As we run
with the land, which is pretty high we were surprised
to see, at this season of the year, some small patches of
snow.'[49] The presence of snow and such volatile weather
at the height of the southern-hemisphere summer would
have mystified the passengers on the First Fleet.

Running along the New South Wales coast, they met
more bad weather and bad luck. Faced with a 'greater
swell than at any other period during the voyage', they
were forced to sail further out to sea when tubs
containing a number of plants for the new colony,
including bananas and grapes, were smashed and lost.[50]
During the storm six of the seven ships in the second
convoy were damaged. According to Arthur Bowes
Smyth:

> [T]he sky blackened, the wind arose and in half an
> hour more it blew a perfect hurricane, accompanied
> with thunder, lightening and rain . . . I never before
> saw a sea in such a rage, it was all over as white as
> snow . . . Every other ship in the fleet except the *Sirius*
> sustained some damage . . . During the storm the
> convict women in our ship were so terrified that most
> of them were down on their knees at prayers.[51]

Less than a week away from Botany Bay all of the food
for the animals was exhausted and there was 'nothing on
board for the stock to eat but sea bread'.[52]

The second convoy finally arrived at Botany Bay on the
evening of 19 January 1788. At ten minutes before eight
the next morning the *Sirius* was in the bay and anchored,
and the other transports 'were all safe in' by nine
o'clock.[53] Captain Hunter was surprised to learn that
Phillip and the *Supply* had reached Botany Bay only two
days beforehand and Shortland and the three fast
transports had only arrived the previous day. Phillip was
later to complain that the '*Supply*, sailing very badly, had
not permitted my gaining the advantage hoped for'.[54]

Phillip's failure to arrive earlier would cause many
problems, as he had not had the several weeks he'd hoped
for to clear land and build secure storehouses before the
bulk of the convoy arrived. But, more importantly, he had
insufficient time to examine alternative sites to Botany
Bay. Just as he had feared, Botany Bay had to be
abandoned within days because it was unsuitable.

Under pressure to empty and release the contracted
ships in the fleet, Phillip only had time to hurriedly
explore Port Jackson, twelve kilometres further north of
Botany Bay. While a better option, it would nonetheless
be a struggle to establish a viable settlement there.

9

ARRIVAL

*We set out to observe the country, on inspection rather
disappointed our hopes, being invariably sandy and
unpromising for the purposes of cultivation . . . Close
to us was the spring at which Mr Cook watered but
we did not think the water very excellent, nor did it
run freely. In the evening we returned on board, not
greatly pleased with our discoveries.*

After a remarkably successful voyage the fleet arrived in
Botany Bay without losing a ship and with fewer deaths
than most of the convoys that would bring convicts to
Australia over the next fifty years. Their joy at surviving the
voyage in such good shape was, however, short-lived when
they realised that Botany Bay was totally unsuitable for the
new settlement; it had to be abandoned in a matter of a few
days. While the British would continue to refer to Botany
Bay for many decades as the site of the penal colony in New
South Wales, no convicts ever actually settled there.

Phillip had arrived at Botany Bay on the *Supply* at a
little after two in the afternoon on 18 January 1788 and
anchored on the north side so that 'the ships that are
following might not miss the harbour'.[1]

Later the same afternoon he and his officers went
ashore to inspect the site they had been sent to colonise.

As was the custom, the naval officers in their smart uniforms were rowed to the edge of the shore, where the seamen would wade the last few metres carrying the officers on their backs to prevent them from getting wet.

Once on shore, some of the officers examined the south of the bay, while Phillip examined the northern side where, unarmed, he made contact with a group of Aboriginal people who had been watching the arrival of the Europeans from the shore. They were naked and armed with spears but, according to Philip Gidley King, proved friendly and 'directed us, by pointing, to a very fine stream of fresh water'.[2]

The next day they were 'very agreeably surprised' to see the three transports the *Alexander*, the *Scarborough* and the *Friendship* arrive safely and anchor nearby. To their even greater surprise and some consternation, at eight o'clock the following morning, Sunday 20 January, they saw 'the *Sirius* and all her convoy coming round Point Solander'.[3] The *Sirius* and the slower ships of the second convoy had in fact reached the outside of Botany Bay the night before. Had they not left their entry until the next morning, they would have arrived on the same day as the three transports.

Arthur Bowes Smyth was aboard the women's convict ship the *Lady Penrhyn*, which arrived with the second part of the fleet. He recorded the excitement and relief of those on board at finally reaching their destination:

> Saturday 19th. This morning I arose at five o'clock in hopes of seeing land, but was disappointed – The *Sirius* and all the fleet made sail about four o'clock in the morning and at 7 a.m. we discovered land about forty miles distant. The joy everyone felt upon so long wished for an event can be better conceived than expressed, particularly as it was the termination of the voyage to those who were to settle at Botany Bay, and:

it is ten weeks on Monday since we left the Cape of
Good Hope; the longest period of any we had been at
sea without touching at any port. – The sailors are
busy getting up the cables and preparing all things for
anchoring.[4]

The following day he recorded his happiness on coming
into Botany Bay and seeing the four ships of the first part
of the fleet all safely at anchor:

Sunday 20th. The *Sirius* made sail at four o'clock this
morning with a fine breeze . . . – About eight o'clock
we came abreast of Point Solander and . . . arrive at
[the] Bay, where we were very happy to find the four
ships who had parted with . . . us, all safe at anchor.
The *Supply* brig got there on Friday night, but the
Alexander, *Scarborough* and *Friendship* reached it
but the evening before us![5]

Of the more than fourteen hundred people who had
embarked, only sixty-nine had died. Many of the deaths
had occurred before the ships left Portsmouth and in the
first few weeks of the voyage, predominantly among the
old and the sick, who should never have been considered
for the journey in the first place.

On the day he arrived in Botany Bay, Arthur Phillip
had noted that they were in no way threatened by the
local Aboriginal population. When the balance of the
transports arrived, however, the newcomers witnessed a
more threatening gesture from a large band of Aboriginal
people who stood on Cape Solander shouting and waving
their spears over their heads in a way that suggested the
newcomers were not welcome.

After less than two days looking for a suitable spot to
establish their new town, the leaders of the First Fleet
were forming the opinion that Botany Bay was totally

unsuitable. It had insufficient fresh water and the bay was open to the region's strong southerly and easterly winds, which would not have provided the ships of the fleet with the necessary shelter. The only significant fertile soil was found by Phillip's colleagues on the south side of the bay, in a spot Cook had named Point Sutherland after one of his seamen who was buried there.

Several months later Phillip was to provide a long report to Lord Sydney explaining why he had so quickly abandoned Botany Bay and settled for Port Jackson.[6] Although Cook had suggested that the harbour was 'tolerably well sheltered from all winds',[7] Phillip disagreed:

> I began to examine the bay as soon as we anchored, and found, that though extensive, it did not afford shelter to ships from the easterly winds; the greater part of the bay being so shoal [shallow] that ships of even a moderate draught of water are obliged to anchor with the entrance of the bay open, and are exposed to a heavy sea that rolls in when it blows hard from the eastward. Several small runs of fresh water were found in different parts of the bay, but I did not see any situation of which there was not some strong objection.[8]

Phillip's colleagues were equally unimpressed with what they saw at Botany Bay. Captain Watkin Tench had this to say:

> We set out to observe the country, on inspection rather disappointed our hopes, being invariably sandy and unpromising for the purposes of cultivation . . . Close to us was the spring at which Mr. Cook watered but we did not think the water very excellent, nor did it run freely. In the evening we returned on board, not greatly pleased with our discoveries.[9]

Surgeon Bowes Smyth also quickly realised that Botany Bay was not the fertile paradise they had been led to expect, when he went ashore on the first night his ship arrived:

> Upon first sight one would be induced to think this a most fertile spot, as there are great numbers of very large and lofty trees, reaching almost to the water's edge, and every vacant spot between the trees appears to be covered with verdure: but upon a nearer inspection, the grass is found long and coarse, the trees very large and in general hollow and the wood itself fit for no purposes of building, or anything but the fire – The soil to a great depth is nothing but a black sand which, when exposed to the intense heat of the sun by removing the surrounding trees, is not fit for the vegetation of anything even the grass itself, then dying away, which, in the shade appears green and flourishing; add to this that every part . . . is in a manner covered with black and red ants of a most enormous size.[10]

Phillip was in Botany Bay for only three days before he set off to search for an alternative location for the new settlement. With the fleet in Botany Bay and the convicts and cargo still aboard, he departed on Monday 21 January with John Hunter, James Kelty, Judge David Collins and a number of other officers to examine Port Jackson, twelve kilometres to the north.[11]

They had very little idea what to expect at Port Jackson, as the only information about it was a brief mention in Cook's journal from eighteen years ago. Cook had made only a passing observation about what he named Port Jackson[12] as they sailed past several miles out to sea:

> Having seen everything this place [Botany Bay] afforded we at day light in the morning weighed with

a light breeze . . . [and] steered along the shore NNE
and at noon we were by observation . . . about two
or three miles from the land and abreast of a bay or
harbour wherein there appeared to be safe anchorage,
which I called Port Jackson.[13]

Phillip's three small boats reached the mouth of Port
Jackson in the early afternoon and rowed through the one
and a half kilometre gap between the north and south
headlands into the harbour. That night they pitched tents
in the small inlet on the south side, which is still called
Camp Cove today.

One of the oarsmen on Phillip's boat was the American
sailor Jacob Nagle, who recalls that on their first day in
Port Jackson he caught some fish, watched by the
governor: '[Phillip] Observed the fish I had hauled in and
asked who had caught that fish. I recollect he said that
you are the first white man that ever caught a fish in
Sydney Cove.'[14]

Mindful that more than fourteen hundred people and
many starving animals were still aboard ships in Botany
Bay awaiting instructions, Phillip quickly explored a
number of coves that might be suitable.

Later on the second day and some six kilometres
deeper into Port Jackson Phillip discovered a sheltered
bay about eight hundred metres long and four hundred
metres wide, which had fresh water running into it. He
decided it was here, and not Botany Bay, that the settlers
would found the new colony. He was to describe Port
Jackson as the 'finest harbour in the world'[15] and named
the site of the proposed settlement Sydney Cove after the
home secretary, Lord Sydney.

While he was examining Sydney Cove, a group of
Aboriginal people had come down to see the Europeans.
They appeared friendly and curious, and were fascinated
at seeing food being cooked in a metal pot.[16]

While Sydney Cove would provide a sheltered harbour and apparently more fresh water, Phillip was forced to make a hurried decision and had no time to consider what might have been better options further along the coast. In a letter to Lord Sydney he was later to explain:

> My instructions did not permit me to detain the transports a sufficient length of time to examine the coast to any considerable distance, it was absolutely necessary to be certain of a sufficient quantity of fresh water, in situation that was healthy, and which the ships might approach within a reasonable distance for the . . . landing of stores.[17]

Meanwhile, some of the convicts back in Botany Bay had been assigned to clearing land for a settlement in case Phillip was unable to find a better alternative. But, according to Surgeon White, even the best place they could find in Botany Bay was unsuitable:

> Although the spot fixed on for the town was the most eligible that could be chosen, yet I think it would never have answered, the ground around it being sandy, poor, and swampy, and but very indifferently supplied with water. The fine meadows talked of in Captain Cook's voyage I could never see, though I took some pains to find them out; nor have I ever heard of a person that has seen any parts resembling them.[18]

While waiting for Phillip's return, some of the officers went ashore to see the Aboriginal people who had come down to the bay carrying spears and shields. White fired a pistol to frighten them, and his shot pierced a shield that was standing in the sand. This, White recorded, had the desired effect, because the Aboriginal people immediately learned to 'know and dread the superiority of our arms'.

He describes how 'from the first, they carefully avoided a soldier, or any person wearing a red coat, which they seem to have marked as a fighting vesture'.[19]

Phillip and his party returned on the evening of Wednesday 23 January to find that the land clearing in Botany Bay was not going well, and he gave instructions for the entire fleet to immediately sail for Port Jackson, less than a week after its arrival in the bay.

On the morning of 24 January strong headwinds were blowing and the English decided to wait until the following day before trying to sail out of Botany Bay. While they were waiting, the crews were shocked to see two strange ships appear outside the bay. Captain Watkin Tench, on board the *Sirius*, had woken at dawn and was getting dressed when he heard the news:

> Judge my surprise on hearing from the sergeant, who ran down almost breathless to the cabin where I was dressing, that a ship had been seen off the harbours mouth. At first I only laughed but knowing the man who spoke to me to be of great veracity and hearing him repeat his information, I flew upon the deck, on which I barely set my foot, when a cry 'another sail' struck on my astonished ear.[20]

At first it was thought the ships were British, although, as the surgeon Worgan noted, 'By noon, we could by the help of our glasses discern that they had French colours flying.'[21] The ships were the *Astrolabe* and the *Boussole*, under the command of Captain La Perouse. They had been on a remarkable exploration voyage for nearly three years, having left Europe nearly two years before the First Fleet in June 1785. The two ships kept being blown to the south of the mouth of Botany Bay and were to be just as thwarted in getting in that day as the British were in getting out.

On 25 January the entire British fleet was still being blown around the bay, and all bar one of the ships again had to abandon their efforts. The ship that succeeded where the others had failed was the nimble little *Supply*. It got out at midday, carrying Phillip, a number of officers including Philip Gidley King, some marines and about forty convicts. It sailed that afternoon up to Port Jackson, where it anchored for the night. King recorded it as follows in his journal:

> The wind blowing strong from the NNE prevented . . .
> our getting out . . . [O]n the 25th . . . we were obliged
> . . . to wait for the ebb tide and at noon we weighed
> and turned out of the harbour.[22]

It seems that Governor Phillip sighted the French as the *Supply* successfully navigated its way out of Botany Bay but decided that dealing with them could wait till after the fleet was settled at Sydney Cove.

Early on the morning of the 26th Phillip and his party were rowed ashore to the spot he had chosen a few days earlier. Here the flag was planted and a little ceremony took place. Possession was taken for His Majesty, whose health, that of the queen and the Prince of Wales, and the success of the colony was drunk. A *feu de joie* was fired by a party of marines and the whole group gave three cheers.[23]

Only a few dozen marines, officers and oarsmen participated in the new country's christening ceremony, while others, including the forty convicts, witnessed it from the deck of the *Supply*.

While Phillip and his party were marking the start of the settlement of Sydney, the bulk of the fleet was still trying to sail out of Botany Bay to join them. As Surgeon Worgan recorded in his journal:

> Thursday 24th. The wind not favouring our departure
> this morning . . . Friday 25th . . . the wind coming on
> to blow hard, right in to the bay, the *Sirius* and the
> transports could not possibly get out.[24]

On the third day of trying, 26 January, the *Sirius* was the
first of the remaining ships to successfully clear the bay,
but, before it left, Captain John Hunter made brief
contact with the commander of the French ships. Hunter
had sent a lieutenant in a boat across to the French and,
shortly afterwards, Captain de Clonard came across and
introduced himself and the ships to Hunter.

Meanwhile the remaining English ships were still
having great difficulty getting away, as the wind was
blowing hard and, in the words of Ralph Clark on
the *Friendship*, there was 'a great sea rolling into the
bay'.[25] The *Charlotte* was blown off course, dangerously
close to the rocks; the *Friendship* and the *Prince of
Wales* 'could not keep in their stays' and became
entangled, which resulted in the *Friendship* losing its jib
boom and the *Prince of Wales* its mainmast staysail and
topsail.

According to Clark it was only good luck that they
were not blown onto the rocks and 'the whole on board
drowned for we should have gone to pieces. Thank God
we have got clear out as have all the ships'.[26]

Later the *Charlotte* collided with the *Friendship*, and
the surgeon Arthur Bowes Smyth claimed that his ship,
the *Lady Penrhyn*, also nearly ran aground. Bowes Smyth
was to blame the near calamity on Arthur Phillip for
insisting the fleet head immediately for Sydney Cove
when it was dangerous to do so:

> Every one blaming the rashness of the Governor
> in insisting upon the fleets working out in such
> weather, and all agreed it was next to a miracle that

some of the ships were not lost, the danger was so very great.[27]

At three in the afternoon the fleet had finally cleared Botany Bay and by four had entered Port Jackson for the eight-kilometre run up to Sydney Cove. There, according to Lieutenant Bradley of the *Sirius*, they anchored 'at the entrance to the Cove in which the *Supply* was laying and where the marines and convicts that came in her were camped. The convoy all anchored in and off the Cove before dark.'[28]

Finally, on a fine summer Saturday evening of what was to become Australia Day, 26 January, the entire fleet had anchored in and around Sydney Cove, more than eight months after leaving England.

10

STRUGGLE

*Thursday 31 January – what a terrible night it was of
thunder and lightening and rain – was obliged to get
out of my tent with nothing on but my shirt to slacken
the tent poles . . . Friday 1 February. In all the course
of my life I never slept worse . . . than I did last night –
what with the hard ground spiders, ants and every
vermin that you can think of was crawling over me.
I was glad when morning came.*

The struggle to build a new life in the harsh and
unfriendly Australian bush was about to begin. For the
next few years life would be uncomfortable, to say the
least, and most of the settlers would have no chair to sit
on, no table to eat at and no bed or cot to sleep in.

However, the first recorded impressions of Sydney
Cove were in fact quite favourable and gave no
indication that the newcomers had any inkling of the
problems that lay ahead. Chief Surgeon White was even
more effusive than Arthur Phillip when he described
Port Jackson as the finest harbour 'in the universe'. Its
many deep, protected coves would, he wrote, be capable
of providing 'safe anchorage for all the navies of
Europe'.[1]

Judge David Collins said the harbour was so naturally

beautiful that it was a shame to dump England's worst on its shores:

> If only it were possible, that on taking possession of nature as we had done, in her simplest purist garb, we might not sully that purity by the introduction of vice, profaneness and immorality, but this is not so much to be wished, was little to be expected.[2]

The unloading of the ships began in earnest on the morning of Sunday 27 January. Many of the convicts were stepping onto solid ground for the first time in more than a year.

Collins wrote of chaotic scenes as hundreds of people began to scramble out of the little rowboats and onto a shore where the dense vegetation came down almost to the water:

> The disembarkation of the troops and convicts took place from the following day, until the whole were landed. The confusion that ensued will not be wondered at, when it is considered that every man stepped from the boat literally into a wood. Parties of people were everywhere and seen variously employed; some in clearing ground for the different encampments; others in pitching tents. Or bringing up stores as were immediately wanted. And the abode of silence and tranquillity was now changed to that of noise, clamour and confusion.[3]

On that first day Captain Watkin Tench recorded an eagerness in all to begin work on the difficult task of clearing land, pitching tents and covering the unloaded stores:

> Business now sat on every brow . . . In one place a party cutting down the woods; a second setting up a

blacksmiths forge; a third dragging along stones or
provisions; here an officer pitching his marquee, with
a detachment of troops parading on one side of him,
and a cooks fire blazing up on the other.[4]

There was a particular urgency about unloading the
livestock as many cows, horses and sheep had already
died after the last of the fresh fodder had run out. On
the day the fleet had arrived in Botany Bay, fresh grass
had been cut and rowed out to the ships to keep the
weakened surviving animals alive. As soon as the fleet
arrived in Sydney Cove, the livestock were clumsily
lowered by rope into boats, rowed ashore and left to
graze on its eastern side.

Earlier in the day the governor had 'marked out the
lines for the encampment'.[5] Phillip and some of his
officers were to be camped on the eastern side, with the
freshwater stream and most of the marines on the western
side, and the convicts further to the west. The western
side of the cove was steeper and rockier, and was later to
be known as The Rocks. It was on this side that the tent
hospital of the early colony was also established.

As everyone who could be landed was working on
clearing land and pitching tents, the usual Sunday
religious observances were ignored. It was not until the
following week that the chaplain, Reverend Richard
Johnson, conducted the first church service, under a large
tree overlooking the harbour.

The following day the last of the marines and their
wives and children were brought ashore,[6] but it was to
be another ten days before the majority of the female
convicts were unloaded from their transports and rowed
to the shore, by which time a large number of tents had
been pitched for them.[7]

A number of the women convicts had somehow
managed to keep some good clothing and were rowed to

shore on their first morning in Sydney dressed in colourful dresses and pretty bonnets.

Only five convict women had been brought ashore earlier – women 'who sported the best characters on board' – to act as cooks and domestic servants. Phillip thought that landing all of the women straight away would be a distraction to the men, some of whom had been on male-only convict transports and would not have seen a woman for the best part of a year.

Phillip's caution turned out to be not unwise, because the women's eventual landing resulted in wild scenes and debauchery that shocked many of the officers. Surgeon Bowes Smyth, who had already made critical comments in his diary about the convict women, described what happened during that day, and especially during that night after the seamen later came ashore during a tumultuous storm, bringing grog with them:

> At five o'clock this morning all things were got in order for landing the whole of the women and three of the ships long boats came alongside us to receive them. The men convicts got to them very soon after they landed, and it is beyond my abilities to give a just description of the scene of debauchery and riot that ensued during the night . . . The scene which presented itself at this time and during the greater part of the night, beggars every description; some swearing, others quarrelling others singing, not in the least regarding the tempest, though so violent that the thunder that shook the ship exceeded anything I ever before had a conception of.[8]

Captain Watkin Tench spelled it out more clearly:

> While they were on board ship, the two sexes had been kept most rigorously apart; but when landed their

separation became impracticable, and would have been perhaps, wrong. Licentiousness was the unavoidable consequence, and their old habits of depravity were beginning to recur. What was to be attempted? To prevent their intercourse was impossible.[9]

The next morning, Thursday 7 February, when just about everyone was finally ashore, many with hangovers, the battalion 'under arms' was marched on parade to a piece of cleared land with colours flying and pipes playing. The convicts were forced to stand in line while the formal declaration of the colony was made.

It began with Judge David Collins' lengthy reading of Governor Phillip's commission. A number of officers were surprised at the apparent broadth of powers given to him. Ralph Clark noted that he had 'never heard of any one single person having so great a power invested in him as the Governor has by his commission'.[10]

This was followed by a speech from Phillip in which, according to Judge Collins, the governor promised good treatment of those convicts who deserved it and threatened severe punishment and execution for wrongdoers:

> He should ever be ready to shew approbation and encouragement to those who proved themselves worthy of them by good conduct and attention to orders; while on the other hand, such as were determined to act in opposition to propriety, and observe a contrary conduct, would inevitably meet with the punishment they deserved.[11]

Phillip also recommended to the convicts that they marry each other and threatened that those guilty of 'indiscriminate and illegal intercourse would be punished with the greatest severity and rigour'.[12] Bowes Smyth described Phillip's speech as a 'harangue':

He also assured them that if they tried to get into the women's tents of a night there were positive orders for firing upon them, that they were idle, not more than two hundred out of six hundred were at work; that the industrious should not labour for the idle; if they did not work they should not eat. In England thieving poultry was not punished with death, in consequence of their being so easily supplied but here a fowl was of the utmost consequence to the settlement, as well as every other species of stock, as they were reserved for breed, therefore stealing the most trifling of stock or provisions should be punished with death; that however much severity might mitigate against his humanity and feelings . . . justice demanded such rigid execution of the laws.[13]

After the parade the officers were invited to the governor's tent for a celebratory dinner at which 'many loyal and public toasts were drank'.[14] Lieutenant Ralph Clark felt the occasion was spoiled by the maggots in the cold collation of mutton that had been killed the day before and complained that 'nothing will keep 24 hours in this country'.[15]

Unloading the stores and provisions would take many weeks. Initially some were simply put on the ground and covered until storehouses could be built, but the theft of food and grog was an immediate problem, which severe punishment and even executions failed to prevent. Much of the food stored on the ground was also lost to insects and parasites, many of which were completely new to the European settlers.

A week after landing in Port Jackson, on 1 February, Arthur Phillip asked Lieutenant King to pay a courtesy call on the French captain La Perouse, who was still anchored in Botany Bay. King left at 2 am on 2 February, to be rowed in a cutter with Lieutenant Dawes and a marine escort, and had been instructed that when he met with La Perouse he was to 'offer him whatever he might have occasion for'.[16] It took eight hours to row the twelve kilometres to Botany Bay, and they reached the French ships at around ten o'clock that morning.

King recalled that the English delegation 'were received with the greatest politeness and attention' by La Perouse and his fellow officers aboard the *Boussole*.

He was informed that he was not the first of the English to visit; a number of convicts had already walked the twelve kilometres overland from Port Jackson to Botany Bay and had been refused the opportunity of escaping on the French ships.

The French thanked King for the offer of assistance and made exactly the same offer of help to the English. La Perouse said he expected to be back in France in fifteen months but had enough supplies on board to last three years and would be happy to provide Phillip with anything he needed.

During their cordial meeting King learned of the remarkable voyage of the French since they had left the French port of Brest three years earlier. They had sailed around Cape Horn and up the Pacific coast from Chile to California and Kamschatka in eastern Siberia before sailing south to Easter Island, Macao in China, Manila in the Philippines, the Friendly Isles, the Sandwich Isles and Norfolk Island.

When the French ships had been in Kamschatka, they had been told that the British intended establishing a colony at Botany Bay, and so La Perouse was surprised to see nothing there when he arrived except the English fleet attempting to leave. As Judge David Collins noted:

> It must naturally create some surprise in M. de la
> Perouse to find our fleet abandoning the harbour at

the very time when they were preparing to anchor in it. Indeed he afterwards said, that 'until he had looked round him in Botany Bay he could not divine the cause of our quitting it . . . having heard at Kamschatka of the intended settlement, he imagined he should have found a town built and a market established.[17]

King was also told of how a number of French officers and crew had been massacred and many others wounded by natives on Mauna Island in the Isles des Navigateurs less than two months before, on 11 December. Among the thirteen who were killed were the captain of the *Astrolabe*, M. De Langle, eight officers, four seamen and a boy.

La Perouse explained that the French had been on good terms with the islanders for a period of several days, during which the French had 'furnished . . . every article of stock in the greatest profusion for barter'[18] and trading had taken place. Then, when everything was ready for their departure, De Langle asked La Perouse if they could collect more fresh water from the island, and two longboats and two smaller boats were duly sent ashore.

On landing the boats were surrounded by locals who 'were armed with short heavy clubs by which means they rendered the French arms useless'.[19] The order to fire the muskets was given and the French believe about thirty natives were killed, but not before many of their own were also killed.

A number of the French managed to swim from the longboats and scramble onto the two rowboats before making their escape back to their ships.

La Perouse had also lost twenty-one crew when two boats were destroyed in the surf off the Alaskan coast in July 1786.

Despite these tragic losses La Perouse said that not a single person had died on the French ships from scurvy during their three years at sea, suggesting that the French were even more effective at managing the disease than the English.

King describes the French vessels as having been 'fitted out with the greatest liberality'. Governor Phillip had had to fight the bureaucracy for all his supplies and had left Portsmouth short of many essentials, but La Perouse's situation, according to King, had been very different:

> Monsieur de La Perouse told me that the king told him to get whatever he wanted and added that if he was now at Brest and had to equip his ships for the remainder of his voyage, that he could not think of any article that he should be in need of.[20]

King was particularly impressed with the array of scientists on the French expedition, which included botanists, astronomers and natural historians and an impressive range of astrological and navigational equipment. The French also carried three timepieces on each ship, whereas the English carried only one for the entire fleet.

After dining with La Perouse and his fellow officers, King and his colleagues were taken ashore to where the French had established a stockade with two cannons around a number of tents housing a range of scientific equipment.

King said his farewells on the night of 4 February and at five o'clock the next morning left to row back to the English settlement in Port Jackson. The return boat trip took even longer, as they were 'obliged to row all the way against the wind and a great swell', and King and his party did not reach Sydney Cove until 7 pm, some fourteen hours later.

Over the next few weeks there was little further contact between the English, busy trying to establish their new home, and the French, who were preparing for the next leg of their long voyage of exploration. However, shortly before the French left Botany Bay Captain John Hunter of the *Sirius* paid them an informal visit and, like King, was impressed by the cordiality and hospitality of his hosts:

> At the beginning of March at which time . . . the two French ships were preparing to leave the coast, I determined to visit M de La Perouse before he should depart, I accordingly with a few officers sailed around to Botany Bay in the *Sirius* long boat. We stayed for two days on board the *Boussole* and were most hospitably and politely entertained and very much pressed to pass a longer time with them.[21]

At the very time that Hunter and his party had gone to visit the French, Judge David Collins described how the captain of the *Astrolabe*, Monsieur de Clonard, came from Botany Bay 'to bring round some dispatches from Monsieur de La Perouse, which that officer requested might be forwarded to the French ambassador at the court of London, by the first transports that sailed for England'.[22]

Within two more weeks the French quietly left Botany Bay, with the two commanders, Phillip and La Perouse, never having met. The *Astrolabe* and the *Boussole* were never seen again and were believed to have sunk off the coast of the New Hebrides with all the crew drowned.

Back in Sydney the new settlers were shocked by the harshness and volatility of the climate, even though it was the middle of the southern-hemisphere summer. Less than a week after arriving, five sheep belonging to the lieutenant-governor and quartermaster were killed by lightning under a tree during a heavy storm. Phillip noted that the branches and trunk of the tree 'were shivered and rent in a very extraordinary manner' and was later to report that nothing had prepared them for the savageness of the weather: 'This country is subject to very heavy storms of thunder and lightening, several trees have been set on fire and some sheep and dogs killed in the camp since we landed.'[23]

A number of the other members of the First Fleet, including the surgeon from the *Sirius*, George Worgan, also recorded their surprise at the violence of the local climate, for which they were totally unprepared:

> The thunder and lightning are astonishingly awful here, and by the heavy gloom that hangs over the woods at the time these elements are in commotion and from the nature and violence done to many trees we have reason to apprehend that much mischief can be done by lightning here.[24]

Lieutenant Ralph Clark of the marines recorded in his journal how difficult it was to sleep in the first week during the kind of tumultuous summer storms that he had never experienced in England:

> Thursday 31 January – what a terrible night it was of thunder and lightening and rain – was obliged to get out of my tent with nothing on but my shirt to slacken the tent poles . . . Friday 1 February. In all the course of my life I never slept worse my dear wife than I did last night – what with the hard ground spiders, ants and every vermin that you can think of was crawling over me. I was glad when morning came.[25]

Watkin Tench was later to describe the fierceness and changeability of the hot summer winds, which were 'like a blast from a heated oven'.[26] The temperature one day 'peaked at a hundred and nine degrees farhenheight, which killed some of the vegetables that had been planted'. He went on:

> It is changeable beyond any other I have ever heard of;
> but no phenomena sufficiently accurate to reckon upon
> are found to indicate the approach of alteration ...
> clouds, storms and sunshine pass in rapid succession.
> Of rain, we found in general not a sufficiency, but
> torrents of water sometimes fall. Thunderstorms in
> summer are common and very tremendous.[27]

The settlers were having great difficulty clearing the tough
Australian bush. They found that many of the tools they
had brought with them from England were not strong
enough, particularly the wood-cutting tools, for the
gnarled hardwoods of Australia. Joseph Banks may have
been right in saying there was 'abundant timber', but, as
Phillip was to report, the new settlers were to find the
Australian gum trees far from ideal for building with:

> The timber is well described in Captain Cooks voyage
> but unfortunately it had one very bad quality, which
> puts us to great inconvenience; I mean the large gum
> tree, which splits and warps in such a manner when
> used green and to which necessity obliged us, that a
> store house boarded up with this wood rendered it
> useless.[28]

Captain Tench said that the local timber was close to
unusable and described how it had delayed the construction of buildings:

> The species of trees are few, and, I am concerned
> to add, the wood universally of so bad a grain as to
> almost preclude a possibility of using it; the increase
> of labour occasioned by this in our buildings has been
> such, as nearly exceed belief.[29]

Surgeon White also noted the lack of suitable building
materials in his journal in March 1788:

The principal business going forward at present is erecting cabbage-tree huts for the officers, soldiers, and convicts; some storehouses, &c.; and a very good hospital; all which in the completion will cost a great deal of time and trouble, as the timber of this country is very unfit for the purpose of building. Nor do I know any one purpose for which it will answer except for fire-wood; and for that it is excellent: but in other respects it is the worst wood that any country or climate ever produced, although some of the trees, when standing, appear fit for any use whatever, masts for shipping not excepted. Strange as it may be imagined, no wood in this country, though sawed ever so thin, and dried ever so well, will float. Repeated trials have only served to convince me that, immediately on immersion, it sinks to the bottom like a stone.[30]

The landscape was foreign and the newcomers had no knowledge of how best to exploit the natural resources. In another contrast with the La Perouse expedition, which brought scientists and botanists, Phillip, although an experienced farmer, was later to confess that his lack of knowledge of this strange new environment was making the task of establishing the colony more difficult:

I must beg leave to observe, with regret, that being myself without the smallest knowledge of botany, I am without one botanist, or even an intelligent gardener in the colony; it is not therefore in my power to give more than a superficial account of the produce of this country, which has such a variety of plants that I cannot with all my ignorance help being convinced that it merits the attention of the naturalist and the botanist.[31]

Sydney had two great advantages over Botany Bay: fresh water and a sheltered harbour. However, very soon the settlers were to realise that not only was the timber virtually unusable, but the local soil was poor and they would have trouble trying to grow their own food.

After only a few weeks the general health of the settlers began to deteriorate and there was an outbreak of the scurvy that had been kept at bay for so much of the long voyage from England. There were already too few workers available to help build the new settlement, and the few skilled carpenters were committed to repairing the transport ships that were soon to return home to England:

> The people were healthy when landed but the scurvy has for some time appeared among them and now rages in the most extraordinary measure. Only sixteen carpenters could be hired from the ships and several of the carpenters were sick. It was now the middle of February; the rains began to fall very heavy and pointed out the necessity of hutting people; convicts were therefore appointed to assist the detachment in this work.[32]

The tent hospital established on the western side of the cove was soon filled with cases of camp dysentery and scurvy. Chief Surgeon John White said of the patients, 'More pitiable objects were perhaps never seen.'[33]

Back in London, when botanist Joseph Banks heard of the outbreak of scurvy in that first winter he was critical of the settlers' ability to cope. He suggested that the colony should learn to find and eat the local 'culinary vegetables': 'They must by degrees learn more and more the use of those [vegetables] which are found wild in the country. I think it will be useless to send out essence of malt to them as a medicine.'[34]

But Surgeon White protested that while he had found a 'small berry like a white current' and a native blueberry called *Leptomeria aceda* that proved to be a good antiscorbutic, it is 'far from sufficient to remove the scurvy', which 'prevails with great violence'.[35]

The newcomers could have learned something from the local inhabitants, but a belief of racial superiority prevented them from taking any lessons from the Aboriginal people, who had survived here – despite the scarce resources – for thousands of years.

The new settlers had, as mentioned earlier, encountered local Aboriginal people on the first day they had landed in Botany Bay, and again when they first came to Port Jackson. On both occasions there had been no violence, which gave Phillip and his colleagues confidence that the Aboriginal people would not be a problem when they moved to Sydney Cove.

In the instructions given to Phillip the British Government had made it clear that it wanted good relations, if possible, with the locals, 'and to conciliate their affections, enjoining all our subjects to live in amity and kindness with them'.[36]

Over the first few months of the new settlement there was little contact, but as the year progressed there were a number of incidents where convicts died, and similar incidents where Aboriginal people died, which would add to increasing hostility between the white and black peoples. This hostility would shape relationships not only for those who arrived with the First Fleet but also for the settlers of the next two centuries.

Erecting buildings proved difficult and slow. It took days for a team of men to cut down a single tree, drag it to the saw pit and cut it into usable strips of timber. There were only sixteen ship's carpenters, most of whom were kept busy on their ships before leaving for their return journey

within a few months of arriving. This left the fledgling
colony with only twelve convicts with carpentry skills.

Initially the entire settlement lived in tents, and even
after two years most settlers had only graduated to living
in crude shacks made of timber beams against which they
would lay bark from the local cabbage tree.

These 'little edifices'[37] proved to be ineffective shelters
in the heaviest weather, when rain would pour through
the doors and cracks. In the early years there was no
sewerage system and no established roads, and during
heavy rain the paths would become fast-running filthy
streams that would undermine and flood the little
dwellings. More than two years after arriving, Judge
David Collins witnessed the devastation caused by floods,
as heavy rains washed many of the convicts' hovels away:
'The rain came down in torrents, filling up every trench
and cavity, which had been dug about the settlement, and
causing much damage to the miserable mud tenements,
which were occupied by the convicts.'[38]

The building of better accommodation was delayed; it
was a higher priority to erect public stores that would
provide security from theft, insects and the weather. It
would be several months, nevertheless, before the first
storehouse could be built. Measuring one hundred feet
long and twenty-five feet wide (thirty by seven and a half
metres), it was used for Sydney's first church service under
shelter before the provisions were moved in.

It had been expected that religion would play a big
role in the new colony, and the responsibility for faith
was vested in the chaplain of the settlement, Reverend
Richard Johnson. Johnson soon became one of the
busiest men in the colony. He held services, either in
the open air or in a storehouse, performed all the
functions of the church – baptisms, marriages, burials –
attended the execution of condemned men and worked
hard among the convicts.

It would be more than five years before a temporary church of wooden posts, wattle and plaster was built, before which Johnson had no place to conduct divine services except for any hut that happened to be empty.[39]

The reverend was to marry a number of convicts within months of arriving. Judge David Collins said that while the marriages were encouraged, many took place for the wrong reasons:

> It was soon observed, with satisfaction, that several couples were announced for marriage; but on strictly scrutinising the motive, it was found in several instances to originate in the idea, that the married people would meet with various little comforts and privileges that were denied to those in a single state; and some, on not finding those expectations realised, repented, wished and actually applied to restore their former situations.[40]

Still, many marriages lasted. Mary Parker had been convicted in the Old Bailey in April 1786 for stealing some clothing and cloth valued at three pounds, two shillings and sixpence and sentenced to seven years' transportation. She sailed on the First Fleet on the *Lady Penrhyn* and met and married John Small in Sydney. He had been convicted in Devon for assault and robbery in March 1785 and had sailed to the settlement on the *Charlotte*.

When they were married by the Reverend Johnson under a tree in Sydney Cove in October 1788, more than fifty weddings had already been performed in the new colony.

Mary and John would have seven children, and their descendants would become one of the largest of a number of convict families in Australia today who can still trace their ancestry back to the First Fleet.[41]

The marines had been promised a barracks, but when it still had not been built at the onset of winter they built

their own shelter with the help of some of the ships'
carpenters, as Tench described:

> As winter was fast approaching, it became necessary
> to secure ourselves in quarters which might shield us
> from the cold . . . The erection of barracks for the
> soldiers was projected and the private men of each
> company undertook to build for themselves two
> wooden houses of sixty-eight feet in length and
> twenty-three feet in breadth.[42]

The first substantial buildings were rectangular timber
structures measuring about twelve feet by nine feet (three
and a half by two and three-quarter metres). The corner
posts were about six inches (fifteen centimetres) square
and buried deep in the ground, with other posts placed at
intervals of about three feet (almost one metre) to hold up
the timber wall panels. The roofs were of thatch, or of
reeds spread between timber 'battens'.

By the middle of the first year there were only four of
these buildings completed, which Phillip needed to secure
the stores behind strong walls and under lock and key.

The construction of brick or secure stone buildings
would take even longer. Although there was plenty of
good stone and clay for bricks, there was no known local
source of lime, traditionally used to make the cement that
would bind the bricks together. Crushed and burned
oyster shells were used as a substitute.[43]

Even the governor lived in a framed tent for the first
eighteen months of the colony. His tent, made by Smith &
Company in St George's Fields and brought out from
England, was set up on the eastern side of Sydney Cove.
Phillip complained it was 'neither wind nor water
proof'.[44]

Finally Phillip was able to leave his tent, as the first
brick building to be completed was the governor's house.

It was officially opened on the king's birthday, in June 1789, nearly eighteen months after the fleet arrived. When building had begun, Phillip had laid a foundation stone with the inscription:

> ARTHUR PHILLIP, ESQ.
> Captain General in and over his Majesty's territory of New South Wales, and its dependencies;
> Arrived in this country on the 18th day of January, 1788, with the first settlers;
> And on the 15th day of May, in the same year, the first of these stones was laid.

The imposing two-storey, double-fronted house, with its nine large windows across the front and two smaller windows on either side of the arched doorway, would be the governor's official residence for fifty-seven years, before it was demolished and replaced with an even larger dwelling a few hundred metres away. Some of the foundations of the original house remain today, under the corner of Bridge and Phillip Streets.

Because there was no architect in the colony, the governor's house was designed and built by the convict brickmaker James Bloodsworth. In addition to the governor's residence Bloodsworth was responsible for the early establishment of the colony's first brickworks, about a mile from Sydney Cove at what later became the Haymarket at the end of Darling Harbour. The First Fleet had only brought out five thousand bricks, but with abundant clay and plenty of water the Brickfield, as the site was called, was quickly producing a large quantity of bricks.

Brickmaking was back-breaking work, and as there were no carts the completed bricks had to be carried nearly two kilometres from the brickworks to the building site at Sydney Cove. George Worgan was

impressed with how quickly the brickworks had been
established:

> I walked out today as far as the brick grounds, it is a
> pleasant road through the wood about a mile or two
> from the village for from the number of little huts and
> cots that appear now, just above the ground, it has a
> villatick [village like] appearance. I see they have made
> between twenty and thirty-thousand bricks and they
> were employed in digging out a kiln and for the
> burning of them.[45]

No doubt grateful for the fine house, Governor Arthur
Phillip pardoned Bloodsworth in 1790 and appointed him
superintendent of the colony's buildings.

James Bloodsworth had been convicted in the Kingston
on Thames court of stealing and sentenced to seven years'
transportation in October 1785. In the colony he was to
partner Sarah Bellamy. Although it is not known if they
ever married, they had eight children together. Sarah was
only 17 years old when she was convicted in the Worcester
Assizes for stealing money and sentenced to seven years'
transportation, only a few months before Bloodsworth.

Bloodsworth decided against returning to England at
the end of his sentence and chose to stay in Sydney. When
he died in 1804, he was afforded a flattering obituary in
the *Sydney Gazette*, Sydney's first newspaper:

> On Wednesday last died, generally lamented Mr.
> James Bloodsworth, for many years Superintendent of
> Builders in the Employ of the Government. He came
> to the colony among its first inhabitants in the year
> 1788 and obtained the appointment shortly after his
> arrival. The first house in this part of the Southern
> Hemisphere was by him erected and most of the
> public buildings since have been under his direction.[46]

After six months a few buildings other than the storehouse had been completed, including a blacksmith's shack and a guardhouse on the eastern side of Sydney Cove. The governor's house was also under construction. Nearby were less substantial huts for the Reverend Richard Johnson and his wife Mary, Judge David Collins and a number of other officials.

Phillip now wanted the more permanent buildings to be positioned in a less haphazard manner and had plans for the building of an orderly city, with streets up to sixty metres wide. However, the plans were never implemented.

While building work was forging ahead slowly but steadily, moves towards self-sufficiency in the production of food were progressing rather less well. The settlers had only limited success at growing food and exploiting the local natural resources.

Everyone was issued a weekly food ration, convicts and marines alike, although the marines were also given their grog ration. In the early days the officers fared better, especially on celebratory occasions such as the king's birthday in June, where they were treated to a feast of mutton, pork, duck, fowl, port Madeira and good English porter. The king's birthday was a major event in the colony's calendar, and even the convicts were given rum.

To begin with the food ration included salted beef, salted pork, rice, peas and flour. However, over the next two years the allocation would be progressively reduced as the colony ran out of food. Eventually even the officers would be forced to accept starvation rations.

The seeds that had been brought from Rio de Janeiro and the Cape, including lemons, limes, figs, grapes and oranges, were sown but fared badly. Surgeon George Worgan recorded that:

> Indigo, coffee, ginger, castor nut oranges, lemons and limes, firs and oaks, have vegetated from seed, but whether from an unfriendly deleterious quality of the soil or the season, nothing seems to flourish vigorously long.[47]

Worgan's own attempt to grow vegetables was equally unsuccessful:

> I put peas and broad beans in, soon after I arrived (February) the peas podded in three months, the beans are still in blossom (June) and neither plants are above a foot high, and out of five rows of the peas each three foot in length, I shall not get above twenty pods, however my soil is too sandy.[48]

Many of the other officers also developed their own small plots of land, but these too proved to be unproductive in the poor soil around Sydney and were 'successively abandoned'[49] as farming moved west of Sydney.

The settlers had found some local wild vegetables to supplement their diet but only a limited amount, not enough to sustain a colony of well over a thousand people. What they found included a plant resembling sage near the seashore, a kind of wild spinach and a small shrub with greenish leaves.

Arthur Phillip established government farms and gardens on which the convicts were obliged to work during the week. However, due to the quality of the soil, they did not prove as productive as hoped.

The settlers had only limited success at fishing. A number of species that had been part of the local Aboriginal diet were rapidly depleted when extensively harvested to feed the new settlement, which had many more mouths to feed. This certainly seems to have been the case with the giant stingrays that in Cook's time had been so prevalent that he initially called Botany Bay 'Stingray Bay'. When Cook had anchored in the bay, some of the rays were so heavy that they needed to be gutted in the water and still weighed hundreds of pounds when pulled aboard.

Captain Tench, who regularly fished all night when the colony was short of food, described the slim pickings thus: 'the universal voice of all professional fishermen is that they never fished in a country where success was so precarious and uncertain'.[50]

Occasionally the pot was improved by the addition of a bird or an animal (including emus and kangaroos), but these too soon became scarcer around Sydney.

One local plant that attracted the newcomers was the sarsaparilla vine, which looked like a bay leaf, tasted a little like liquorice root and was found to be a good substitute for tea. Chief Surgeon White used it medicinally, finding it to be a good 'pectoral', for clearing the respiratory tract.[51]

'Sweet tea', as it became known, was thought to have a number of restorative and health benefits. John Nicol, who was to sail as a steward on the *Lady Juliana* in the Second Fleet, found it was already being widely used in Sydney when he arrived and brought some back to England via China:

> They have an herb in the colony they call sweet tea. It is infused and drank like the china tea. I liked it much; it requires no sugar and is both bitter and sweet. There was an old female convict, her hair quite grey with age, her face shrivelled, who was suckling a child she had born in the colony. Everyone went to see her, and I among the rest. It was a strange sight, her hair quite white. Her fecundity was ascribed to the sweet tea. I brought away with me two bags of it, as

presents for my friends; but two of our men became
quite ill of the scurvy, and I allowed them the use of
it, which soon cured them, but reduced my store.
When we came to China, I showed it to my Chinese
friends, and they bought it with avidity, and impugned
me for it, and a quantity of the seed I had likewise
preserved. I let them have the seed and only brought a
small quantity of the herb to England.[52]

The sarsaparilla leaves would attract a lot of attention in
London after the publicity surrounding the First Fleet
convict Mary Bryant, who escaped from Sydney with her
husband, two children and seven other convicts. The
party managed to reach Koepang in Timor before being
recaptured, and Mary Bryant was one of five who
survived and were eventually returned to London. Her
sensational story generated support and sympathy and
she was eventually pardoned with the help of James
Boswell. She famously gave him as a thank-you present
some sarsaparilla leaves that she had somehow kept
throughout her ordeal.

The small amount of produce that was locally grown
or caught notwithstanding, the weekly ration was less
than adequate from the start, and many convicts ate all
their food before the next issue and then resorted to
stealing to survive. This left those who had had their food
stolen with little option but to steal from someone else.

Almost all the crimes committed in the early days of
the colony involved the theft of food. Captain Tench
noted that it was surprising how 'few crimes of deep rye,
or a hardened nature have been perpetuated during the
first few years'.[53]

The first criminal court in the new colony was
convened only two weeks after landing, on Monday
11 February, to hear charges against a number of convicts.
One was found guilty of assault and sentenced to one

hundred and fifty lashes, and a second was banished for a week on a small rocky island with only bread and water for stealing a biscuit from another convict. The third was found guilty of stealing a plank of wood and sentenced to fifty lashes but later forgiven, and the sentence not carried out.

Judge David Collins said the mildness of the first punishments seemed to have encouraged rather than deterred others from committing more serious offences. Before the end of the month the court was reconvened to hear evidence of a plan by some convicts to rob the public stores. One of the convicts, Thomas Barrett, was the first to be hanged in the new colony, but his colleagues were given a last-minute pardon. As Surgeon John White recorded in his journal:

> February 27th. Thomas Barrett, Henry Lovell, and Joseph Hall, were brought before the criminal court and tried for feloniously and fraudulently taking away from the public store beef and pease, the property of the crown. They were convicted on the clearest evidence, and, sentence of death being passed on them, they were, about six o'clock the same evening, taken to the fatal tree, where Barrett was launched into eternity, after having confessed to the Rev. Mr. Johnson, who attended him, that he was guilty of the crime, and had long merited the ignominious death which he was about to suffer, and to which he said he had been brought by bad company and evil example. Lovell and Hall were respited until six o'clock the next evening. When that awful hour arrived, they were led to the place of execution, and, just as they were on the point of ascending the ladder, the judge advocate arrived with the governor's pardon, on condition of their being banished to some uninhabited place.[54]

Within a week convicts Daniel Gordon and John Williams were tried and convicted of stealing wine. Because Williams was regarded as an 'ignorant black youth', the court recommended that the governor show him mercy, and he was accordingly pardoned. Gordon, who was also black, was sentenced to death, but at the gallows this was changed to banishment.[55]

The following day James Freeman was tried for stealing seven pounds of flour from another convict. He was convicted and sentenced to be hanged, but while under the ladder, with the rope about his neck, he was offered his free pardon on condition of performing the duty of the common executioner as long as he remained in the country, 'which, after some little pause, he reluctantly accepted'. William Shearman, his accomplice, was sentenced to receive 'on his bare back, with a cat-o'-nine-tails, three hundred lashes, which were inflicted'.[56]

Within six months of arriving, as the thieving escalated, Collins argued that harsher punishments were unavoidable:

> Exemplary punishments seemed about this period to be growing daily more necessary. Stock was often killed, huts and tents broken open, and provisions constantly stolen, particularly about the latter part of the week; as many of those unthrifty people, taking no care to husband their provisions through the seven days that they were intended to last them, had consumed the whole by the end of the third or fourth day.[57]

The floggings were savage but were not designed to incapacitate the convicts. As a later account describes, unless it was night time, the convict was expected to go back to work immediately after the punishment:

He was immediately sent to work, his back like
bullocks liver and most likely his shoes full of blood
and not permitted to go to the hospital until next
morning when his back would be washed by the
doctors mate and a little hog's lard spread on with a
piece of tow, and so off to work . . .[58]

It was the theft of food that led to the decision to grow
vegetables on what was to become known as Garden
Island, about two kilometres out from Sydney Cove in
Port Jackson. It was felt that the vegetables would have a
better chance of being harvested on the island, as it was
more difficult for thieves to reach.

For most of the convicts life in the new settlement was
harsh, with poor accommodation and inadequate food
that lacked nutrition. Conditions were crowded, with
more than a thousand people packed into an area of little
more than two square kilometres. It was little different
from living in a prison; there were no bars and fences, but
equally there was nowhere to go except into the seemingly
endless bush.

Most of the convicts felt no commitment to the building
of a new society. For most, beginning a colony on the other
side of the world would have been daunting. They had
been banished from their homeland. Few believed they
would ever see their home or loved ones again.

While many wanted to return to England after their
sentences had been served out, Britain made it clear that
they were not wanted and that they should be provided
with no assistance or cooperation if they tried to arrange
a passage home. Governor Phillip was told in no
uncertain terms that the government thought the convicts
were incapable of living honestly in Britain and should be
encouraged to stay away. Phillip was also told that the
convicts would have to arrange and pay for their own

passages home – which was extremely unlikely, because practically none of them had money for the fare.

After the transport ships that had brought the convicts out to New South Wales had left for their journey home, the convicts would have despaired all the more of ever getting back to England.

11

FRICTION IN THE SETTLEMENT

*We have laboured incessantly since we arrived here to
raise all sorts of vegetables and even at this distant
period we can barely supply our tables, his Excellency
not excepted. This together with the miserable state of
the natives and scarcity of animals, are convincing proofs
of the badness of the country. You will no doubt have a
flattering public account but you may rely on what I
have advanced. Every gentleman here, two or three
excepted, concur with me in opinion and sincerely wish
the expedition may be recalled.*

Between the convicts and their masters was a wide
cultural and social chasm. The officers showed little com-
prehension or understanding of the convicts, whom they
regarded in every respect as inferior. The differences
extended even to language, as many of the convicts spoke
different dialects and often could not be understood by
the officers. Captain Watkin Tench refers to a number of
the convicts who spoke a 'flash' or 'kitty' language and
required a translator when they were being tried in the
colony's criminal court, which was now up and running.[1]

The officers' low opinion of the convicts worsened the
longer they were forced to coexist in the struggling
settlement. Several months after arriving in Sydney,

Surgeon John White said that the convicts were so hardened in wickedness and depravity that many were totally insensible to the fear of corporal punishment, or even death itself.[2]

The convicts were assigned to work from 7 am till 3 pm each day and on Saturday until 12 pm, usually on construction or on the vegetable farms. Outside these hours they were free to work for themselves. However, Phillip was to complain that the convicts were lazy and not useful for the building of the new settlement: 'The convicts, naturally indolent, having none to attend them but overseers drawn from amongst themselves and who fear to exert any authority, makes this work go on very slowly.'

Within six months of arriving, Phillip had written to Nepean asking for more thought to be given to selecting the convicts who were sent out: 'In our present situation I hope that few convicts will be sent out for one year at least, except carpenters, masons and bricklayers, or farmers who can support themselves and assist in supporting others.'[3]

The convict women had even fewer skills to contribute to the building of the colony. Captain Tench was moved to remark that most of the women 'lived in a state of total idleness, except for a few who are kept at work in making pegs for tiles, and picking up shells for burning into lime'.[4]

Phillip, in a letter to Lord Sydney, stated that he thought the colony had no future as a convict settlement and suggested that free settlers, who could use the convicts to develop the place, were what was needed. He had no confidence that the convicts at work could be effectively supervised by the military, but thought settlers with an interest in their own enterprises would be able to get more out of them:

> Your Lordship will, I hope judge it expedient to send out settlers to whom a certain number of convicts may

be given; they my Lord, will be interested in cultivating the land and when a few carpenters and
bricklayers are sent out who will act as overseers, and
have some little interest in the labour of the convicts
who are under their care, a great deal of labour will
be done by them who are employed on public works.[5]

Phillip had written to Evan Nepean with the same
message: 'If fifty farmers were sent out with their families
they would do more in one year in rendering this colony
independent of their mother country as to provisions,
than a thousand convicts.'[6]

The low opinion they held of the convicts did not
prevent a number of the officers from living with
convict women and having children, even if the officers in
question had a wife and other children waiting back in
England.

At the end of their sentenced terms the male convicts
could be granted land to become farmers. They were
allowed forty acres of land and an additional four acres
for each of their children. Women convicts were ineligible
for land grants when their term expired; they could either
marry someone with land or return to England. All those
who took land were obliged to live on it and cultivate it,
during which time they could continue to draw rations
from the public store for twelve months.

Phillip had his doubts about the ability of the convicts
to make good farmer settlers. Few had a background in
farming and fewer felt any commitment to building a new
life in this land, where they had been forced to live.

A further complication arose when an increasing
number of convicts came to Phillip claiming their term of
sentence had expired, only to find that their freedom
could not be confirmed because the record of their convictions had not been sent out from England:

The masters of the transports having left with the
agents the bonds and whatever papers they received
that related to the convicts, I have no account of the
time for which the convicts are sentenced, or the dates
of their convictions; some of them, by their own
account, have a little more than a year to remain,
and, I am told, will apply for permission to return to
England.[7]

The convicts were understandably unhappy. Phillip
rejected their claim that they should be paid wages and
suggested Judge Collins take their details until the matter
could be settled.

Even two years later the situation was still not
resolved. On 15 April 1790 Phillip again sought instructions as to what he should do with convicts who claimed
their sentences were up:

I have to request that the necessary instructions may
be sent out respecting those convicts who say their
terms of transportation are expired of which we have
a very great number, very few who are being desirous
of becoming settlers in this country.[8]

Four months later he was to write again to say that there
were now thirty convicts claiming they had served their
time and would want passages back to England.

The first convict to seek a grant of land in the new
colony was James Ruse, who as a 22-year-old had been
convicted of stealing in the Cornwall Assizes in July 1782
and sentenced to death. He was reprieved to be transported for seven years to Africa but spent almost all of the
next five years aboard the *Dunkirk* hulk in Plymouth
before being sent with the First Fleet on the *Scarborough*.
In July 1789 he claimed his sentence had expired and
requested a land grant so he could become a farmer. He

was one of the minority of convicts who had some
farming experience.

In the absence of Ruse's records, however, Arthur
Phillip would not initially grant him land. He relented in
November 1789 and allowed him to farm an allotment
until he could be given title when proof of his freedom
arrived. With the help of Phillip he was given clothes,
food, seeds, livestock, a hut and some help to clear the
land. Ruse proved to be industrious and managed to
make a success of farming.

Although not the first person to cultivate land in the
colony on his own behalf, Ruse was the first ex-convict to
seek a grant, as most of the other emancipated convicts
showed no inclination to take up agriculture. Undeterred by
famine, drought and the depredations of convict life, Ruse
applied himself diligently to his task and proved not only
a hard worker but also, by local standards, a successful
farmer. By February 1791 he was able to support both himself and his wife, Elizabeth Perry, a convict whom he had
married on 5 September 1790. In April 1791 he received the
title to his land, the first grant issued in New South Wales.

Phillip's first report back to England about the new
colony was dated 15 May 1788, almost four months after
the fleet had arrived. In this report he outlined some of
the difficulties facing the early settlement and foreshad-
owed something of the looming food crisis. His long
handwritten account was put aboard the returning ships
of the fleet that would reach England in March the
following year.

In his report Phillip explained that Botany Bay had been
quickly abandoned as a site for the colony because there
was insufficient water, much of the coastal land was
unhealthy swamp and the harbour provided too little
shelter for ships.

He explained that he was forced to settle on Sydney
Cove due to the instructions to unload the ships and

release the vessels at the earliest possible date, even though this site, too, had been found to have limited water and available fertile soil.

Phillip admitted that progress in establishing the new colony was slow. Having been a farmer, he recognised that the harsh vegetation, the rocky ground and the absence of fertile soil would make things difficult: 'The necks of land that form the different coves and bear the water for some distance are in general so rocky that it is surprising such large trees should find sufficient nourishment.'9

Even at this early stage there were warning signs that the new colony was not going to be able to produce enough food:

> The great labour in clearing the ground will not permit more than eight acres to be sown this year with wheat and barley. At the same time an immense number of ants and field mice will render our crops very uncertain. Part of our livestock brought from the Cape, small as it was, has been lost and our resources in fish is also uncertain. Some days great quantities are caught but never enough to save any part of the provisions; and at times fish are scarce.10

Phillip added that the *Sirius* would soon sail north to purchase more livestock. Within months, however, the food shortage would be so great that the more immediate need of grain caused plans to change. The flagship would instead be sent on an urgent run to collect food from the Cape of Good Hope.

The challenges and problems of the new settlement in Sydney did not absorb Arthur Phillip to the extent that he forgot his orders, which included an instruction to colonise Norfolk Island, some fifteen hundred kilometres

KING GEORGE III, PAINTED BY SIR WILLIAM BEECHEY: George III authorised the sending of convicts to New South Wales and was to sit on the throne for fifty years. He was first believed to have gone mad in 1788, the year the First Fleet settled at Sydney Cove. (© National Library of Australia: AN2280932)

SIR JOSEPH BANKS, ENGRAVED BY S. W. REYNOLDS AND S. COUSINS AFTER THOMAS PHILLIPS: Aristocrat botanist Joseph Banks was to be a major influence in sending the convicts to Botany Bay, which proved to be totally unsuitable for settlement and had to be abandoned within a few days. Banks had visited the bay in 1770 with Captain Cook on the *Endeavour*. (© National Library of Australia: AN9283211)

LORD SYDNEY, ENGRAVED BY JOHN YOUNG AFTER GILBERT STUART: Lord Sydney was variously described as enlightened and progressive and a politician who scarcely rose above mediocrity. He was responsible for finding a solution to the convict problem as secretary of state for the Home Office in the government of William Pitt the Younger. (© National Library of Australia: AN10038055)

ARTHUR PHILLIP, ENGRAVED BY WILLIAM SHERWIN AFTER FRANCIS WHEATLEY: There was nothing particularly outstanding in his career when Arthur Phillip was plucked from semi-retirement at nearly 50 years of age to lead the expedition as the first governor of New South Wales. His appointment was criticised by the Admiralty, but he was to prove a good choice. (© National Library of Australia: AN9846227)

DAVID COLLINS, ENGRAVED BY ANTOINE CARDON AFTER JOHN THOMAS BARBER: David Collins, at 31, took on the job as the first judge in the new convict colony even though he had no formal legal qualifications. He left his wife in England and, although still married, had two children to a young convict woman in Sydney and another two to the daughter of convicts later in Hobart Town. (© National Library of Australia: AN9483647)

REVEREND RICHARD JOHNSON, PAINTED AND ENGRAVED BY G. TERRY: Sailing as chaplain on the First Fleet, Reverend Richard Johnson, the 34-year-old Anglican, took with him more than four thousand religious pamphlets, books and Bibles to help straighten the twisted souls of the convicts, most of whom couldn't read. (© National Library of Australia: AN9594799)

JOHN SHORTLAND, ENGRAVED BY SAMUEL SHELLEY AND PUBLISHED BY J. STOCKDALE: John Shortland was the naval agent responsible for the transport of convicts on the voyage to Botany Bay. He was to be the senior naval officer on the ill-fated return voyage to England of four ships of the First Fleet, the *Alexander*, the *Friendship*, the *Prince of Wales* and the *Borrowdale*. (© State Library of Victoria: PB000254)

THE *SIRIUS*, PAINTED BY FRANK ALLEN: The flagship *Sirius* carried supplies and one hundred and sixty passengers, including Arthur Phillip and the senior officials for the new settlement. On the voyage it leaked badly and many of its timbers below the waterline were found to be rotten. (© Frank Allen)

THE *ALEXANDER*, PAINTED BY FRANK ALLEN: This was the largest convict transport but the unhealthiest ship of the fleet, on which convicts began to die before it left Portsmouth. The *Alexander* carried almost two hundred male convicts, some marines and the ship's crew. (© Frank Allen)

THE *SUPPLY*, PAINTED BY FRANK ALLEN: Only twenty-one metres long and a third of the weight of the *Sirius*, the tiny *Supply* was the smallest but fastest ship in the fleet. One of the naval officers complained it was too small for the voyage and not able to carry many provisions. (© Frank Allen)

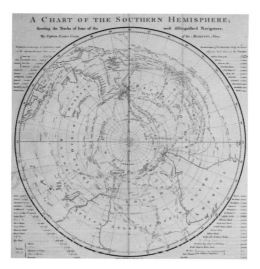

CHART OF THE SOUTHERN HEMISPHERE, BY CAPTAIN JAMES COOK: Captain John Hunter
probably used this 1770 map when he circumnavigated the globe in the *Sirius* to find
food for the hungry colony. (© National Library of Australia: NK2456-15)

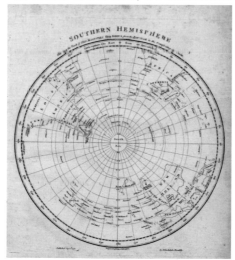

CHART OF THE SOUTHERN HEMISPHERE, ENGRAVED BY BENJAMIN BAKER: This map shows
the route taken by Captain John Hunter in the *Sirius*. He left Sydney in October
1788 and sailed under New Zealand, then below Cape Horn to the Cape of Good
Hope at the tip of southern Africa. After loading food, he sailed back through
the Great Southern Ocean and under Tasmania to reach Sydney in May 1789.
(© National Library of Australia: NK2456-16)

A FAMILY OF NEW SOUTH WALES

A FAMILY OF NEW SOUTH WALES, ENGRAVED BY WILLIAM BLAKE AFTER PHILIP GIDLEY KING (TOP), AND CAPTAINS HUNTER, COLLINS AND JOHNSTON WITH GOVERNOR PHILLIP, SURGEON WHITE ETC., PUBLISHED BY ALEXANDER HOGG: The new settlers had virtually no knowledge or understanding of the local inhabitants beyond the brief observations of Cook and Banks, who had stayed in Botany Bay barely a week almost eighteen years earlier. Relations between the new settlers and the Aboriginal people were based on a mutual incomprehension that gradually worsened. (© National Library of Australia: AN7691834, AN7890412)

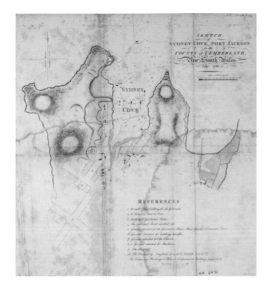

SKETCH OF SYDNEY COVE IN JULY 1788, ENGRAVED BY THOMAS MEDLAND AFTER LIEUTENANT WILLIAM DAWES AND CAPTAIN HUNTER: At the time Sydney was mostly a collection of huts, but this map includes planning for roads, a church and a farm. (© National Library of Australia: NK02456-124)

PART OF THE CREW OF HMS *GUARDIAN* ENDEAVOURING TO ESCAPE IN THE BOATS, PAINTED AND ENGRAVED BY ROBERT DODD: On hearing the convict settlement was running out of food, the British Government dispatched the *Guardian* with almost a thousand tons of supplies, but the ship was wrecked when it crashed into a giant iceberg in the Great Southern Ocean on 24 December 1789. (© National Library of Australia: AN9537928)

JOHN HUNTER, PAINTED BY WILLIAM MINEARD BENNETT: A loyal and effective deputy to Governor Phillip, the 50-year-old bachelor John Hunter commanded the flagship *Sirius* until it was shipwrecked under his command. (© National Library of Australia: AN2272205)

THE MELANCHOLY LOSS OF HMS *SIRIUS* OFF NORFOLK ISLAND, 19 MARCH 1790, PAINTED BY GEORGE RAPER: The loss of the *Sirius* was devastating news to the Sydney settlement, which was now running out of food and left with only the tiny ship the *Supply* for contact with the outside world. (© National Library of Australia: AN21511971)

north-east of Sydney. Phillip's instructions, signed by King George III, had explicitly called for the early settlement of Norfolk Island:

> Norfolk Island . . . being represented as a spot which may hereafter become useful, you are as soon as circumstances will admit of it, send a small establishment thither to secure the same to us, and prevent it being occupied by the subjects of any other European power.[11]

The British wanted to secure the island, which had been noted by Cook on his voyage eighteen years earlier, as part of the empire. It was believed it could produce a superior hemp or flax for sails and canvas – both vital for the Royal Navy.

Accordingly, on 1 February, within a week of arriving in Sydney Cove, Arthur Phillip asked his young protégé Lieutenant Philip Gidley King to organise to take the *Supply* with a small group to settle the island.[12]

Before leaving for Norfolk Island, King was issued with detailed written instructions from Phillip. 'After having taken the necessary measures for securing yourself and people, and for the preservation of the stores and provisions',[13] he was to grow the flax plant and cotton, corn and other grains with the seeds they had taken with them. They were to be left with six months' provisions but were expected to procure vegetables and fish locally. Labour for the development of the colony was to be provided by the convicts, 'being servants of the Crown till the time for which they are sentenced is expired, then labour is to be for the public'. Finally King was ordered to ensure that religion was observed and prayers of the Church of England were to be read 'with all due solemnity' every Sunday.

At 7 am on 14 February King set sail to his new post on the tiny tender the *Supply* with perhaps the smallest ever party to establish a colony of the British Empire. His group of twenty-three included a surgeon, a carpenter, a weaver, two marines, eight male convicts and six female convicts. The 33-year-old surgeon, Thomas Jamieson, was an Irish Protestant who had sailed as surgeon's mate with the *Sirius* in the First Fleet. Jamieson would stay on Norfolk Island for eleven years before taking up the post of senior surgeon in New South Wales.

The little party took two weeks to sail the fifteen hundred kilometres to Norfolk Island on the seventy-foot long HMS *Supply*, which was commanded by Lieutenant Henry Ball. On the way they passed an island where they observed giant turtles. Ball was to name the island Lord Howe, after one of the lords of the Admiralty.[14]

The *Supply* spent a week sailing around the rocky shores of Norfolk Island in high seas trying to find somewhere to land, until at last King discovered a small gap in the reef. It seems that Cook had encountered the island on an uncharacteristically calm day eighteen years previously, as he had managed to anchor in a reef on the north side of the island.

For two years King supervised this little establishment, organising the clearing of land and struggling against grubs, rats, hurricanes and occasionally troublesome convicts. Thanks to the fertile soil he was able to report favourably on the island's prospects, although when the *Supply* left to return to Sydney he had not found the promised flax, which had been the major reason for the settlement: 'We have not seen a leaf of flax or any herbal grass whatever, the ground being quite bare, which is rather extraordinary as Captain Cook says that flax is more luxuriant here than in New Zealand.'[15]

Phillip then had to report the absence of flax to London, noting that the French commander La Perouse had also failed to find it when he had called in on Norfolk Island the year before:

> The small quantity of flax that has been procured is
> sufficient to show the quality but the flax plant
> described by Captain Cook I have never met with, nor
> had the botanists that accompanied Mons La Perouse
> found it when I saw them, and which was sometime
> after they arrived.[16]

King believed that Cook may have mistaken another
local plant for flax. However, a year later he was able to
report that they had finally found flax growing on the
island, but that 'it in no manner resembles the flax of
Europe'. It was never to become a significant crop on the
island.

Having put King and his party safely ashore, Ball
returned to Sydney on the *Supply*. He again travelled via
Lord Howe Island. The island is about a thousand
kilometres south of Norfolk Island and about the same
distance east of Sydney. It is about eight kilometres in
length and was uninhabited but with plentiful bird life
and at that time of year abundant with turtles. This time
Ball took sixteen of the giant turtles back to Sydney.

Among the convict women who had been taken to
Norfolk Island was Ann Inett, who, at the relatively
mature age of 31, became Philip Gidley King's house-
keeper and lover. She had been convicted in 1786 in the
Worcester Court of stealing a petticoat, two aprons, a
pair of shoes, five handkerchiefs, a silk hood and other
clothing, with a total value of a little under one pound.
Initially condemned to be hanged, her sentence was
commuted to seven years' transportation to New South
Wales. Ann Inett went on to have two children with King,
both boys, who were named Norfolk and Sydney.

When King returned to England for a short time two
years later, he married and brought his new wife back
with him to Norfolk Island. He was to have three more
children with her, named Phillip, Maria and Elizabeth.

Nevertheless he continued to care for his first two boys, both of whom eventually became officers in the navy.

In October 1788 Phillip sent more convicts to Norfolk Island on the store ship *Golden Grove* before it returned to England with the *Fishburn*. By that time King was able to report some success with growing food on the island. Unlike the settlers in Sydney they had managed to grow a variety of vegetables, and after an initial failure they looked forward to a good harvest of grain. King reported that the soil was good, the people were healthy and that he felt the island could be self-sufficient in food production within two years, as long as they were provided with some cattle.

Towards the end of the first year of the settlement of Norfolk Island there was a mass escape plan involving most of the convicts. When next the *Supply* came to the island, the plotters intended abducting the ship's surgeon then sending a message for the marines aboard to come and rescue him. Once the marines had come ashore, they planned to send another message to the remaining marines on the *Supply* saying that the first boat with their colleagues had hit a reef and they should come to help. This, they hoped, would enable the convicts to then seize the now defenceless ship.

The scheme was discovered when the plotters tried to recruit Lieutenant King's gardener, and the convict woman who was living with the gardener told King of the plan. Forewarned, King was able to quickly round up the ringleaders, and the escape was thwarted.

In his second major report back to England, in July 1788, Arthur Phillip stated that the settlement around Sydney Cove was still struggling. He said that he had hoped to have given 'a more pleasing account of our present situation'. However, the building program was going too slowly, the convicts needed proper supervisors, they could find no limestone for cement, more cattle had died or had been lost in the bush and they still had stores to unload from the ships but did not yet have the storehouses to secure them.

Phillip warned Nepean that it would take the colony a long time to become self-sufficient and that for some years it would be heavily dependent on supplies from England for its survival:

> At present no country can afford less support to the first settlers, or to be disadvantageously placed for receiving support from the mother country, on which it must for a time depend. It will require patience and perseverance, neither of which will, I hope be wanting.[17]

The problems the settlers were having establishing the colony did not prevent Phillip telling the British Government what they wanted to hear. He wrote that he had no doubt 'but that this country will prove the most valuable acquisition Great Britain ever made'.[18]

However, Major Robert Ross, the commander of the marines, strongly disagreed. In a letter sent back to the Admiralty at the same time as Phillip's, Ross said that Sydney was destitute and could never support a self-sufficient colony:

> Might I presume to intrude an opinion on their Lordships with respect to the utility of settlement upon this coast, at least upon this part of it, it should be that it never can be made to answer the intended purpose or wish of Government, for the country seems totally destitute of everything that can be an object of a commercial nation, a very fine harbour excepted, and I much fear that the nature of the soil is such as will not be brought to yield more than

sufficient sustenance for the needy emigrants whose desperate fortunes may induce them to try the experiment. Here I beg leave to observe to their Lordships that the above is but a private opinion.[19]

In September Phillip wrote to Lord Sydney to explain why he had not followed the instruction he had received before leaving London to go and fetch women from one of the Pacific islands in order to address the shortage of women in Sydney. Continuing in his previous vein, he said that the colony was in no shape to accommodate the women: 'With respect to sending to the islands for women, your Lordship will, I believe, think that in the present situation of this colony it would be only bringing them to pine away a few years in misery.'[20]

Captain Tench wrote candidly in his journal after the first few months that the colony had little commercial value to Britain other than as a refuge for unwanted convicts. In a chapter titled 'Some thoughts on advantages which may arise to the mother country from the forming of a colony', Tench said the settlement was 'unequalled' for a place to send convicts but 'when viewed in a commercial light, I fear its insignificance will appear very striking'.

For the colony to be self-sufficient in food, he said, the British Government would need to send out a 'sufficient military force' to cultivate the ground, and even then the 'parent country will still have to supply us for a much longer time with every other necessity of life'.[21]

While Phillip was continuing to report favourably on the potential of the colony throughout the year, Ross may not have been the only officer who was sending back different accounts. An unsigned letter from a marine officer sent in November 1788 claimed that Sydney was struggling and that flattering reports being sent to London should be disregarded. The letter claimed that

almost all the officers in the settlement wanted the
venture abandoned and the men recalled to England:

> We have laboured incessantly since we arrived here to
> raise all sorts of vegetables and even at this distant
> period we can barely supply our tables, his Excellency
> not excepted. This together with the miserable state of
> the natives and scarcity of animals, are convincing
> proofs of the badness of the country. You will no
> doubt have a flattering public account but you may
> rely on what I have advanced. Every gentleman here,
> two or three excepted, concur with me in opinion and
> sincerely wish the expedition may be recalled.[22]

Towards the end of the year, and faced with failed
harvests in Sydney, Phillip authorised the settlement of
Rose Hill, some twenty-five kilometres to the west of Port
Jackson, where the soil was more fertile.

By the end of the year a few more buildings had
been erected in Sydney: a small stone house was built
for Major Robert Ross, the lieutenant-governor and
commander of the marines, two storehouses had been
completed and the hospital was still under construction.

An observatory had also been established on the point
of the western side of Sydney Cove, near the current-day
southern approach to the Sydney Harbour Bridge.
Lieutenant Dawes, the marine officer and astronomer,
had set up equipment to observe a comet that had last
been seen in 1661 and that would, according to calcula-
tions, return in 1788. The point was named Maskelyne
Point after the astronomer royal who had arranged for
the instruments to be sent with the First Fleet, but it later
became known as Dawes Point. This is where the Sydney
Observatory building stands today.

As the settlers approached Christmas of the first year,
there were still only a few solid structures in Sydney Cove,

with most people living in shacks or tents. There were no solid roads. Only a quarter of the settlers were involved in cultivating the land for food, the first harvests had failed and they remained almost totally dependent on the food brought from England. Relations with the local Aboriginal people had deteriorated, the marines were disaffected and the convicts generally showed no interest or motivation in the building of a new world.

The management of the struggling colony was made more difficult by the increasing friction between Governor Phillip and the Marine Corps, headed by Major Robert Ross. Central to the problem was lack of clarity as to the duties and responsibilities of the marines.

Phillip had very few officers at his disposal for supervising the convict workers, and he had expected the cooperation of the officers of the Marine Corps in ensuring the convicts worked effectively at farming and building the new settlement.

The marine officers, on the other hand, believed they were there to maintain order among the convicts and provide protection from any possible assault from hostile natives. They saw their role as military, not civil.

Phillip felt frustrated by what he saw as a petty lack of cooperation from the start, writing to Lord Sydney:

> The officers who compose the [marine] detachment are not only few in number, but most of them have declined any interference with the convicts, except when they are employed for their own particular service. I requested soon after we landed that officers would occasionally encourage such as they observed diligent, and point out for punishment such as they saw idling or straggling in the woods. This is all I desired, but the officers did not understand that any interference with the convicts was expected, and that they were not sent out to do more than the duty of soldiers.[23]

Phillip also complained in the same letter that the marine officers refused to sit on the criminal court: 'The sitting as members of the Criminal Court is thought a hardship by the officers, and of which they say they were not informed before they left England.'

The marines and their commander Major Ross, on the other hand, felt they were not afforded the respect or regard they deserved. In a letter to London Ross criticised Phillip for not consulting with anyone else in the colony, saying, 'from our Governors manner of expressing himself . . . he communicates nothing to any person but to his secretary'.[24]

Ross and some of his fellow officers were also resentful that the fortress they had expected to be constructed in Sydney had not been. It had always been part of the plan for the new settlement and was intended to form the centre of the marines' barracks.

However, Phillip had judged very early on that an assault by the Aboriginal people was unlikely and that constructing accommodation, storehouses and other civic buildings was a higher priority. Ross complained directly to the Admiralty:

> Here in justice to myself and the detachment under my command, I must observe to their Lordships that the detachment is at this hour without any kind of place of defence to retire to in case of an alarm or surprise, though I have in justice to myself repeatedly mentioned and urged his Excellency to get something or other erected for this purpose.[25]

Ross also complained that the entire marine detachment was still living in tents and that not enough was being done to build their barracks:

> We still remain under canvas, no habitations being provided for either officers or men but what they

themselves with the assistance of four carpenters and
a few others, convicts (of all trades) has been given me
for the use of the detachment, were for some time
erecting and when any of them will be finished . . . is
impossible for me to say.

These were not even the first sources of friction between
Ross and Phillip. Quite early on in the first year Ross had
wanted to arrest five of his marine officers who had
refused to reconvene a court martial involving a marine.
The case involved an allegation that a marine private,
Joseph Hunt, had struck another marine, William
Dempsey. A third, Thomas Jones, had intervened and was
abused by Hunt. The court found Hunt guilty and
sentenced him to either ask for a public pardon from
Dempsey or receive a hundred lashes.

Ross was outraged by the decision, saying that a
prisoner could not be permitted to choose his own
punishment and that the court should reconvene and
decide one punishment or the other. Captain Watkin Tench,
who had convened the court with his four lieutenants,
insisted the law did not allow a reconsideration of a court
martial and effectively disobeyed his superior's orders.

Ross wanted the five officers arrested and court-
martialled but, as there were only four captains and
twelve lieutenants in the whole settlement, Phillip felt
there were already too few officers in service and didn't
want the matter to go any further.

In the end there were not enough officers to reconvene
the court martial. Tench and his colleagues resumed their
normal duties and that is where the matter rested, except
for the damage to the marines' morale and the standing of
Ross with his colleagues.

While these arguments were taking place, Phillip had
written to London protesting that he had 'used every
means in my power to prevent a general court-marshal,

the inconveniences of which were obvious' but his proposal was 'declined' by Ross.[26]

Robert Ross also wrote to London insisting that his authority and the morale and good order of the marines required that the formal disciplinary procedures be followed. Without this 'decisive step', he wrote, it would be 'absolutely impossible' for any commanding officer to properly carry out his duties.[27]

The original incident involving a private in the marines may have been relatively trivial, but it demonstrated to the British Government that the two most senior officers in the colony of New South Wales could not resolve their differences and work in harmony.

Ross believed that the Marine Corps was being treated no better than the convicts. In the same letter to the Admiralty he protested that the marines were forced to survive on exactly the same rations as the convicts, except for receiving a ration of rum that was close to undrinkable:

> I shall take the liberty of mentioning to their Lordships the quantity of the provisions served to myself, the officers and men of the detachment, in which there is now no difference between us and the convicts, but in half a pint per day of Rio spirits, which in taste and smell is extremely offensive.[28]

The marines also complained that they were punished as much and often more severely than the convicts. Phillip had demonstrated from the first week of the voyage that he did not want to provoke a convict uprising through the imposition of excessive punishments on them. His subsequent interventions secured more lenient punishment of convicts, while the punishments of the marines went ahead. They tended to come from the same lower social classes as the convicts and were accustomed to stiff justice and rough discipline, so this resulted in an obvious disparity that would have created much resentment among the marines.

Major Robert Ross does not appear to have been a very popular figure in Sydney with any group, though. Judge David Collins claimed an 'inexpressible hatred'[29] for him, which is somewhat understandable, given Collins' closeness to Governor Phillip.[30] However, some of Ross' own officers, including his deputy, Ralph Clark, also recorded that relations between Ross and others became so strained that he ceased to be on speaking terms with his senior colleagues.[31]

12

THE FLEET GOES
HOME

*The scurvy had now arrived to such a height among the
crew that eleven were unable to move and the remaining
part were so exceedingly feeble from the effects of it as
scarcely to be able to navigate the ship so that our
situation was become extremely critical . . .*

In the months following the arrival of the fleet and the
unloading of the convicts and supplies, the nine
contracted ships had to leave to return to England. Those
left behind watching their last connection with the world
they knew sail over the horizon had the sense of being 'cut
off . . . from the rest of civilized nature' and a feeling of
profound desolation.[1]

The nine ships would have mixed fortunes on their
voyages home. As there was a shortage of fresh food in
Sydney, all of them set off with inadequate provisions.

According to Phillip all of the contracted ships –
except the *Fishburn* and the *Golden Grove* – were
completely unloaded of their cargo and cleared to go
before the end of May, but they all needed major
work to be made seaworthy for the journey home. It
was found that 'the worm had so much destroyed
their sheathing to have worms eating the timber'[2] and it
was necessary that the ships be pulled up and put on

their sides so the carpenters could replace the wooden supports.

The *Charlotte*, the *Lady Penrhyn* and the *Scarborough* were the first to be 'discharged from Government service', in late March, but it took another six weeks for the necessary repairs to be carried out so the ships could set sail. They departed in early May after being at the settlement for a little over three months, and while they were the first ships to leave they would not be the first to reach England.

The *Lady Penrhyn* left Sydney on 5 May 1788, and the *Scarborough* the following day. The *Charlotte* left early on 6 May and by mid-morning was heading down Port Jackson, according to its captain, Thomas Gilbert, 'with light breezes and frequent showers of rain'.[3] Before being cleared to go, the ship was twice searched for any convicts who may have hidden away below decks.

Captain Gilbert had decided to take a more easterly route through the Pacific Ocean to China than had ever been undertaken before, and with 'no chart to guide me and with dangers of which I was entirely unacquainted' kept a record of the voyage.[4] Having unloaded its cargo of supplies and more than a hundred convicts in Sydney, the almost empty ship was on its way to pick up its cargo of tea with a crew 'not exceeding thirty',[5] several of whom were only boys.

Within a week of leaving Sydney and with no fresh food, the crew began to contract scurvy. Captain Gilbert headed straight for Lord Howe Island, which was the closest place to Sydney where he could stop for provisions and find some fresh food.

Arthur Phillip had ordered Gilbert before he left not to seek provisions on Lord Howe Island, saying that the available fresh food on the island should be for the settlers in Sydney Cove. As Captain Gilbert wrote, Phillip told him that Lieutenant Ball, standing off the island in the *Supply* at that point, 'had directions to prevent my landing on this newly discovered land of promise'.[6]

Gilbert said that his crew had tried to find enough food in Sydney and had fished 'as often as possible' before leaving, but that fish, while 'palliative', would not 'altogether alleviate' scurvy:

> The situation of my ships company rendered it necessary that I should if possible procure a supply of fresh provisions and vegetables as the scurvy had begun to make a rapid progress amongst them. I was determined to endeavour to surmount every difficulty and land upon the island.[7]

When he reached the island and was trying to find a spot to anchor, he saw the *Supply* and also the *Lady Penrhyn*, which had left Sydney the day before his ship. To Gilbert's surprise Lieutenant Ball of the *Supply* sent for him to come over, telling him that the island 'afforded plenty of turtle, fowls, fish, cocoa nuts and cabbages'.

The following day Gilbert and members of his crew went ashore but without Ball, who did not want it 'supposed that he conducted us to the island'. Once on the island they found large fat birds 'walking with less fear and concern than geese in a farm yard' as well as large eggs, fat pigeons, partridges in 'great plenty' and cabbages.

The uninhabited Lord Howe Island was the home of some unique animal life. While briefly there, the surgeon on the *Lady Penrhyn*, Arthur Bowes Smyth, made the earliest known drawing of the now extinct white gallinule. He also observed the bell magpie, or currawong, and four now rare or extinct birds that have been identified as the Lord Howe Island pigeon, the booby, the Lord Howe Island rail or woodhen and an extinct species of parakeet. Bowes Smyth kept a valuable journal of the First Fleet voyage and early settlement, as well as recording much of the wildlife in the new colony. He was believed to have been the first white man to have seen an emu, which he included in his illustrations. He died shortly after arriving back in England in April 1790 and was buried at his home town of Tolleshunt D'Arcy in Essex.

The next day the *Scarborough* appeared at the island. It had been agreed in Sydney that the three ships would rendezvous off Lord Howe Island and sail together to China, but a few days later, according to Gilbert, 'when daylight broke we found the *Lady Penrhyn* gone'.[8] Now abundantly supplied, the *Charlotte* and the *Scarborough* headed off together for Norfolk Island, almost another thousand kilometres further to the north.

On the way there Gilbert was shocked to learn that two deserters from the *Sirius* were aboard the *Charlotte*, having stowed away before it left Sydney – this despite the ship having been searched twice by the marines before leaving. Gilbert said he protested 'against their conduct' but that they had sailed too far to take the men back and said he would 'swear an affidavit' to the British authorities at the earliest opportunity – though there is no record that he did.

A week later the two ships were off Norfolk Island. Here Gilbert had intended landing to collect timber for ships' masts that he hoped to sell in China but, finding 'a tremendous surf on all sides of the island',[9] they decided against trying to land and continued on their journey.

For the next month the ships sailed further north in 'hot and sultry'[10] weather with occasional calms and rainy spells, until they came across some islands, one of which Gilbert named Gilbert Island after himself. He named the Marshall Islands after the captain of the *Scarborough*. While among the islands, they invited aboard

a number of natives who had paddled their canoe alongside and despite language difficulties managed a friendly
exchange of nails and fish hooks for some local matting
and seashells.

Deciding against accepting an invitation to go ashore
with the natives, the two captains sailed on past other
new islands that Gilbert was to name Daniel's, Pedder's
and Arrowsmith, and through a passage he would name
Fordyce's Passage.[11] He suggested in his journal that all
the islands he was passing might 'prove to have safe and
convenient harbours' and such 'necessities' as to allow
regular trade between New South Wales and China.[12]

They had now been sailing for two months, and
despite the fresh food from Lord Howe Island and a little
more from the Gilbert and Marshall islands, scurvy again
became a problem. As Gilbert wrote: 'Captain Marshall
informed me that ten of his men were down with scurvy.
Having been for so long without procuring refreshment
from on shore, that disorder, so fatal to seamen, now
began to grow alarming in both ships.'[13]

The ships were now in a difficult position. Gilbert
admitted he had sailed too far north and calculated that
with the onset of the south-west monsoon they would not
be able to reach Formosa (Taiwan) and then China until
the later north-east monsoon, which was some months
away. He also thought that because of the 'sickly state of
the crew' they would be unable to reach Japan, where the
currents 'were rapid and uncertain' anyway. With no
other choice, he decided to turn around and head south.
'I never intended to have gone so far northward. There
being no alternative but that of returning southward
while we had it in our power to do so.'[14]

A week later Captain John Marshall sent the *Scarborough*'s boat across to inform Gilbert that Marshall's
brother was dangerously ill with scurvy. Gilbert went
across himself with what medicines they had on board.

Neither ship had a surgeon, as most of the surgeons who had sailed on the First Fleet were now in Sydney and surgeon Bowes Smyth was on the *Lady Penrhyn*, which they had last seen off Lord Howe Island. Gilbert found the situation aboard the *Scarborough* to be serious:

> Mr. Marshall's case was however very obstinate; he had languished some time under that disorder and as we were not able to make any land, where the sole effective remedy against it could only be obtained, from the benefit of air on shore and from the use of fruit and vegetables, it had now arrived to such a height to deprive him of life.[15]

Over the next two weeks the number of cases of scurvy increased and another seaman died. The *Charlotte* was in as bad a condition as the *Scarborough*, and as they reached a critical stage Gilbert decided to head for Tinian Island in the Northern Marianas, more than two thousand kilometres south of Japan and about two thousand kilometres east of the Philippines:

> The scurvy had now arrived to such a height among the crew that eleven were unable to move and the remaining part were so exceedingly feeble from the effects of it as scarcely to be able to navigate the ship so that our situation was become extremely critical, which induced me to make the best of my way to the island of Tinian, and this I signified to Captain Marshall.[16]

A week later they reached the island, where they quickly found some oranges, coconuts and cabbages and put the sick ashore 'to receive the benefit of land air as soon as possible'. Tarpaulins and sails were used to make a shelter for them, while those who were fit enough went inland to kill wild pigs and birds.

After only three days, and worried about the high surf and the reef, they 'with great difficulty' brought the sick aboard again. In the high seas there were not enough able-bodied men to pull in the anchor, so instead the chain was cut. Gilbert noted that this drastic action was taken in the nick of time:

> Had the ship remained a quarter of an hour longer in the bay, I am fully persuaded, and my officers and the whole ships company are of the same opinion, that she must inevitably have driven ashore upon the reef.[17]

The *Scarborough* made a similarly quick departure, prompting Gilbert to admit that he had been 'obliged to forego all the benefits' he had hoped for as they had left before collecting enough fresh food, and the sick had not had time to recover.

Three weeks later the *Lady Penrhyn* would also stop at Tinian Island and find the *Charlotte*'s anchor buoy.

For the next few weeks the two ships sailed on towards China, treating their sick with wine and 'such other anti scorbutic' as they had on board.[18] On 3 September, almost four months after leaving Sydney, they sighted Bashi Island, north of the Philippines and south of the islands of Formosa and Grafton. According to Gilbert Bashi Island had been named by Captain James King, who had taken command of the *Resolution* on his way back to England after Cook had been killed in 1779 in Hawaii. A week later, on 9 September, the *Charlotte* reached Macao.

Macao was the Portuguese island port on the mouth of the river leading to Canton. Gilbert noted that the city, like most of the Portuguese Empire, was in decline, having been 'formerly richer and more populous than it is at present' and having 'lost much of its ancient consequence'.[19]

The *Charlotte* would soon be joined there by the *Scarborough* and, in the following month, by the *Lady Penrhyn*. They would load up a 'valuable cargo of teas and china ware' and sail for England.[20]

Incredibly, despite the scurvy that afflicted and killed many on the other ships, Gilbert was to boast that not one crew member had died of the disease on the *Charlotte*. His only fatality occurred after the ship reached Macao, when the boatswain died and was buried on Dean's Island. This death, Gilbert insisted, had less to do with the ship and more to do with the boatswain's excessive drinking once they had reached the shore.

The *Lady Penrhyn*, which had left Sydney for China the day before the *Charlotte* and the *Scarborough* and arrived in Macao a month later, had experienced its own difficulties en route.

Lieutenant John Watts, aboard the *Lady Penrhyn*, kept an account of the journey. He had sailed as a midshipman with Captain James Cook's third voyage on the *Resolution*, being promoted during the expedition to able seaman. According to the *Naval Chronicle* of 1801 Watts had been tattooed all over his body by natives of the Pacific islands he had visited in the course of the voyage with Cook.

Watts recorded that a month after leaving Sydney and passing the islands that were to be named the Macaulay Islands and the Curtis Islands, scurvy broke out on the *Lady Penrhyn* and disabled almost the entire crew:

> The scurvy now began to spread very fast among the crew, and by the 6th, they had nine men unable to get out of their hammocks, and many others complained very much: swelled gums, the flesh exceeding black and hard, a contraction of the sinews, with a total debility; were the general appearances. Wine was daily served out to them, and there was sour-krout on board, but the people refused to eat it. From this to

the 17th they had little variety; by that time the people
were in a deplorable state, for with every person on
board, the Captain included, they could only muster
ten men able to do duty, and some of them were in a
very weakly state: sour-krout, which before had been
refused, now began to be sought after, and they had
all the Captain's fresh stock, himself and officers
living solely on salt provisions.[21]

A few days later, and despite being almost halted by a lack
of wind followed by frequent heavy storms, the ship
managed to reach Tahiti. Its men were told they were the
first white people to visit the island since Cook had been
there more than a decade earlier. The natives, who remembered Cook, were pleased to see the *Lady Penrhyn* and
brought fresh food to the stricken crew:

When anchored they had only three men in one
watch, and two in the other besides the mates, and
two of these ailing; the rest of the crew were in a truly
deplorable state.

Their first care was naturally to procure some
refreshments, and it was a pleasing circumstance for
them to see the natives flock round the ship, calling
out '*Tayo Tayo*,' which signifies *friends*; and '*Patri no
Tutti*,' Cook's ship; and bringing in very great plenty
cocoa nuts, bread-fruit, plantains and taro, and a fruit
known by the name of the Otaheite apple; they also
brought some hogs and fowls.[22]

The Tahitians' friendliness was in spite of the fact that
they had suffered from the earlier visit of the English.
According to Watts:

Great numbers of the natives had been carried off by
the venereal disease, which they had caught from their

connections with the crews of the *Resolution* and
Discovery; nor were the women so free from this
complaint as formerly, especially the lowest class,
the better sort seemingly not wishing to hazard the
catching so terrible a disorder.[23]

Within a few weeks and with access to plenty of fresh food,
the diseased crew, 'who had recovered in a most astonish-
ing manner', were once again able to work the ship. The
Lady Penrhyn was by no means the first ship to enjoy
sexual experiences with the Tahitians, and it was with the
crew's 'great reluctance' that Captain Sever ordered the
ship to depart on its next leg to the Society Isles.

After stopping at a number of other nearby islands, the
ship loaded a huge amount of food, including sixty large
pigs, fifty piglets, a hundred and fifty chickens, a large
quantity of coconuts, green vegetables, sugar cane, taro and
yams, and about a hundred pumpkins. Watts said the crew
were not only perfectly recovered, but also, with so much
fresh food aboard, they had every 'reason to hope that they
would not be any more alarmed for their safety'.[24]

On 15 September they stopped on Saypan Island in the
Marianas, having seen bullocks grazing on the shore, and
brought aboard a young steer. Ten days later they reached
Tinian Island and saw in the water a buoy with a severed
anchor chain and a sign identifying it as belonging to the
Charlotte, indicating it had passed this way some time
before. Stopping again, they loaded aboard more fresh
food, including pigs and chickens and some green
breadfruit and guavas, limes and 'sour oranges',[25] which
was enough to last them until they reached Macao on
19 October. In all, their journey from Sydney had taken
them a little more than five months.

Finally, loaded with their East India Company cargo
of chinaware and tea, the three ships sailed from Macao
in November 1788 and arrived back in London the

following April. This was a month later than three of
the other ships of the First Fleet, which had left Sydney
the previous July and sailed a more direct route to
England.

These three ships were the *Alexander*, the *Prince of
Wales* and the *Borrowdale*. They sailed from Sydney on
13 and 14 July 1788 with the *Friendship,* but the latter
ship would not reach England.

When planning their route back to England, the
masters of the four ships had considered going south from
Sydney, east under New Zealand and then below Cape
Horn at the southern tip of South America. However, the
season was thought to be too far advanced for them to
attempt this southern course, and the passage by Cape
Horn was objected to by the governor. It was winter in
the southern hemisphere and the ships would not be able
to sail in the high latitudes, so it was decided they should
head north up the east coast of Australia, then west either
through the Endeavour Straits or even further north
above New Guinea.

When the ships reached the top of Australia, they
took the more northerly course, tracking the route
charted by Captain Carteret of the Royal Navy some ten
years earlier. This would take them between New Britain
and New Ireland, off the east coast of Papua New
Guinea.

Although the dangers of scurvy were well known, the
settlement in Sydney was itself already short of fresh
food when the ships departed, and, like the *Charlotte*,
the *Lady Penrhyn* and the *Scarborough*, they were
unable to take with them any food that would have
helped keep scurvy at bay. All the ships had left England
with portable soup, but even this was now almost totally
exhausted. Portable soup was made from boiling meat,
offal and vegetables into a thick paste, which was then
dried out and cut into cakes, like modern-day stock

cubes. The soup was prepared on board by dissolving the tablets in boiling water.

It was presumed that the four ships would regularly stop after leaving Sydney and collect fresh vegetables and fruit on the islands they passed. For various reasons this did not occur, and it was to have terrible consequences.

The ships were under the command of Captain John Shortland, the First Fleet's naval agent, who sailed on the *Alexander*. The *Friendship*, the *Prince of Wales* and the *Borrowdale* went ahead, as the *Alexander* required some last-minute preparations. It was agreed that the ships would rendezvous at Lord Howe Island.

Two days after leaving Sydney, the ships were struggling against the wind and spent the day and evening tacking first into a north-west wind and later to the east-south-east. By midnight the *Alexander* could see only the *Friendship* and had lost sight of the *Borrowdale* and the *Prince of Wales*.

Shortland, although still hoping to join up with the other ships, decided to press on in an easterly direction. However, after encountering more difficult weather, he abandoned the planned rendezvous and headed off with the *Friendship* in a more northerly direction. They were not to sight either the *Prince of Wales* or the *Borrowdale* for the rest of the voyage.

Shortland ordered the *Alexander* and the *Friendship* to head north to Carteret Harbour in New Ireland, which had been discovered and charted by Captain Phillip Carteret in 1768.

After being at sea for nearly four weeks, they arrived at the harbour to be met by a number of canoes carrying natives bearing 'rind of an orange or a lemon, the feathers of tame fowls and other things that might be procured on shore'.[26] One of the natives handed up to Captain Shortland what he thought to be a breadfruit.

Despite their fresh food being all but exhausted and knowing that a variety of fruit could be purchased here, Shortland decided to press on, failing to see how vital the food would ultimately become to his crew. This was a big mistake, as Shortland was later to confess:

> From what was seen in the possession of these people, there can be no doubt that their land produces cocoa-nuts, breadfruit bananas, and most other vegetables of the Society and Friendly Isles. Nor was it without the greatest regret that [I] declined the invitations of the natives and proceeded without touching for refreshments, which doubtless might have been obtained in plenty but the length and uncertainty of [the] passage seemed to forbid the least delay; nor was it at this time foreseen how much superior to every other consideration the acquirement of a wholesome change of diet would be found.[27]

So the ships pressed on with their food stocks depleted, and Shortland continued with the detailed mapping of his route. A month later they passed through the straits that separate the Bougainville and Choiseul islands, on the northern end of the Solomon Islands chain.

Inevitably the scurvy arrived with a vengeance, affecting first the crew of the *Alexander* and then those on the *Friendship*. Five of the *Alexander*'s crew were unable to work and complained of soreness in their legs and difficulty breathing. Their gums were sore and bleeding and their teeth so loosened they could only eat the rice and flour from their rations with difficulty.

As they approached the equator and the weather became hotter and more sultry, the scurvy on the *Alexander* spread among the crew, despite efforts to control it including smoking the ship and washing it down with vinegar, and issuing the crew increased rations of beer, port and wine.

They passed the Palau Islands on 11 September and, seeing cocoa palms on a small island, lowered a boat from each of the ships to fetch fresh fruit and vegetables for the sick. Duncan Sinclair, the master of the *Alexander*, was on one of the boats and complained that they were only able to acquire about thirty green coconuts before he felt sufficiently threatened by the natives on the island that he 'returned as expeditiously as I could'.[28]

By the end of September most of the *Alexander*'s crew were now disabled with the illness and men began to die. The *Friendship*, which till now had fared better, was also reporting that fewer men were able to work.

On 27 September the *Alexander* neared Mindanao in the southern Philippines. Two weeks later the fleet was to the west of Borneo when the *Friendship* struck a reef but was pulled off without incurring any serious damage.

By now eight men on the *Alexander* had died and the ship was reduced to two men in each watch; there were only four men and two boys still fit for duty. The *Friendship* had only five men left who were able to work the ship. In an attempt to get as many of the sick to work as possible, the crew were offered double pay when the ship reached Batavia (present-day Jakarta).

By the time another two weeks had passed, it was no longer possible to sail both ships any further. The masters of the ships, Duncan Sinclair of the *Alexander* and Francis Walton of the *Friendship*, agreed to abandon the smaller *Friendship* and transfer all the surviving crew to the *Alexander* on condition that Walton be allowed half the freight of the *Alexander* when the ship reached England.

It took four days for the remaining able-bodied men to transfer the supplies across from the *Friendship* to the *Alexander*, then the *Friendship* was bored with holes and set adrift to sink.

The *Alexander* sailed on and passed Pamanookan on northern Java on 5 November. They had now been at sea for almost four months with virtually no fresh food, and by now only one sailor and the officers were physically capable of going aloft to handle the ship's sails.

To add to their woes, later that day four boats flying Dutch and Portuguese colours chased them. Three of the boats had eighteen oars and the other either twelve or fourteen, and Shortland says he had no doubt they meant to seize the *Alexander*. Throughout the day every effort was made, by both the healthy and the sick, to hoist more sail and outrun their pursuers. Shortland eventually ordered the ship's guns to be fired over the pursuers' heads, after which they pulled away and headed for shore.

On 19 November, as they limped towards the port of Batavia, the fatigued crew were unable to sail further when the wind dropped. The *Alexander* dropped its anchor between the islands of Alkmara and Leyden at the mouth of Batavia, fired its gun and signalled for assistance. At first no help came, but the next day a passing Dutch ship sent six sailors over to help sail the stricken ship into port, and the following day it sent over fresh food.

When the ship finally moored in Batavia, the sick were sent to the local hospital, 'where several of them died, being too far gone for any accommodation or skill to recover'.[29] The *Alexander* finally left Batavia on 6 December on the next leg of its journey to Cape Town, with only four of the original crew – the rest were either dead or had not yet recovered.

When the *Alexander* reached Cape Town on 18 February 1789, its crew encountered the *Sirius*, which had left Sydney the previous October, some three months after the *Alexander*. The *Sirius*, under the command of Captain Hunter, had already been in Table Bay for six weeks, picking up urgently needed food to take back to Sydney.

Hunter had heard reports of the misfortune of the *Alexander* and the *Friendship* from a Dutch frigate that had earlier arrived in Cape Town from Batavia:

> On the 19th [January] a small Dutch frigate arrived here from Batavia from which I learned Lieutenant Shortland had arrived at that port with a single ship, about the beginning of December in a very distressed condition, that he had buried the greatest part of the ships company and was assisted by the officers and the company of the above frigate to secure his vessel and hand the sails, which could not have been done without assistance, and that he had been reduced to the necessity, some time before his arrival, to sink the other vessel, which was in company with him for the purpose of managing one out of the remaining part of the two ships companies, without which he never could have reached Batavia with either: for when he arrived there he had only four men, out of two crews who were capable of standing on deck.[30]

A month later, as Hunter was leaving Table Bay, the *Alexander* limped into the port:

> On the 18th of February, to my no small satisfaction (for I was preparing to sail the next day), Mr. Shortland arrived in the *Alexander* transport. I was going off from the shore, when I discovered the ship coming round Green Point; I rowed directly on board, and his people were so happy to see their old friends in Table-Bay, that they cheered us as we came alongside. I now received from Mr. Shortland an exact confirmation of all the intelligence which I had received concerning him from the officers of the Dutch frigate.[31]

Hunter had also heard what had happened to the other two ships, the *Prince of Wales* and the *Borrowdale*, which had become separated from the *Friendship* and the *Alexander* off the New South Wales coast some seven months earlier. Two English ships had been seen in Rio de Janeiro, and their crews were also in a terrible condition. From the description given to him, Hunter was in no doubt that the ships were the *Prince of Wales* and the *Borrowdale*:

> A Dutch ship arrived here from Rio de Janeiro. By this ship I received information of the arrival at that place of two vessels from the east coast of New Holland, that had arrived singly, and in very great distress, from sickness, and death of many of their people, that the first which arrived, had her name on her stern (*Prince of Wales* – London) from which circumstances there could be no doubt of its being one of our transports. The other vessel was also well described that I knew it to be the *Borrowdale* store ship. The officers of this India ship observed further that they were so weak that had they not been boarded by boats without the harbour, they had been unable to bring their vessels to safety.[32]

The *Borrowdale* and *Prince of Wales*, after losing contact with the *Alexander* and *Friendship*, had taken the other route after all. Even though it had been decided in Sydney before they left that they should return to England by heading west back to Cape Town, the two private transports had gone the easterly route around Cape Horn.

Hunter was told that there was so much 'sickness and death' on the ships in Rio de Janeiro that the crew were unable to sail any further and had to be helped into Rio's harbour.

The *Borrowdale* and the *Prince of Wales*, with their depleted crews and some additional seamen they signed on in Rio de Janeiro, would finally reach England in March 1789. The *Alexander* left Table Bay on 16 March 1789 and arrived at the Isle of Wight in England on 28 May.

By any measure the voyage of the *Alexander* and the *Friendship* had been calamitous. They had lost contact with the other two ships, the *Prince of Wales* and the *Borrowdale*, within two days of leaving Sydney; they had failed to rendezvous at Lord Howe Island; and they had also failed to ensure they were carrying sufficient quantities of fresh food. These events and mistakes saw almost all of the crew dead or incapacitated and required the scuttling of a perfectly good ship, the *Friendship*. Shortland, however, would be congratulated on his leadership because he was able to provide detailed charts and maps of his journey – even though earlier explorers, including Carteret and Bougain, had mapped much of it before.

The arrival of the *Prince of Wales* and the *Borrowdale* in England, with the first news of the First Fleet since its arrival in Botany Bay more than a year before, attracted widespread public interest and extensive coverage in the newspapers in England. The first news had been brought back on the *Prince of Wales*, but England would have to await the arrival of the *Borrowdale* to read Arthur Phillip's more extensive dispatches.

The *General Evening Post* reported on 24 March that 'The *Prince of Wales* from Botany Bay arrived at Falmouth, brings an account of the fleet being all safe arrived at Botany Bay'. The same day the *Whitehall Evening Post* reported that 'The two ships of war, the *Sirius* and the *Supply*' and the convict transports 'had made good their voyage to Botany Bay'. The paper went on to say that Arthur Phillip's dispatches for the British Government were on the *Borrowdale*, which had not yet reached England. Similar stories ran the same day in the *Evening Advertiser* and the *London Advertiser*, and in *The Times* three days later.

Within two days the *Borrowdale* arrived carrying Arthur Phillip's reports and dispatches, and far more detailed stories appeared in a number of papers, including the *General Evening Post*, the *London Chronicle*, the *Advertiser* and the *Whitehall Evening Post*. The reports covered details of the voyage of the First Fleet, the decision to abandon Botany Bay, the clearing of land in Sydney Cove for the new settlement, a description of the 'bushy' bearded and 'fuzzy' haired Aboriginal people, kangaroos ('as big as sheep'), bird life, soil and climate.

On 27 March the *Evening Advertiser* reported that a copy of Phillip's first dispatches was being sent to King George III, 'by royal command, for the perusal of his Majesty'.

Until now all the stories had reported positively on the expedition. Indeed, on the same day as the story above, the *London Advertiser* got a little carried away with its description of Sydney, 'where Natures gifts appeared equal to all their wishes – the verdure strong and rich, and the springs of the best water'. However, on 28 March *Felix Farley's Bristol Journal* reported that the information brought back on the *Borrowdale* indicated that all was not well in the new settlement:

> The accounts they bring are far from favourable, they lost all their livestock, the soil is not so good as represented, nor can they prevail on the natives to converse with them, or supply them with provisions, of which they are short.

Book publishers were quick to cash in on the public excitement. On 28 March an advertisement appeared in the *World* for the first of many journals to be published by officers who had sailed on the First Fleet: 'In a few days will be published: A Narrative of the Expedition to Botany Bay. By Captain Tench of the Marines. Printed by Debrett.'

At this time Tench was still in Sydney and he would not return home to England for another three years. He had nevertheless managed to complete his first manuscript and have it taken back on the first available ship for publication in London.

The government was quick to react to the news from New South Wales and the positive spin given to the venture in the newspapers. On 30 March it was reported in the *Public Advertiser* that the government had 'come to the resolution to send out all convicts sentenced to transportation, and all respites, in the next fleet that is to sail for Botany Bay, in order that his Majesty's gaol in the Kingdom may be once cleared'.

The last two ships to leave Sydney to return to England were the store ships, the *Golden Grove* and the *Fishburn*.

Their release had been delayed by the need to build secure storehouses to receive the provisions still held on the ships, particularly on the *Fishburn*, which had a large quantity of rum aboard that was most at risk of theft.

The *Fishburn* was finally unloaded and ready to depart at the end of September. The *Golden Grove*, which had been cleared earlier and was waiting on the readiness of the *Fishburn*, had in the meantime been sent with more settlers to Norfolk Island, returning on 10 October.

On 19 November these last two ships left to return to England via Cape Horn. They were the only two contracted ships of the First Fleet that would return without encountering serious misadventure. After reaching England, the *Golden Grove* worked carrying freight on the London to Jamaica run until it disappeared from the records in 1804. There are no surviving records as to what happened to the *Fishburn* after its return home.

Back in the colony, with all the contracted ships departed and the *Sirius* off to fetch food, only the little *Supply* remained, which only added to the sense of isolation felt by the thousand settlers who were struggling to survive at the end of their first year in Sydney.

13

THE ABORIGINAL PEOPLE

[T]he natives revenge by attacking any stragglers they meet . . .

Relations between the new settlers and the Aboriginal people were characterised by a mutual incomprehension that gradually worsened. The settlers had virtually no knowledge or understanding of the local inhabitants beyond the brief observations of Cook and Banks, who had stayed barely a week in Botany Bay almost eighteen years earlier.

The first European encounter with the Aboriginal people on the east coast of Australia came on the day Cook landed in April 1770:

> As we came in, on both points of the bay, several of the natives and a few huts, men women and children on the south shore abreast of the ship, to which place I went in the boats in hopes of speaking with them, accompanied by Mr. Banks, Dr. Solander, and Tupia [a native Polynesian who had voluntarily joined Cook on the *Endeavour* at Tahiti] – as we approached the shore they all made off, except two men, who seemed resolved to oppose our landing. As soon as I saw this I ordered the boats to lay upon their oars, in order to

speak to them; but this was to little purpose, for
neither us nor Tupia could understand one word they
said. We then threw them some nails, beads, etc.,
ashore, which they took up and seemed not ill pleased
with, in so much that I thought that they beckoned to
us to come ashore; but in this we were mistaken, for
as soon as we put the boat in they again came to
oppose us, upon which I fired a musquet between the
two, which had no other effect than to make them
retire back, where bundles of their darts lay, and one
of them took up a stone and threw at us, which
caused my firing a second musquetload, with small
shot and although some of the shot struck the man,
yet it had no other effect than to make him lay hold a
target. Immediately after this we landed which we had
no sooner done than they throwed two darts at us this
obliged me to fire a third shot soon after which they
both made off, but not in such haste but what we
might have taken one, but Mr. Banks being of opinion
that the darts were poisoned made me cautious how I
advanced into the woods.[1]

Later the same day, when Cook encountered them again,
he said they 'all fled at my approach' and in his journal he
was later to record that 'I do not look upon them to be a
warlike people, on the contrary I think they are a timorous
and inoffensive race, no ways inclinable to cruelty.'[2]

Banks concurred but in harsher terms. After observing
the lack of aggression in the Aboriginal people over a five-
day period from the end of April to early May 1770, even
when the English provoked them, he was to record in his
journal, 'Myself in the woods botanizing as usual, now
quite void of fear as our neighbours have turned out such
rank cowards.'[3]

As we have seen, he elaborated on this theme nine
years later when giving evidence to the House of

Commons inquiry that had examined Botany Bay as a site
for the transportation of convicts:

> [Banks] apprehended there would be little possibility
> of opposition from the natives, as during his stay there
> in the year 1770, he saw very few and did not think
> there were above fifty in the neighbourhood, and had
> reason to believe the country was very thinly pop-
> ulated, those he saw were naked, treacherous, and
> armed with lances, but extremely cowardly.[4]

The Gadigal Aboriginal people around Sydney Cove had
no knowledge of the Europeans. The short visit by Cook's
party in 1770 had been to Botany Bay, which was mainly
inhabited by different tribal groups, and it is unlikely that
any of those living around Port Jackson ever saw one of
Cook's men.

There were almost thirty different Aboriginal groups
living within about a forty-kilometre radius of Sydney at
the time of the arrival of the First Fleet.[5] There were about
ten groups around Port Jackson, with the Gadigal
language group predominant around Sydney Cove and on
the south of the harbour.

There is no reliable count of the local Aboriginal
population at the time. Cook had said they were not
numerous, and Phillip reported that there might have
been about fifteen hundred spread out through the entire
Sydney region, including Botany Bay, Port Jackson and
Broken Bay and 'the intermediate coast'.[6]

Certainly the Aboriginal population in the area was in
the hundreds rather than the thousands. The arrival of a
thousand European settlers concentrated on Sydney
Harbour was to have a devastating impact on the local
environment – causing not only a scarcity of resources but
also the introduction of diseases that the Aboriginal
people had no immunity to. An outbreak of smallpox

wiped out a large number of the local people a year after the settlers arrived.

Each group or tribe had its own language or dialect and was distinguished by its bodily decorations, songs, dances, tools and weapons. It is believed that there was some migration north and south along the coast, which meant that any one group could understand and communicate with another. There was less mixing between the hinterland and the coast. When the Aboriginal Bennelong, who was from the coastal Wangal group, went with a party of settlers twenty-five kilometres west to Parramatta in 1789, he was unable to understand what the locals were saying.

In Governor Phillip's original written instructions from King George III the settlers had been ordered to develop friendly relations with the Aboriginal people:

> You are to endeavour by every possible means to open an intercourse with the natives, and to conciliate their affections, enjoining all our subjects to live in amity and kindness with them. And if any of our subjects shall wantonly destroy them, or give them any unnecessary interruption . . . it is our will and pleasure that you do cause such offenders to be brought to punishment according to the degree of the offence.[7]

Phillip had himself written of the importance of good relations with the Aboriginal people in his 'vision' of the colony before leaving England:

> I think it is a great point gained if I can proceed in this business without having any dispute with the natives, a few of which I shall endeavour to persuade to settle near us and who I mean to furnish with everything that can tend to civilize them, and to give them a high opinion of the new guests.[8]

Part of this civilisation would require clothing the black man. Within months of arriving Phillip was to write to England seeking food, clothing and blankets for an increasingly desperate colony. At the same time he asked the British Government to send out clothing to cover the Aboriginal people:

> Clothing for the natives, if sent out will I daresay be very acceptable to them when they are among us. I should recommend long frock and jackets only, which will equally serve men and women.[9]

On arrival in New South Wales the governor had given instructions that the Aboriginal people were to be treated in a friendly way. The surgeon George Worgan wrote in his letter of 12–18 June 1788:

> The governor gave strict orders, that the natives should not be offended, or molested on any account, and advised that wherever, they were met with, they were to be treated with every mark of friendship. In case of their stealing any thing, mild means were to be used to recover it, but upon no account to fire at them with ball and shot.[10]

Phillip's colleagues saw little to justify the respect he wanted shown to the locals. Almost all of them were to record negative views about the Aboriginal people, and when their journals were published back in England they would help shape a European view of the Aboriginal people that would last for the next two centuries.

Surgeon Arthur Bowes Smyth believed they were stupid and lazy, and reflected this attitude in comments in his journal:

> Upon our landing seven or eight of the natives came close up to us – They were all provided with lances of

a great length pointed with the bone of a sting ray at one end and a piece of oyster shell at the other, grown or rubbed to a fine edge and one of them had a heavy bludgeon which I persuaded him to exchange with me for a looking glass. They were all perfectly naked rather slender, made of a dark black colour, their hair not wooly but short and curly. – Every one had the tooth next the fore tooth in his upper jaw knocked out, and many of them had a piece of stick about the size of a tobacco pipe and six or eight inches in length run through the septum of the nostrils, to which from its great similitude we ludicrously gave the name of a Sprit Sail Yard. They all cut their backs bodies and arms which heal up in large ridges and scars.

They live in miserable wigwams near the water which are nothing more than two or three pieces of the bark of a tree set up sideways against a ridge pole fastened to two upright sticks at each end – they are about two or three feet high, and few amongst them are to be found which are weather proof. Their principal food consists of fish which they in general eat raw – Sometimes they feast upon the kangaroo, but I believe them to be too stupid and indolent a set of people to be able often to catch them: from the appearance of many of the lofty trees we saw, some way up the country having regular steps chopped at about two foot asunder in the bark of the tree quite up to the top where the tree begins to branch out, there is reason to suppose they mount these with large stones where they lie in ambush till some kangaroos come under to graze when they heave the stone upon them and kill them.[11]

The 37-year-old Bowes Smyth was one of the first who had sailed with the First Fleet to return to England and publish his journal. He was only in New South Wales for four months before he sailed back on the *Lady Penrhyn*, which returned to England via Lord Howe Island, Tahiti and China.

American seaman Jacob Nagle also provided an early indication of the views of the white settlers about the Aboriginal people:

> The natives here are the most miserable on the sea coast I ever saw . . . They have some huts of bark but when the weather is cool, they generally get on the lee side of the harbour in the caves and hollow rocks and they always carry their fire with them to kindle a small fire at the entrance or otherwise in the middle of the cave. They chiefly live on fish. I have seen them have yellow root but it was so noxious and slimy that I could not bear it in my mouth.[12]

Not all of the assessments of the Aboriginal people were condescending and dismissive. Watkin Tench acknowledged that the lack of 'advancement and acquisition' might support the view that they 'were the least enlightened and ignorant on earth', but he argued that on more detailed inspection they 'possessed acumen, or sharpness of intellect, which bespeaks genius', citing some of their tools and weapons the manufacture of which 'display ingenuity'.[13]

Tench described them as more diminutive and slighter than Europeans, 'especially about the thighs and legs' and doubted that any reached the height of six feet. They wore no clothes, did not wash and if they did, it would 'not render them two degrees less black than an African Colony'.[14]

They lived in crude huts that 'consist only of pieces of bark laid together in the form of an oven, open at one end and very low',[15] although long enough for a man to lie full length. They carried lances and stone hatchets and manufactured small fishing nets.

The canoes they used to fish were as crude as their huts, 'being nothing more than a large piece of bark tied up at both ends by vines',[16] yet they were experts at paddling for miles out into the open sea. Tench noted that they made their fire by 'attrition', friction from rubbing wood together, and nearly always they carried a fire in the base of the canoes for the immediate cooking of the fish they caught.[17]

They cultivated no food and were entirely hunters and gatherers. Tench said that meat was rarely eaten raw, 'unless pressed by extreme hunger', but broiled, with their vegetables, on an open fire.[18] They used no cooking utensils and were fascinated, as has been mentioned earlier, when they first saw meat cooking in a pot on one of the settlers' fires.

Their diet was based on fishing, and when fish could not be caught they would collect the oysters and other shellfish around the shores. Tench said they also dug up and ate fern roots and a number of different wild berries.

He observed that the Aboriginal people were often hungry, and to alleviate the sensation of hunger they tied a vine ('ligature') tightly around their stomachs. Tench had seen English soldiers do something similar.

When given bread by the Europeans, they chewed it before spitting it out. They liked the salted pork and beef they were given, but most would not drink alcohol a second time. Many kept domesticated dingoes.

Tench said the women were distant and reserved and most had the two top joints of the little finger of their left hand cut off.

The men typically had one of their incisor teeth ceremonially removed, and Tench witnessed it being done to a number of them:

> The tooth to be taken out is loosened by the gum being scarified on both sides with a sharp shell. The

end of a stick is then applied to the tooth, which is
struck gently several times with a stone, until it
becomes easily moveable, when the 'coup de grace' is
given by a smart stroke. Notwithstanding these pre-
cautions, I have seen a considerable degree of swelling
and inflammation follows the extraction . . . It is
seldom performed on those who are under sixteen
years old.[19]

The initial contact between the Europeans and the
Aboriginal people had been friendly enough. When the
fleet landed in Botany Bay, and a few days later in Sydney
Cove, the exchanges between them were quite amicable as
the English handed out ribbons and trinkets as gestures of
friendship. Before the fleet had left Portsmouth, 'toys,
ribbons and other trifling articles' were put on board the
ships as presents for the Aboriginal people 'in order to
preserve their friendship that they will live peaceably with
the new settlers'.[20]

After only a few months, however, attacks against the
settlers were on the rise. Surgeon John White believed that
this was in retaliation for the stealing of food and for
assaults on the Aboriginal people:

30th [May 1788]. Captain Campbell of the marines,
who had been up the harbour to procure some rushes
for thatch, brought to the hospital the bodies of
William Okey and Samuel Davis, two rush-cutters,
whom he had found murdered by the natives in a
shocking manner. Okey was transfixed through the
breast with one of their spears, which with great
difficulty and force was pulled out. He had two other
spears sticking in him to a depth, which must have
proved mortal. His skull was divided and comminuted
so much that his brains easily found a passage through.
His eyes were out, but these might have been picked

away by birds. Davis was a youth, and had only some
trifling marks of violence about him. This lad could not
have been many hours dead, for when Captain
Campbell found him, which was among some
mangrove-trees, and at a considerable distance from
the place where the other man lay, he was not stiff nor
very cold; nor was he perfectly so when brought to the
hospital. From these circumstances we have been led to
think that while they were dispatching Okey he had
crept to the trees among which he was found, and that
fear, united with the cold and wet, in a great degree
contributed to his death. What was the motive or cause
of this melancholy catastrophe we have not been able
to discover, but from the civility shewn on all occasions
to the officers by the natives, whenever any of them
were met, I am strongly inclined to think that they must
have been provoked and injured by the convicts.[21]

By July Captain Tench recorded that the Aboriginal
people wanted little to do with the white man. 'They
seemed studiously to avoid us,' he said, 'either from
jealousy, or hatred.'[22]

Eight months after arriving Phillip confessed that the
white men knew little of the Aboriginal people and the
Aboriginal people resented the white man's presence. He
wrote to tell Lord Sydney of an idea he had for the two
groups to learn more about each other:

I am sorry to have been so long without knowing more
of these people but I am unwilling to use any force and
hope this summer to persuade a family to live with us,
unless they attempt to burn our crops, of which I am
apprehensive, for they certainly are not pleased with
our remaining among them, as they see we deprive
them of fish, which is almost their only support; but if
they set fire to the corn, necessity will oblige me to

drive them to a greater distance, though I can assure
your Lordship that I shall never do it but with the
greatest reluctance and from absolute necessity.[23]

A month later Phillip was to admit that he thought it
unlikely that an Aboriginal family could be persuaded to
voluntarily join the white community and it might be
necessary to use force to bring them over:

> I now doubt whether it will be possible to get any of
> these people to remain with us, in order to get their
> language without using force; they see no advantage
> that can arise from us that may make amends for the
> loss of that part of the harbour in which we occasion-
> ally employ the boats for fishing.[24]

Shortly after he was to note a further deterioration in
relations, when he recorded that the locals were increasingly avoiding the settlers. He thought it was because the
convicts had been stealing from them, and they in turn
had been attacking and murdering stragglers from the
camp:

> The natives now avoid us more than they did when
> we first landed and which I impute to the robberies
> committed on them by the convicts, who steel their
> spears and fizgigs, which they frequently leave in
> their huts when they go a fishing and which the
> people belonging to the transports purchase . . . This
> the natives revenge by attacking any stragglers they
> meet and one of the convicts has been killed since the
> *Sirius* sailed.[25]

On New Year's Eve of the first year of settlement and, in
Tench's words, 'tired of this state of petty warfare and
endless uncertainty',[26] Phillip decided that some of the

Aboriginal people should be abducted and brought into the white settlement. He believed that bringing them into the settlement would help bridge the language and cultural gap and provide the British with someone who could help communicate with the natives.

Lieutenants Henry Ball and George Johnston of the marines were duly ordered to go down to the north side of the harbour to bring back as many Aboriginal people as possible. Watkin Tench described the expedition:

> Pursuant to his resolution, the governor on the 31st of December sent two boats, under the command of Lieutenant Ball of the *Supply*, and Lieutenant George Johnston of the marines, down the harbour, with directions to those officers to seize and carry off some of the natives. The boats proceeded to Manly Cove, where several Indians were seen standing on the beach, who were enticed by courteous behaviour and a few presents to enter into conversation. A proper opportunity being presented, our people rushed in among them, and seized two men: the rest fled; but the cries of the captives soon brought them back, with many others, to their rescue: and so desperate were their struggles, that, in spite of every effort on our side, only one of them was secured; the other effected his escape. The boats put off without delay; and an attack from the shore immediately commenced; they threw spears, stones, firebrands, and whatever else presented itself, at the boats; nor did they retreat, agreeable to their former custom, until many musquets were fired over them.[27]

When they reached Sydney, the captive caused a lot of excitement when he was brought out of the boat tied up: 'the clamorous crowds flocked around him'. After many 'unsuccessful attempts were made to learn his name',[28] he

was called Manly by the Europeans, after the name of the
beach where he was abducted. Watkin Tench, who helped
bath, dress and feed Manly, recorded the episode in considerable detail:

> He appeared to be about 30 years old, not tall but
> robustly made . . . His hair was closely cut, his head
> combed and his beard shaved.
>
> To prevent his escape, a handcuff with a rope
> attached to it was fastened around his left wrist,
> which at first highly delighted him; he called it *Ben-
> gad-ee* (or ornament), but his delight turned to rage
> and hatred when he discovered its use.[29]

The next morning, New Year's Day, Manly was taken in
a boat down the harbour 'to convince his countrymen
that he had received no injury from us'.[30] When they
reached Manly, a number of his people came to talk to
him and asked why he didn't jump from the boat there
and then. 'He only sighed, and pointed to the fetter on his
leg, by which he was bound.'

Perhaps to compensate for his abduction, Manly was
given much more to eat than the standard ration:

> He dined at the side table at the Governors and ate
> heartily of fish and ducks, which he first cooled. Bread
> and salt meat he smelled at but would not taste, our
> liquors he treated in the same manner and could drink
> nothing but water.[31]

Over the next months Manly settled down and managed
to communicate his real name – Arabanoo – but his
continued detention failed to cause any significant
improvement in the relationship between the settlers and
the locals, which, as Tench wrote, had been the entire
justification for the abduction:

> One of the principal effects which we had supposed
> the seizure and captivity of Arabanoo would produce,
> seemed as yet as great a distance as ever; the natives
> neither manifested signs of increased hostility on
> his account, or ask any explanation ... of their
> countryman who was in our possession.[32]

Two months later sixteen convicts left their work at the brick kiln and marched to Botany Bay to steal fishing tackle and spears from the locals. They were attacked. One of the convicts was killed and seven were wounded. Phillip ordered that the survivors be 'severely flogged' in the hope that it would impress the Aboriginal people. However, the gesture backfired, wrote Tench, as the locals were appalled at the sight of the Europeans savagely flogging their own people: 'Arabanoo was present at the infliction of the punishment; and was made to comprehend the cause and necessity of it; but he displayed on the occasion symptoms of disgust and terror only.'[33]

In April 1789, more than a year after the arrival of the First Fleet, there was an outbreak of smallpox that was to kill a large number of the Aboriginal people. Some estimates suggest that as much as half the local population died.[34] Only one European perished, a sailor from the *Supply*.

The first symptoms of smallpox included a fever, headaches, joint and muscle pain and a feeling of exhaustion followed by frequent vomiting. After several days of shivering a rash appeared and developed into skin blisters. In severe cases the blisters became so dense as to coalesce into giant pustules. If the individual survived, the pustules left scars or 'pocks', which resulted in the disease being called the 'speckled monster' in the eighteenth century. Death was slow, painful and probably came as a relief for those who were severely affected. Those who were weaker, the very young and the very old died swiftly.

Smallpox was a greatly feared disease and an outbreak could spread quickly and kill many people. The first recorded epidemic was in ancient Egypt and seems to have reached Europe around the fifth or sixth century AD. By the eighteenth century it was a regular occurrence in Europe and in the colonies of north America.

The process of eradicating smallpox among Europeans had begun with the realisation that survivors could never contract the disease a second time. This led to the process of 'variolation', whereby a healthy person would be deliberately infected with material from someone with the disease in the hope of inducing a mild case of infection and thereby bringing about an immunity. The practice resulted in the death of between two and three per cent of those who were inoculated but saw a dramatic reduction in the number of epidemics.

The Aboriginal people had no exposure or resistance to the disease that was to devastate their population. Arthur Phillip noted that some who were infected had left their camp, saying that the disease 'must have been spread to a considerable distance as well as inland and along the coast'.[35]

The settlers provided some medical help, and Arabanoo went to the aid of as many of his people as possible. The fetter was removed from his leg so he could move around the area but he too was struck down and died six days later. By this stage Arabanoo had become popular among the settlers. He was buried in the governor's garden, and Phillip and all the officers of the settlement attended the funeral.[36]

The white settlers could not account for the outbreak, although it must have been brought into the area by the First Fleet. If it had been carried by one of the new settlers, why hadn't it appeared before now, almost fifteen months after their arrival? And why wasn't it evident among any other of the Europeans?

Arthur Phillip speculated as to how the disease could have arrived in the colony:

> Whether the small pox, which has proved fatal to great numbers of the natives, is a disorder to which they were subject before any Europeans visited this country, or whether it was brought by the French ships, we have not yet attained sufficient knowledge of the language to determine. It never appeared on board any of the ships in our passage, nor in the settlement, until some time after numbers of the natives had been dead with the disorder.[37]

Another possibility is that the disease was released from one of the vials that the surgeons had brought as a source of variolation, but the surgeons denied it.

After the death of Arabanoo the settlers sought a replacement and conscripted two Aboriginal men, Bennelong (also known as Beneelon) and Colbee, into their service. The two men joined two Aboriginal children, Abaroo and Nanbaree, who were taken into the settlement when their parents died during the smallpox epidemic.

Bennelong was to adjust to the white man's environment better than his colleagues. For most of the time he seemed happy to live among the English. He wore their clothes and was an effective liaison between his people and Governor Phillip. As Tench noted, he also enjoyed a drink:

> He became at once fond of our viands [food] and would drink the strongest liquors, not simply without reluctance, but with eager marks of delight. He was the only native we knew who immediately showed a fondness for spirits.[38]

Bennelong went to live in a little house built by the settlers for him in Sydney Cove. The area later became known as

Bennelong Point and provided the site for the Sydney Opera House around a hundred and fifty years later. He was highly regarded by the English, as Tench wrote:

> His powers of mind were certainly far above mediocrity. He acquired knowledge, both of our manners and language, faster than his predecessors had done. He willingly communicated information, sang, danced and capered, told us all the customs of his country, and all the details of his family economy. Love and war seemed his favourite pursuits; in both of which he had suffered severely. His head was disfigured with several scars; a spear had passed through his arm, and another through his leg. Half of one of his thumbs was carried away; and the mark of a wound appeared on the back of his hand.
>
> The cause and attendant circumstances of all these disasters, except one, he recounted to us. 'But the wound on the back of your hand, Beenalon. How did you get that'. He laughed and owned that it was received in carrying off a lady of another tribe by force. 'I was dragging her away. She cried aloud and stuck her teeth into me.'[39]

Despite being held in regard by the settlers, and initially being happy in the white man's world, Bennelong fled back to his own people early in 1790. Some months later Phillip was told that Bennelong had been seen, and he took a boat with armed marines to recapture him across to Manly Cove on the northern side of Port Jackson where the Aboriginal people were feasting on a beached whale.

With the rowers sitting in the boat, Phillip went ashore with his fellow officers carrying gifts for the locals. As a gesture of friendship Phillip withdrew a knife from his belt and threw it on the ground, but it frightened one of the natives, who quickly lifted his spear with his foot and threw it at Phillip. The four-metre lance went through Phillip below the shoulder blade and the barb came out of his back.

Phillip and his colleagues hurriedly stumbled down the beach towards the boat. One of the marines, Lieutenant Waterhouse, tried to pull the spear out but, realising it would cause more damage, broke off the shaft instead. As they pulled Phillip onto the boat, the crew fired off a round from their muskets to aid their escape.

It took two hours to row back up the harbour. Phillip lay on the floor of the boat, conscious but bleeding, and his colleagues expected him to die. When they reached Sydney Cove, the surgeon William Balmain thought at first that his subclavian artery had been severed, but after treating the wound he saw that the injury was not as serious as he had feared. Bennelong, who had not been involved in the wounding of Phillip, expressed concern at the incident and began calling at Sydney Cove asking after the welfare of the governor. Eventually contact was re-established and Bennelong moved back to Sydney Cove.

When Phillip returned to England in 1792, he took Bennelong and another Aboriginal man, named Yemmer-rawanne, with him. Yemmerrawanne was reportedly unhappy in London and became ill and died, but Benne-long seemed to enjoy himself, initially at least. He wore laced shirts and embroidered waistcoats and was a novel figure in British society. In May 1793 he was taken to meet King George III. In London he learned to box, skate and smoke and adopted some of the English manners, including the use of knife and fork, bowing and drinking toasts.

After more than two years Bennelong longed to go home, and he returned to Sydney in September 1795. By now he was drinking heavily and constantly fighting, which resulted in his losing the respect of many of his own people. He died a sad figure aged about 50 in 1813.

The failure of the Aboriginal people and the Europeans in Australia to understand each other was exacerbated by fundamental differences in their respective societies. The Aboriginal people accepted that different groups had rights to different territory. The Europeans, by contrast, treated all of the land as entirely their own; by their law it now belonged to King George III and to his heirs and successors.

Survival in the harsh Australian environment required a sensitive relationship between the people and the land and the sea, yet the First Fleeters took everything they could, depleting the natural food supply and chasing away many of the other animals. The Aboriginal people shared what they had, but the English, committed to the idea of individual property, saw them as scavengers when they asked for food.

Over the next two centuries these fundamental differences would disrupt and destroy a civilisation and culture that had survived for thousands of years.

14

CRISIS

Famine . . . was approaching with gigantic strides, and the
gloom and dejection overspread every countenance. Men
abandoned themselves to the most desponding reflections
. . . Still we were on the tip toe of expectations . . . every
morning from daylight until the sun sank did we sweep the
horizon, in hope of seeing a sail . . . all our labour and
attention were turned to one object – the procuring of food.

The First Fleet settlers had struggled in the early days to establish a new home, but over the next two years a growing food shortage was to create a crisis that would threaten the survival of the entire settlement.

From the start food was rationed, although it was envisaged that the restrictions would gradually be eased as the colony developed its own food supply. The fleet had sailed with only two years' worth of supplies, and having spent the best part of a year on the voyage out from England it was important that sufficient crops were sown immediately on arrival.

But within two months of arriving an assessment of available food stocks resulted in what was to be the first of a series of cuts to the food ration. Over the next two years the standard issue would be progressively reduced to starvation levels.

The shortage of food in the settlement was made worse
by theft from the public stores. Phillip, who had initially
demonstrated a tolerance that raised the eyebrows of even
his most loyal officers, now agreed to the most severe
treatment of those caught taking food. The governor
'signified . . . his resolution that the condemnation of
anyone for robbing huts or stores should be immediately
followed by execution'.[1]

It had been hoped that they might have been able to at
least partially offset the lack of fresh food with turtle meat.
In February of 1788, when Lieutenant Henry Ball had
ferried Philip Gidley King and his small party of settlers to
Norfolk Island on the *Supply*, he had brought back from
Lord Howe Island sixteen large turtles each weighing more
than a hundred and fifty pounds. More of the turtles would
have given the settlement a good source of fresh meat.

In May Lieutenant Ball was sent back to Lord Howe
Island to collect as many as he could load onto the
Supply, only to find that the turtles they had seen there
earlier had already migrated further north for the winter.
According to Surgeon White the return of the *Supply* to
Sydney without any turtles was 'a dreadful disappointment to those who were languishing under the scurvy,
many of whom are since dead, and there is great reason
to fear that several others will soon share the same fate'.[2]

Fishing proved to be erratically successful, and there
was the occasional hunted emu or 'stray kangaroo which
fortune now and then threw in our way', but by the
middle of the first year the settlers became 'utter strangers
to the taste of fresh food'.[3]

By July White was to complain that illness was
aggravated by the lack of vital food. At the time he
reported that a total of one hundred and fifty-four
marines and convicts were too sick to work:

> The distress among the troops, their wives and
> children, as well as among the convicts, who have been

ill for want of necessaries to aid the operation of
medicines has been most materially and sensibly felt . . .
The articles [include] sugar, sago, barley, rice, oatmeal,
currents, spices, vinegar, portable soup and tamarinds
. . . Constantly living on salt provisions without possibility of change make them more necessary.[4]

In the same month Phillip sent the first clear signal to
England that the settlement was heading for crisis.[5] In a
long letter he told Lord Sydney that the original plan that
required the settlers to bring out with them only two
years' provisions, after which they would be self-
sufficient, had failed. Phillip wrote that he had hoped to
'provide a more pleasing account of our present situation'
but that the colony 'must for some years depend on
supplies from England'. In his opinion, 'A regular supply
of provisions from England will be absolutely necessary
for four or five years, as the crops for two years to come
cannot be depended on for more than what will be
necessary for seeds.'[6]

In September Phillip wrote again to say that the first
harvest had failed and yielded only enough food to
support the colony for a 'few days'. Consequently none of
the grain was fed to the settlers but was instead saved as
seed for the following year's sowing:

> It was now found that very little of the English wheat
> had vegetated and a very considerable quantity of
> barley and many seeds had rotted in the ground,
> having been heated in the passage and some much
> injured by weevils. All the barley and wheat likewise,
> which had been put aboard the *Supply* at the Cape
> were destroyed by the weevil.[7]

Phillip also described the sorry state of the colony's
livestock:

> The greatest part of the stock brought from the Cape is dead, and from the inattention of the men who had the care of the cattle, those belonging to the Government and two cows belonging to me are lost ... All my sheep are dead and a few only remain of those purchased for Government. The loss of four cows and two bulls falls very heavy.[8]

Although the pigs and chickens 'thrive and increase fast', he admitted that:

> I have now given up all hopes of recovering the two bulls and four cows that were lost, and one sheep only remains of upwards of more than seventy which I had purchased at the Cape on my own account and on Government's account.[9]

In July Phillip had written that the failure of the new colony to grow any significant food meant that all of the settlers would be largely dependent for another year on the food that was still in two small storage sheds: 'All the provisions we have to depend on until supplies arrive from England are in two wooden buildings, which are thatched. I am sensible to the risk but have no remedy.'[10]

Clothing was also wearing out and replacements running short. As the first winter came, many of the settlers, including the marines, had worn out their shoes and were forced to go about their business barefoot: 'Clothing in this country is full as necessary as in England, the nights and mornings being very cold; and before any supplies can be sent out most of the people will be without shoes, the most necessary article.'[11]

Phillip would complain in September: 'The clothes for the convicts are in general bad and there is no possibility of mending them for want of thread; it is the same with shoes, which do not last a month.'[12]

The settlement also needed 'some kind of covering' for the children, as children's clothing had never been included in the original planning.[13]

The combination of disease and the shortage of food was taking its toll, and more people died in the first eight months after arriving than had died on the eight-month voyage from England: fifty-two had died in the colony by September, compared with forty-eight while sailing from England. Sadly, the dead on land included twenty-three women and children.[14]

The marine captain Watkin Tench admitted that before the end of the first year the settlers were increasingly desperate for supplies and living every day in the hope that ships from England would appear with fresh provisions: 'We had long turned our eyes with impatience towards the sea, cheered by the hope of seeing supplies from England approach, but none arriving.'[15]

In August, while exploring the head waters of the river that ran from the mountains in the west into Port Jackson, Phillip had found fertile soil and decided to establish a settlement at what was to become known as Rose Hill, thinking that this area might be ideal for the colony's food production.

The situation was so urgent in September, though, that with the food stocks declining and 'the fear of not having grain to put into the ground next year', Phillip decided to send Captain Hunter on the *Sirius* to Cape Town to fetch grain and flour. As Hunter was to record:

> In the month of September, Governor Phillip signified to me, that it was his intention very soon to dispatch the *Sirius* to the Cape of Good Hope, in order to purchase such quantities and provisions as she might be capable of taking on board.[16]

Before it could leave, the *Sirius* had to be made shipshape, as its maintenance had 'been much neglected'. For the next month Captain Hunter 'employed an old man, the carpenter's yeoman, and a convict caulker'[17] to help prepare the ship for its voyage.

It had originally been planned that the *Sirius* would be sent to the Cape to collect more livestock, given the losses and death of so much that came with the fleet at the beginning of the year. However, the failure of the first year's harvest in both Sydney and Norfolk Island left the colony with a more immediate need of food; and the *Sirius* was not large enough to carry both livestock and grain.[18]

A month after Hunter left on his quest to southern Africa, the food ration in the colony was reduced by a third.

To reach the Cape of Good Hope and return quickly Hunter decided to circumnavigate the globe by sailing east under New Zealand and then under Cape Horn at the bottom of South America before heading east again to reach Sydney:

> At that season of the year the route to the eastward by Cape Horn promised fairest for an expeditious passage; I therefore steered for the South Cape of New Zealand which I passed on the 12th [November] and made the coast of Terra del Forego on the 26th November.[19]

The voyage was to prove difficult from the start. Within a day of leaving Sydney a major leak was discovered below the waterline that required the water to be pumped out of the *Sirius* all the way to Cape Town:

> On the day I sailed from Port Jackson the ship sprang a leak, which admitted two feet four inches water in the four hours but as before my arrival here we had

discovered it to be about two or three feet below the wale, starboard side, I hope to have it stopped before I sail on my return to the coast of New South Wales.[20]

It appears that the ship's maintenance team of the old man, the carpenter's mate and the convict caulker had not done a good job.

Even though it was now approaching the height of the southern-hemisphere summer the prevailing winds took the *Sirius* in latitudes towards the Antarctic, amid snow and icebergs: 'The weather proved intolerably cold. Ice, in great quantity, was seen for many days; and in the middle of December . . . water froze in open casks upon the deck in the latitude of forty four degrees south.'[21]

By late November the crew began to be disabled with scurvy. As many of the crew had eaten very little fresh food since they had last been in the Cape of Good Hope on their way to New South Wales the year before, the illness came as no surprise to Hunter. He had nothing on the *Sirius* for its treatment except for 'a little essence of malt'. Their only hope, he said, was 'for a speedy passage' to their destination, where they would have access to fresh food that would 'reinstate their health'.[22]

Aboard the *Sirius* the American seaman Jacob Nagle described going around Cape Horn at Christmas and passing dangerously close to more than thirty giant icebergs and large pieces of floating ice, which was 'the most dangerous in the night'. He also said they passed whales that were 'very numerous and that were so thick that we could not count them' and their spouting soaked all the crew on deck with spray.[23]

Nagle was one of the many crew stricken with scurvy who collapsed. He had to be 'carried below three times in one night'. The disease decimated the crew and 'some died in the sight of the Cape'.[24]

The ship finally reached Robben Island, about eight kilometres from the mouth of Table Bay, on New Year's Day 1789. Fresh fruit was immediately brought on board for the sick; the following day they entered Table Bay. Nagle described how he and the others stricken with scurvy tried to eat the fresh fruit: when 'biting an apple, pear or peach the blood would run out of our mouth from our gums'.[25]

By the time they arrived at the Cape of Good Hope after roughly ninety days' sailing, more than half of the crew were too ill to work the ship, according to Hunter:

> When we arrived in this bay, we had just twelve men in each watch, and half that number, from scorbutic contractions in their limbs, were not able to go aloft . . . Immediately after our arrival, I directed that sick quarters should be provided for the sick, which was done, and the invalids, to the number of forty, were landed under the care of Mr. Worgan, the surgeon of the ship.[26]

Hunter was keen to be away with the relief food as soon as possible but was delayed in Cape Town loading the supplies because he had so many sick crewmen. He also had only two little boats to bring the cargo from the shore, 'Governor Phillip having found it necessary to keep the *Sirius*' long boat and a smaller boat for the use of the settlement, which reduced our number to two six oared cutters'.[27] At the time of their arrival Table Bay was very busy and it was difficult to hire additional boats.

Hunter also needed to repair the *Sirius*, which was still leaking badly. He had the ship 'heeled', or put on its side, and a number of holes plugged, but reported that the ship would need major repair work 'below the wales' when they eventually returned to Port Jackson.[28]

Nagle and four other seamen deserted the *Sirius* in Table Bay, objecting, Nagle said, to the behaviour of the young midshipman who was in charge of the boat that was ferrying and loading food onto the ship:

> He begin upon the whole boat crew with his rattan without any provocation and being a stripling not more than 15 years of age I told him we would not be treated in such a manner by a boy. When we got on shore, five out of the six left the boat not intending to return any more.[29]

Nagle was persuaded to return when Hunter admonished the midshipman and confined him for three weeks to his cabin as punishment, but the other four crewmen disappeared and 'never did return'.[30]

Hunter left Table Bay on 20 February 1789, after more than seven weeks in the port. His voyage back to Sydney was even more difficult than that of the previous year, when he had sailed as commander of the slower ships in the First Fleet. This time he did not 'meet with the westerly winds quite so soon as I expected, or as we had done the last time we had made this passage'.[31]

When later on the voyage back they finally met with strong winds, the weather closed in so much that they were unable for some days to calculate their exact position:

> It may not be improper here to observe, that three days had now elapsed without a sight of sun during the day or a star during the night from which we could exactly determine our latitude ... the gale not in the least likely to abate, and the sea running mountain high, with very thick weather, a long dark night just coming on, and an unknown coast I may call it, (for although it has been seen by several navigators, it is not yet

known) close under our lee; nothing was now left to be done but to carry every yard of canvass the ship was capable of bearing, and for every person on board to constantly keep the deck.[32]

After finally rounding Tasmania and heading north, they again encountered strong headwinds and did not reach Port Jackson until early May, having been away seven months. Tench described the relief felt by everyone in the settlement on seeing them:

> May 1789. At sunset, on the evening of the 2nd instant, the arrival of the *Sirius* Captain Hunter from the Cape of Good Hope was proclaimed and diffused universal joy and congratulations. The day of famine was at least procrastinated by the supply of flour and salt provisions she brought us.[33]

The *Sirius* had brought vital relief to Sydney, but, after the initial excitement, reality set in. Its cargo of flour was not enough to make up for all the other declining food stocks of the colony. David Collins captured the disappointment: 'The *Sirius* brought one hundred and twenty seven thousand weight of flour for the settlement . . . but this supply was not very flattering as the short space of four months at a full ration, would exhaust it.'[34]

If the first year for the colony had been difficult, the second year was to be much worse. Theft of food from the stores and from other people was rife, as was pillaging from the vegetable gardens before the food was ripe for harvest. Increased punishments, including executions, could not control it.

In March 1789 six marines were caught stealing large quantities of food and grog from the public store. Nobody seemed to notice that the stores had been gradually depleted for 'upwards of eight months'[35] or that the marines had excessive amounts of alcohol that they shared with some of the convict women.

The scheme was uncovered when one morning the commissary was conducting the usual inspection of the food store and found a broken piece of key stuck in the lock. The locksmith identified it as belonging to a marine private named Joseph Hunt, who had regularly been in trouble in the settlement. Hunt turned and gave evidence against the other marines. They had had the key made so that when one of them was posted at night to guard the store, he would allow the others entry to steal food and grog. If a night patrol passed the store while the thieves were inside, 'the door was found locked and secure' with the guard outside and the 'store apparently safe'.[36]

On Friday 27 March all six marines were hanged on a scaffold that had been built between the storehouses.

In August a convict called John Harris persuaded Judge David Collins and Arthur Phillip to establish a night watch from among the more trusted convicts – and so Australia's first police force was formed, though it is not clear if it made any difference to the level of thefts.

By the beginning of November in the second year of the settlement the standard rations of flour, salted meat and peas or rice were reduced again. By now everyone knew that the settlement was in a state of crisis, and all attention was focused on where the next intake of food would come from. Watkin Tench wrote:

> Famine . . . was approaching with gigantic strides, and the gloom and dejection overspread every countenance. Men abandoned themselves to the most desponding reflections, and adopted the most extravagant conjectures. Still we were on the tip toe of expectations . . . every morning from daylight until the sun sank did we sweep the horizon, in hope of seeing a sail. At every

fleeting speck which arose from the bosom of the sea,
the heart bounded and the telescope was lifted to the
eye . . . all our labour and attention were turned to one
object – the procuring of food.[37]

By the end of 1789, two and a half years after leaving
England and nearly two years after arriving at Sydney, the
only food in addition to that which had been brought
with them had been the few months' supply of flour
brought by the *Sirius* and some very small harvests of
locally grown crops.

The settlement was running out of other supplies as
well. Towards the end of 1789 the colony ran out of
candles 'so that everyone was obliged to go to bed the
moment it was dark'.[38]

On 1 November 1789, following a calculation of the
remaining food, a decision was made to further cut
the food ration: '[E]very man from the Governor to the
convict' had their ration cut by a further third – except for
women feeding babies.[39]

By the end of December the new settlement at Rose
Hill had, thankfully, registered its first decent harvest –
two hundred bushels of wheat and thirty-five bushels of
barley. By comparison Sydney Cove only produced
twenty-five bushels of grain, which vindicated Phillip's
decision to establish the new settlement.

Welcome though the harvest was, for the hungry
mouths of Sydney it was not to be enough. By early in the
new year the flour they had brought from England had
completely run out and they were forced to begin eating
into the modest supply that had been brought back from
the Cape of Good Hope. By May the following year
almost all the food in the colony would be gone.

In the letters written from Sydney Cove in 1788 Phillip
had asked for the urgent supply of additional food and
provisions but also for convicts who had skills required in

the colony and overseers to supervise the convicts at work.

In April 1789 Lord Sydney had written to the lords of the Admiralty to say that King George III had authorised the urgent dispatch of a supply ship to relieve the colony:

> The letters which have been received from Captain Phillip Governor of New South Wales representing that a great part of the provisions sent out with him to the settlement lately made upon the coast has been expended and that there is an immediate occasion for a further supply, together with certain articles of clothing, tools, implements for agriculture, medicines etc. His Majesty has given orders that one of his ships of war of two decks, with only her upper tier of guns, shall forthwith be got ready to carry out the said provisions and stores.[40]

Within a month the Admiralty had responded by appointing Lieutenant Edward Riou as captain of the HMS *Guardian*, which would take fresh supplies to New South Wales. The *Guardian* had been built five years earlier in the Limehouse shipbuilding docks in London, a big forty-four-gun naval frigate. At one hundred and forty feet long (forty-two and a half metres), it was bigger than all the ships of the First Fleet. When it was converted for transporting cargo, and the guns on the lower decks taken out, it was capable of carrying more than nine hundred tons of food and other supplies.

The 27-year-old Riou had joined the navy as a 14-year-old midshipman in 1776 and had sailed with Cook on his third great voyage up the west coast of America. He later served on the *Romney* under Vice-Admiral John Montague in the British North Atlantic station and was promoted to lieutenant in 1780.

The Admiralty had also instructed that twenty-five convict tradesmen and farmers be sent out in response to Phillip's request for more convicts with skills to further the development of the settlement. This was to be the first time that convicts were chosen because they might be suited to serving out their sentences in the new colony.

Another of Phillip's concerns was addressed by the Admiralty, who had been asked by Lord Sydney to ensure that convict overseers also be sent on the *Guardian*. Phillip had complained that the convicts had no effective supervision, since the marine officers refused to oversee the convicts at work and relying on other convicts as supervisors had not succeeded:

> About eight to ten persons should also be engaged and take their passage in the said ship, to be employed as overseers of the convicts. These measures . . . have been strongly recommended by Captain Phillip . . . from having found by experience that the convicts placed as overseers have not been able to enforce their orders and carry that command which persons in a different situation would be likely to do.[41]

The overseers who sailed on the *Guardian* included Philip Divine and Andrew Hume, who had been supervisors of convicts in the hulks at Woolwich, John Barlow, who had served as an officer in the army, and John Thomas Dodge, a former surveyor, gardener and commander of an American merchant ship.

In addition to being loaded with food and other provisions the *Guardian* was to have a special shed built on its quarterdeck for trees and plants that were to be transplanted in Sydney. This addition was the result of botanist Joseph Banks' direct lobbying of King George III, who gave instructions for it to be built and two gardeners sent on the ship:

> Having laid before the King a letter from Sir Joseph
> Banks, proposing that a small coach may be erected on
> the quarterdeck of the *Guardian* for the purpose of
> conveying to Port Jackson in pots of earth such plants
> and trees as will be useful in food or physique and
> cannot conveniently be propagated by seed . . . I am
> commanded to signify your Lordships pleasure . . . that
> you do give orders that it may be immediately erected.[42]

It took several months to organise, transport and load the
supplies onto the *Guardian* – almost a thousand tons in
all. The cargo included a large amount of grain, ninety-
three pots containing vegetables, herbs and fruit, and
livestock, including sheep, horses, cattle, goats, rabbits
and poultry. Also on board were the twenty-five
'artificers', or qualified convict tradesmen, and ten agricultural supervisors, or overseers.

The *Guardian* had been due to sail at the end of
June 1789[43] but was delayed and did not leave until
12 September. By the time the *Guardian* left Portsmouth,
the *Lady Juliana*, the first of the Second Fleet ships,
carrying more than two hundred women convicts, had
already been gone a month. However, by sailing the more
direct route down the African coast rather than going
across the Atlantic, the *Guardian* was able to overtake the
Lady Juliana and reached Cape Town on 24 November
while the *Lady Juliana* was still in Rio de Janeiro.

At the Cape of Good Hope Riou was made further
aware of the plight of the colonists in New South Wales
when he was told how John Hunter had been there in the
Sirius earlier in the year, using Admiralty bills of credit to
buy much-needed food before hurrying off with the
supplies for the hungry settlement.

Realising the urgent need for his relief supplies, Riou
wasted no time in topping up, loading the ship with more
cattle and horses as well as one hundred and fifty fruit

trees, before leaving Cape Town on 11 December. They had stayed in port for only two weeks.

As Christmas approached, the *Guardian* was making good time. It was more than a thousand kilometres to the east and south of Cape Town, deep in the Great Southern Ocean, sailing in fresh breezes and surrounded by fog and large 'islands of ice', as Riou described.[44]

On the afternoon of Christmas Eve, in need of drinking water for both the crew and the livestock, the *Guardian* lowered its small boats over the side. According to the master of the ship, Clements: 'The cutter and the jolly boats were hoisted out and sent with a petty officer and a boats crew in each to gather up the broken pieces of ice, which were floating at a distance from the main body.'[45]

The ship's captain, Edward Riou, was well aware of the hazards of sailing in these waters and noted the conditions in his journal:

> We found the great emission of fog from this mountain of ice darken the hemisphere to the leeward of it . . . The horizon became clouded all around and in less than a quarter of an hour we were again shut up in a thick, close general mist and scarce able to see the ship's length before us. From this it was apprehended there were many more such islands of ice floating in these seas, which appeared very dangerous.[46]

At 7.45 pm, as the watch was changing, the *Guardian* crashed into an iceberg. Clements recalls that as it happened he was handing over the watch to Mr Harvey, the master's mate, and had just remarked 'how much more dreadful it would be to be ship wrecked before an island of ice than among rocks, when the noise reached the cabin and gave the fatal signal of failure'.[47]

As the ship shook from end to end, Riou ran immediately up onto the deck. '[T]he scene appeared abysmal beyond relief';[48] the front of the *Guardian* had wedged under a giant iceberg that appeared to be twice as tall as the mainmast of the ship.

It was quickly established that the rudder had broken away and the tiller was broken in two places, but the extent of any damage below the waterline was not yet apparent. As Clements was to later recall:

> When at last the sails filled she began to forge off but struck again and continued crashing on the ice underneath her until she at last got clear . . . The wind was blowing hard [and] we soon lost sight of the ice. Our spirits then gained new vigour and served to supply fresh strength.[49]

The joy was short-lived, however, because within half an hour it was discovered that there was more than two feet of water in the hold, and the water level was rising fast. All available hands were put to the pumps, but they were unable to stem the rise.

To lighten the ship Riou immediately ordered the crew to jettison as much of the cargo as possible that was destined for New South Wales: 'All hands that could be spared were set to work to clear the deck of cattle, booms, the hay, gun carriages, bows and spare anchors, and below decks aft, of provisions.'[50]

By nine o'clock at night the pumps were all at work but the water level had risen in the hold to over three feet and gaining. At ten the water reached five feet and men were tiring at the pumps, so they were split into two shifts to work alternately every half-hour, with breaks in between:

> The captain ordered refreshments to be allocated to each man, taking particular care that the grog should not be made too strong. Every man received the first

supply with biscuits and cheese, which seemed to give
them fresh spirits to return to their laborious duty.
The rum was soon nearly expended but the captain
thought it would be extremely dangerous to open the
hold to get at more, for fear the men's getting at it;
wine and water was accordingly given in lieu of it.[51]

At midnight the water level reached six feet and 'it
was blowing a strong gale and an immense sea was
running'.[52] All night long the crews continued to pump
and by sunup the next morning – Christmas Day – at last
the water level below decks began to fall. By that
afternoon the crew were exhausted: 'About this time the
crew became almost unable to perform any duty, from
their limbs being benumbed by the frequent transition
from the heat of labour and having rested in wet
clothes.'[53]

By five in the afternoon the water had risen again, and
Riou severely bruised his hand when it was crushed by a
crate they were endeavouring to throw over the side. By 4
am on Boxing Day the water level was nearing seven feet
for the first time. To make matters worse, during the night
the topsails, which had been left unattended, were torn to
pieces 'by the violence of the wind and the ship was left
to the entire mercy of a most tremendous sea'.[54]

Up to this point the crew had not been told of the seri-
ousness of their predicament, but around six o'clock on
the morning of Boxing Day the ship's carpenter came up
and reported that the water was as high as the orlop, or
lowest deck, and gaining about a foot every hour. A
number of the crew, already exhausted, resigned themselves to the inevitable sinking of the ship and certain
death and broke into the rum store: 'A few of the more
profligate escaped with utmost vigilance and secreted
themselves below, where they got intoxicated with liquor
and became insensible of their danger.'[55]

Amazingly, while all this was going on, Riou went to his cabin and wrote a letter to the Admiralty in which he declared 'there seems to be no possibility of my remaining many hours in this world' and praised all the crew for their honourable conduct. No mention was made of the fact that a number of crew were comatose with alcohol:

> If any part of the officers or crew of the *Guardian* should ever survive to get home, I have only to say their conduct after the fatal stroke against an island of ice was admirable and wonderful in everything that related to their duties, considered either as private men or on his Majesty's service.[56]

By evening, when the water was up to the lower gun deck and it appeared the ship was about to sink, everyone on board was given the option of abandoning ship and going aboard one of the five small boats. Riou decided to go down with his ship: 'As for me, I have determined to remain in the ship and shall endeavour to make my presence useful as long as there is any occasion for it.'[57]

The boatswain was ordered to make sure every little boat had oars, a mast and a sail, a compass, a cask of water and 'other necessities', but their loading proved to be extremely difficult and resulted in panic and chaos. A number of the little boats were buffeted against the side of the ship in the high seas:

> We then set to work and hoisted out the cutter on the starboard and lee side and afterwards the other boats on the booms; they were all fortunately got into the water with very little damage but the sea was immensely high and it was with great difficulty they were kept from being stove to pieces along side.[58]

The largest boat was quickly adrift of the *Guardian*. It had only seven men aboard, but no food or water. In desperation a number of the men jumped into the icy water trying to reach the boats. According to Riou, 'If these men lived out the day it would be the utmost: indeed, I am inclined to think they could have survived a few minutes.'[59]

Clements, on one of the boats, watched one of the others sink and then lost sight of another.

Sixty-two men of the original one hundred and twenty-three[60] stayed on board the *Guardian*, either because they could not safely board one of the lifeboats or because they thought their chances of survival were better trying to keep the *Guardian* afloat. Among those who stayed was Thomas Pitt, the nephew of the prime minister, two midshipmen, the ship's carpenter, the surgeon's mate John Fairclough, thirty seamen and boys, twenty-one convicts and three of their supervisors.

Of the five small boats, only one was ever heard of again. Among its fifteen survivors was Clements, who would later record their nine-day ordeal in an open boat in freezing conditions. He described how they boarded late in the afternoon on Boxing Day in squally and cloudy conditions and tried to head 'as much northward as the sea would allow' but finally lost sight of the only other boat that they still had contact with.

There was very little drinking water, so they rationed it out in the bottom of a tobacco canister at the rate of about two gills, or a little less than a quarter of a litre, for each person each day. After four days they were running out of food and divided 'our last fowl . . . and received a small thimble of rum each'.

By New Year's Eve, according to Clements, they were so thirsty that 'many people this day drank their urine'. There was still some cheese and ham on board but it remained uneaten:

We could not eat the smallest crumb till supplied with additional measure of water to moisten our lips. We dropped our bit of biscuit into the water and afterwards sipped a little of it with each mouthful to force it down.[61]

On 4 January 1790 they sighted a ship about four hundred kilometres east of Natal off the east coast of Africa:

> One day more of such misery as we suffered in the last twelve hours, would have certainly terminated the lives of some, and the others must soon after have paid their debts to nature. At day break the gunner, who was then at the helm, discovered a ship at a little distance from us . . . Our joy at this sight was great beyond expression.[62]

It was a French ship, the *Viscountess of Brittany*, which was on its way to the Cape from India. Fifteen days later the survivors were landed safely back in Table Bay, which they had left nearly two months earlier.

Meanwhile, it was thought that the *Guardian* had sunk, and when the news reached London *The Times* reported that 'The Captain made every exertion possible to save the ship' but 'with the rest of the crew are all supposed to have perished'.[63]

However, Riou and sixty-one of the remaining crew who had stayed on the waterlogged ship somehow stayed afloat for two months, travelling without an effective rudder at a maximum speed of barely four knots. By the end of the first week in January the water was above the lower deck as the exhausted crew continued to pump it out. For several weeks the ship drifted across the Indian Ocean to the south of Cape St Mary in Madagascar and back towards Africa.

On 21 February, two months after it began sinking, the
Guardian was seen by a passing Dutch packet boat that
was carrying mail from the Spice Islands and Batavia back
to Europe. The Dutch ship was 'providentially steering
a high southerly latitude' and assisted the half-sunken
Guardian back to the Cape of Good Hope.

The ship was now beyond repair, with a large part of
its hull missing and much of its structure torn away. Riou
reported to the Admiralty that repairing the ship would
be pointless, the 'cost would be so immense, together with
refitting her, as to exceed the value of a new ship'.[64]

On 12 April the disabled vessel was torn from its
moorings in a fierce gale and beached, and the cargo that
had not been thrown overboard was salvaged and put
ashore. Over the next three months first the *Lady Juliana*
and then the three convict transports from the Second
Fleet – the *Neptune*, the *Surprize* and the *Scarborough* –
arrived in Cape Town and were ordered to take aboard
some of the *Guardian*'s salvaged supplies 'from Lieutenant Riou for use in the colony'.[65]

Salvaged items that finally reached Sydney included
leather, clothing, linen and two hundred casks of flour,
but much of what was vitally needed in the colony,
including salt, rice, oatmeal, sugar and medicines, was
'perfectly spoilt and useless', according to Riou's letter to
Lord Stephens of the Admiralty.[66]

In the same letter Riou praised the surviving twenty
convicts who had stayed on the stricken ship and who
were now to be sent on with the Second Fleet to Sydney
to complete their sentences.[67] As a result of these representations the British Government authorised their
pardons, provided they did not return to England until
their time for transportation was completed.[68]

Of the overseers and qualified convict tradesmen who
had been sent on the *Guardian* at Phillip's request, only
five made it to Sydney on the *Lady Juliana*:

Of the five superintendents who have arrived only one is a farmer, two say they were used to the farming business when they were 17 and 19 years of age but they cannot . . . instruct the convicts or direct a farm; and we are in great want of a good master carpenter, brick and tile master.[69]

Prior to the arrival of the *Lady Juliana* in early June 1790 the Sydney Cove settlers had been forced to cut the food rations again. The previous November the ration had been cut by a third. In April, in the absence of any relief, it had been cut to half the standard ration, and many in the colony were too hungry to work:

The settlement had been at two thirds of the established rations from the 1st of November and now it was reduced to something less than half a ration, consequently little labour could be expected from the convicts and they are only employed for the public in the mornings leaving the afternoons to attend their gardens.[70]

Everyone was given the same: a small amount of flour, pork and rice. Even with the reduced ration the food was expected to totally run out later in the year – the pork by July, the rice in the first week of September and the flour in November.

15

A WAITING GAME

[W]e were surprised to see a boat, which was known to belong to the Supply, rowing towards us. On nearer approach, I saw Captain Ball make an extraordinary motion with his hand, which too plainly indicated that something disastrous had happened . . . A few minutes changed doubt into certainty and to our unspeakable consternation we learned that the Sirius had been wrecked on Norfolk Island . . .

At the beginning of the third year of the settlement the *Supply* had returned from Norfolk Island with news from Philip Gidley King that the settlement there had reaped a successful harvest of grain and that the vegetable gardens were also doing well. On receiving the news, and aware that Sydney was rapidly running out of food, Phillip decided to send two hundred convicts and a force of marines with their families to Norfolk Island, where their prospects for survival would be much better. King, who by this time had been on Norfolk for more than two years, had reported that the soil was good and they had managed to harvest good crops of vegetables and other crops. He also said there were plenty of birds and fish.

Phillip was able to use the venture as an opportunity to recall his protégé, Philip Gidley King, in order to send him back to England to comprehensively report on the settlement. At the same time he would rid himself of his nemesis Major Robert Ross, who would replace King as commander of Norfolk Island, since the greatly enlarged colony there would need a proportionately enhanced force of marines.

In justifying his decision to send Ross, Phillip said that the marine commander was so hot-tempered that he would only talk to him when it was absolutely necessary:

> I readily acknowledged the assistance I received, but the warmth of temper, which has been the source of many discontents, has obliged me for some time past to avoid, as far as the service permits, calling on the Lieutenant Governor otherwise than as the commandant of the detachment.[1]

Some of Phillip's colleagues were equally delighted to be rid of the unpopular marine commander. Judge David Collins, who despised Ross, later wrote to his father detailing the happy news and suggesting Ross' day of retribution had arrived: 'Since Major Ross went from here, tranquillity may be said to have been our guest . . . While here he made me the object of his persecution – if a day will come – a day of retribution.'[2]

To take such a large party and supplies to Norfolk Island required both of the remaining two ships left in the colony – the *Sirius* and the *Supply* – and would leave Sydney with no ships at all.

On a cool and cloudy morning, 3 March 1790, the marines and their officers boarded the two ships, and the following morning nearly two hundred convicts were put aboard. The next day the ships were seen leaving Port Jackson heads with their two hundred and seventy passengers and heading into huge seas that almost blew them onto the rocks at North Head.

After that rocky start the two ships made good time, however, and reached Norfolk Island after only eight days' sailing, but the now familiar huge surf prevented them from landing in Sydney Bay on the south side of the island. Both ships sailed round to Cascade Bay on the northern side and managed with some difficulty to unload most of their passengers over the next two days, before high winds blew the ships back out to sea. They had not yet managed to unload all of the provisions for the new settlers.

Realising they were unlikely to be able to unload their cargo in Cascade Bay, the ships returned to the south side and Sydney Bay. Early on the morning of 19 March, despite high seas and strong winds, Hunter managed to steer the *Sirius* into the bay, where it met up with the *Supply*, which had already arrived there.

Later in the morning the crews had started loading the stores onto the small boats to be rowed to shore when the *Sirius* was caught in the surf and dragged onto the reef.

Captain Hunter was well aware of the dangers of trying to anchor the *Sirius* off Norfolk Island – which was renowned for not having anything resembling a natural harbour – but felt that those on the island were desperate for the unloading of their provisions:

> We had put on shore from the *Sirius* and the *Supply* two hundred and seventy people, and had no opportunity of sending any stores with them, as we were now driven out of sight of the island. I knew the exhausted state of stores there; I was also acquainted with the many difficulties which Lieutenant Ball, commander of the *Supply*, had met with in the different voyages he had made from Port Jackson to this island, with provisions; and the length of time he had, in some of those voyages, been obliged to cruise, before he could have any access to the shore; so con-

tinually does the surf break all round it. These consid-
erations gave me much anxiety and uneasiness.[3]

American seaman Jacob Nagle was on the *Sirius* when it
hit the reef. He described things as fairly calm at the time:

> A fine pleasant day with a light breeze off shore all the
> seamen that could muster hook and line was catching
> gropers not thinking of any danger or at twelve o'clock,
> when thinking of going to dinner, Captain Ball of the
> *Supply* brig hailed us and informed Captain Hunter
> that we were too close in the swell of the surf having
> hold of us . . . and Captain Ball, being at a distance out
> side of us, perceived it sooner than we did. Immediately
> we made sail that we could set, and a light breeze off
> shore, but the wind and swell driving us in.[4]

As the water poured into the torn hull, the crew were
ordered to cut away the masts in an attempt to lighten the
ship and allow it to pull clear of the reef, but the damage
was already too great. When they opened the hatch,
according to Nagle, there was already four feet of water in
the hold. Late in the day it became obvious they were in a
hopeless situation and a pulley was made that allowed the
crew to be taken one by one to the safety of the beach. Over
the next few days the crew worked 'both night and day, so
we had no rest' to salvage as much of the cargo as possible
before the stricken vessel completely broke up.

One of the survivors of the wreck was the second-
lieutenant of the *Sirius*, Newton Fowell, who noted that
some of the officers lost 'part of their clothes and all of
their [live] stock' but that his loss was, luckily, 'not very
great' as he was able to salvage his trunk, even though
most of his clothes were badly stained.[5]

Fowell described how, during the salvage operations,
two convicts went out to the stricken ship to throw dying

livestock – which had been three days without water – overboard. Instead of carrying out this duty, the convicts found some grog, lit themselves a fire and stayed to get drunk. When they ignored the order to come ashore, another convict was sent with the instruction that if they did not obey the order he should throw them both overboard. The next morning they came ashore.

Major Robert Ross now found himself commander of an island with a population of around seven hundred people, which included the original party who came with Philip Gidley King and those who had come since. The new settlers had lost a large proportion of their food and other provisions with the sinking of the *Sirius*, and Ross immediately stamped his authority on his new realm by declaring martial law.

In a letter he sent back to Phillip, he said that the morning after the sinking of the *Sirius* he 'judged it necessary . . . to proclaim marshal law' so as to preserve what food was left and to stop anyone from killing or plundering any livestock.[6] He immediately reduced the food ration and stopped the hunting of wild birds.

Jacob Nagle, who would be stranded on Norfolk Island for almost a year because of the sinking of his ship, was unimpressed with Ross' authoritarian rule:

> Lieutenant Governor Ross was a merciless commander to either free man or prisoner. He had us under three different laws; the seamen were still under navy laws, the soldiers under military laws, besides the civil laws and the marshal laws of his own directions, with strict orders to be attended for the smallest crime, whatever the neglect of duty.[7]

Nagle describes how the crew of the *Sirius* survived on Norfolk Island. Not wishing to live in the barracks with the marines, they built a village of shacks near the beach.

Many of the convict women were assigned to collect rushes for thatching the roofs of the shacks and ended up living with the seamen.

The convicts were assigned to clear land for a garden where, according to Nagle, the ground was 'rich black soil'. They were initially given rations of 'a pound and a half-pound of flour and a pound and a half-pound of grain mixed together and a few ounces of meat' a week, but in only six weeks the meat ran out.

They were easily able to supplement their meat ration by catching birds, however, which were plentiful on the island. To start with they ate the large gannets: 'A sea fowl, apparently as big as a goose, would come open mouthed at you, but destroying a good many, they left the island.' Then they hunted the mutton bird on Mount Pitt on the north-west of the island, which, according to Nagle, was the only reason they survived:

> These bird seemingly as god would have it, was the saving of us, as it was the chief living we had while they lasted . . .
>
> We would start out in the afternoon and reach the mount by dusk. I suppose about four or five miles up hills and down steep valleys . . . when we arrived on the mount we would knock up a fire and wait till the birds begin to fall. There would be sailors, soldiers and convicts, to the amount of fifty or sixty a night. By calculation there would not be less than twelve to fourteen hundred destroyed of a night. When they began to drop, we would go down into the vales and the more we hollered 'ho, ho, ho', the birds would come running, crying out 'ke, ke, ke' thinking it was their mate or their young, and by that means every man would take home what he thought sufficient in his knapsack, which would be twenty or thirty or more. When completed, every man would light his

torch and set out homewards, all in a line, as the path
was small and in this season of the year was heavy
rains. By the time we got to town, would be eleven or
twelve o'clock at night, all wet and muddy.[8]

Nagle said that Ross tried to stop the sailors from
hunting the birds but that Captain Hunter disagreed.
When Ross had one of the seamen flogged, Hunter
ordered his second in command from the *Sirius*,
Lieutenant Bradley, to issue leave passes to any of his
crew who wanted one:

> About this time the Governor issued orders that no
> man dare kill a bird at Mount Pitt . . . he had a
> convict which he sent daily to the mount for birds
> who discovered one of our seamen that had killed two
> or three and the Governor Ross punished him with
> two dozen. Through his tyrannical behaviour,
> Captain Hunter and him did not agree while on the
> island. He would not allow the soldiers or convicts to
> go a foraging and wished the Captain to prevent us
> likewise but as the Governor clapped sentries on the
> roads which led around the island, that no one could
> go anywhere without a pass, the Captain ordered
> Mr. Bradley to give the seamen a pass whenever they
> called upon him for one . . . He [Hunter] told him
> [Ross] he did not wish his men to starve while there
> was anything to be got by foraging around the island.[9]

Ross' tyrannical rule of Norfolk Island would last only
eleven months, as he and the rest of the marines were
recalled by the British Government to be replaced by the
newly formed New South Wales Corps, under Major
Grose, which would arrive on the Second Fleet ships from
June 1790. The instructions terminating Ross' appointment, in a letter written by the home secretary, Grenville,

on Christmas Eve 1789 – some months before Ross went to Norfolk Island – were totally unambiguous:

> Major Grose has been appointed to succeed to the Lieutenant Government of New South Wales and on his arrival you will direct Major Ross and his officers of the marine corps operating under his command together with such of the non-commissioned officers and private men as may be desirous of returning home, to be embarked as soon as possible for that purpose.[10]

The devastating news of the sinking of the *Sirius* was brought back to Sydney by the *Supply*. Watkin Tench recalled being rowed out to meet Lieutenant Ball in Port Jackson with Arthur Phillip:

> The Governor . . . determined to go down the harbour and I begged permission to accompany him. Having turned a point about halfway down, we were surprised to see a boat, which was known to belong to the *Supply*, rowing towards us. On nearer approach, I saw Captain Ball make an extraordinary motion with his hand, which too plainly indicated that something disastrous had happened . . . A few minutes changed doubt into certainty and to our unspeakable consternation we learned that the *Sirius* had been wrecked on Norfolk Island . . .[11]

On the same day that the news of the sinking of the *Sirius* arrived, Arthur Phillip called together his senior colleagues in Sydney to discuss their predicament. Until then Phillip had rarely confided in or consulted with anyone. At the meeting the severity of the food situation was outlined and a decision made to yet again cut the food ration. It was now down to starvation levels. Everyone would receive a weekly ration of one kilogram of now very old salted pork, which had dried out and shrivelled, half a litre of peas and fifty-five grams of rice. The only significant addition to the ration would be whatever vegetables the gardens could deliver and from fishing, which had already proved to be unreliable and irregular.

Phillip of course did not know that the *Guardian*, carrying urgent relief supplies, had been shipwrecked. However, he correctly guessed that because such a long time had passed since he had pleaded for more food that an accident must have occurred: '[F]rom the time which has passed since my letter might be supposed to have been received in England, there was reason to suppose some accident had happened to the store ships sent out.'[12]

As the hungry colony approached its third winter, many of the clothes had been worn out to rags. Captain Watkin Tench tartly observed: 'There is nothing more ludicrous . . . than the expedients of substituting, shifting and patching, which ingenuity devised to eke out wretchedness and preserve the remains of decency.'[13]

Tench went on to describe the severity of the situation:

> The insufficiency of our ration soon diminished our execution of labour. Both soldiers and convicts pleaded such loss of strength as to find themselves unable to perform their accustomed tasks, the hours of public work were accordingly shortened . . . every man was ordered to do as much as his strength would permit and every other indulgence was granted.[14]

Tench also said that a number of people died of starvation and that he witnessed one case himself:

> I was passing the provision store when a man with a wild haggard countenance who had just received his daily pittance to carry home came out. His faltering

gait and eager devouring eye led me to watch him and he had not proceeded ten steps before he fell. I ordered him to be carried to the hospital, where, when he arrived he was found dead. On opening the body the cause of death was pronounced to be inanition [an empty stomach].[15]

In April 1790, after more than two years in the colony, Chief Surgeon John White finally exploded. In a savage and honest letter to a friend in England he described what was not contained in any of the official letters or journals of Phillip or any of the officers, who would have been careful when they wrote not to offend their superiors. The letter, which was published in a number of London newspapers in December 1790 and January 1791,[16] caused a sensation:

> Hope is no more, and a new scene of distress and misery opens our view . . . For all the grain of every kind which we have been able to raise in two years and three months would not support us three weeks. . . . Limited in food and reduced as the people are, who have not had one ounce of fresh animal food since first in the country.[17]

White also lashed out at the British Government. He could not have known at the time that the *Guardian*, hurrying to bring them relief supplies, had been wrecked only weeks away from reaching New South Wales a few months earlier. Nor would he have known that the Second Fleet was on its way; already in Cape Town, it would arrive in Sydney two months later. 'In the name of heaven, what has the ministry been about. Surely they have forgotten or neglected us, otherwise they would have sent to see what had become of us, and to know how we were likely to succeed.'

White believed the whole expedition was a failure, and couldn't understand why the location hadn't been more carefully vetted before settlers were dispatched:

> From what we have already seen we may conclude that there is not a single article in the whole country that in the nature of things could prove of the smallest use or advantage to the mother country or the commercial world . . . It would be wise by the first steps to withdraw the settlement at least such as are living, or remove them to some other place. This is so far out of the world and the tract of commerce that it could never answer.

The Reverend Richard Johnson reflected the desperation of the settlers in a tone perhaps even more bitter than White's: 'Tis now about two years and three months since we first arrived at this distant country. All this while we have been as it were, buried alive . . . our hopes are almost vanished.'[18]

With the *Sirius* lost and with food running out, Phillip had no choice but to send the last surviving ship off to Batavia to hunt for food. Lieutenant Ball, on the tiny *Supply*, was to collect as much food as could fit on the seventy-foot tender and hire any other vessel he could find in Batavia to bring additional supplies.

On board he had Lieutenant Philip Gidley King, who was returning to England at the request of Arthur Phillip to report directly on the colony. In Batavia King was able to board a Dutch packet, the *Snelheid*, which set off less than a month later. Shortly after the ship left the Dutch port, 'a putrid fever made its appearance' and killed many of its crew. This forced it into Mauritius, where King, who was also ill, had to recuperate for most of August and part of September. The ship then resumed its journey via the Cape of Good Hope back to Holland. King was put over the side and into a local English boat as they passed by Beachy Head off the Sussex coast. He reached London four days before Christmas in 1790.

A number of the crew of the *Supply* also became sick when they reached Batavia, a port which was notorious for disease. Lieutenant Newton Fowell, now on the *Supply*, described Batavia in a letter to his father. It was unhealthy, he said, because its many canals were not kept clean and the build-up of waste was 'very offensive'. None of the crew had been sick before they arrived, he wrote, but many became ill within days of anchoring in the city.[19]

Back in Sydney food had become so scarce that dinner invitations took on a new twist, as Tench described:

> If a lucky man who had knocked down a dinner with his gun, or caught a fish by angling off the rocks, invited a neighbour to dine with him, the invitation always ran 'bring your own bread'. Even at the governor's table, this custom was constant observed. Every man when he sat down pulled his bread out of his pocket, and laid it on his plate.[20]

Finally, at 3.30 in the afternoon on 3 June 1790, two and a half years after the arrival of the First Fleet, the signal flag was broken out on Port Jackson's South Head – a ship's sail had been sighted.

Captain Watkin Tench had been alone and, hearing noise, rushed outside to see people running around in a state of excitement:

> I was sitting in my hut, musing on our fate, when a confused clamour in the street drew my attention. I opened my door and saw several women with children in their arms running to and fro with distracted looks, congratulating each other and kissing

their infants with the most passionate and extrava-
gant marks of fondness. I needed no more; but
instantly started out and ran to a hill where, by
the assistance of a pocket glass, my hopes were
realised. My next-door neighbour, a brother officer
was with me but we could not speak. We wrung each
other by the hand, with our eyes and hearts
overflowing.[21]

Despite the heavy rain that began to fall, Arthur Phillip
and a number of his colleagues began to row down the
harbour and out towards the incoming ship. Once he
was satisfied that it was an English ship, Phillip returned
to Sydney Cove in one of his fishing boats. Tench and
Surgeon John White continued until they were alongside
the ship, planning to direct it back up the harbour.

It was the *Lady Juliana*. Because of the heavy weather
it anchored that night inside the North Head and sailed
into a jubilant Sydney Cove the next morning. From the
Lady Juliana the settlers would receive not only food but
their first direct news from England in more than three
years. As Tench reported, 'Letters, letters, was the cry.
They were produced and torn open in trembling and
anticipation.'[22]

They were also to learn of the *Guardian*, which had been
lying wrecked in Table Bay when the *Lady Juliana* had
passed through the Cape of Good Hope three months
before.

The *Lady Juliana* was the first arrival of the Second
Fleet; more convict ships would arrive over the next
few weeks. There were five ships in the Second Fleet: the
convict transports the *Lady Juliana*, the *Surprize*,
the *Neptune* and the *Scarborough*, and the storeship the
Justinian. They had left England with more than twelve
hundred convicts and provisions. While food rationing
would continue, the Second Fleet, with its stores and

provisions, had averted almost certain disaster for the First Fleet settlers.

Three months after the arrival of the *Lady Juliana* and the other ships of the Second Fleet the lookout at South Head signalled the arrival of the *Supply*, which had returned from Batavia with a cargo of food. They had been gone for six months and two days.

Lieutenant Ball reported that he had experienced difficulty buying all the grain he wanted in Batavia so he had bought almost ninety tons, or ninety thousand kilograms, of rice instead. He had also managed to charter a small Dutch ship, the *Waaksamheyd*, that would arrive in Sydney with more food on 17 December. This additional food included items that were not on the *Supply*, including pork, beef and sugar.

The arrival of the Second Fleet also brought relief to Norfolk Island, which also was struggling to find enough food. Having unloaded convicts and supplies in Sydney, the *Surprize* and the *Justinian* were sent with some of the convicts and relief supplies to the island. Jacob Nagle, still stranded there with the other crew members of the shipwrecked *Sirius*, described the arrival of the two ships:

> On one evening four of us was sitting in my hut. We were all messmates and considering the situation we were in at that present time. I think it was a Thursday evening. On the next Saturday our last provisions was to be served out, which was but one half-barrel of flour, to be served amongst seven hundred souls. The birds were destroyed, the cabbage tree likewise all gone, and as for the fish, it was very uncertain . . . We allowed ourselves to be in a wretched situation. The next morning at daylight . . . I walked out on the beach aback of my hut. I cast my eyes around on the ocean and then to the westward of the island, I discovered a ship close under the island.

> I hollered out 'sail ho! sail ho!' . . . By this time the
> whole town was alarmed.[23]

Nagle said that when they boarded the *Surprize,* 'the
Captain, understanding our situation, treated us extremely
well, gave us a hearty meal and some grog'.

Nagle also said that despite the food shortages no one
died of starvation or disease during the eleven months
they were stranded on the island. He suggested that when
the *Supply* finally came to take the *Sirius* crew back to
Sydney some of the seamen would have preferred to stay:

> We now found ourselves comfortable, being on full
> allowance, and I know a great many seamen would
> rather have stayed on the island than to come away. It
> was rather singular, though the hardships and want of
> provisions, while on this island, eleven months and
> seven days, there was neither, woman or child died
> a natural death, excepting one old woman 70 or
> 80 years of age.[24]

Despite the relief brought by the Second Fleet and the
arrival of more food on the *Supply* and the *Waaksamheyd*, the Sydney settlement would continue to
experience shortage. Captain Watkin Tench recorded in
his journal the return of hardship as the settlement
entered its fourth year and the food ration was cut again:
'Notwithstanding the supplies which had recently arrived
from Batavia, short allowance was again proclaimed . . . I
every day see wretches pale with disease and wasted with
famine, struggle against the horrors of their situation.'[25]

Nevertheless, the crisis that had threatened the survival
of the entire settlement had passed. With the arrival of the
Second Fleet, the British Government announced that in
future two convict fleets a year would be sent to New
South Wales and with them additional provisions. At the

same time the farms that had been started in more fertile soil around Rose Hill began to yield good harvests of food, and with this success more and more farms were being started nearby around the Parramatta, Nepean and Hawkesbury Rivers.

16

ARRIVAL OF THE SECOND FLEET

*The landing of these people was truly affecting and
shocking; great numbers were not able to walk, nor
move a hand or foot, such were slung over the ship
side in the same manner as they would sling a cask,
a box or anything of that nature.*

While the arrival of the *Lady Juliana* and the other four
ships of the Second Fleet in June 1790 would be the end
of the crisis that had threatened the survival of the early
convict settlement, it would also mark an infamous
episode in the early history of Australia, one of the worst
chapters in seafaring history.

Of the one thousand and thirty-eight convicts who were
loaded on board the *Surprize*, the *Neptune* and the *Scarborough* in England in 1789, nearly a quarter died before
they reached Sydney. Of the remaining seven hundred and
fifty-six who arrived alive in Sydney, four hundred and
eighty-six were immediately hospitalised in hastily erected
tents. A hundred and twenty-four would die during their
first days in the colony.

Less than six months after the First Fleet had sailed
into Sydney Cove, and unbeknown to Arthur Phillip, the
British Government had begun preparations for sending
a second fleet. The London press carried reports that

Home Secretary Lord Sydney had issued orders for another 'Botany Bay fleet' to be prepared, even though the government had not yet received any news from Sydney.[1]

The first ship commissioned for the Second Fleet was the four-hundred-ton *Lady Juliana*. In November 1788 the loading of convicts and supplies began. It was planned that if no good news came back from New South Wales, the ship would instead be sent to Nova Scotia, in what was referred to in the press as the Quebec Plan.[2]

In March 1789, nearly two years after the First Fleet had left England and more than a year after it had arrived in Sydney, the government received the first reports from Governor Phillip. These gave them sufficient confidence to send more convicts to New South Wales.

The first ship of the Second Fleet, the *Lady Juliana*, with two hundred and twenty-six women convicts and supplies on board, took almost a year to reach Sydney. It left England six weeks before the *Guardian*, on 29 July 1789, but was still in Rio de Janeiro harbour – where it would spend a leisurely six and a half weeks – when the *Guardian* reached Cape Town. By the time the *Lady Juliana* finally reached Cape Town, the wreck of the *Guardian* was back in Table Bay, having struck the iceberg almost two months before.

It has been suggested that part of the reason for the slow passage of the *Lady Juliana* was that the entire crew had partnered with the convict women aboard the ship and were in no hurry to reach the penal settlement. In the words of John Nicol, a steward on the ship:

> When we were fairly out to sea, every man on board took a wife from among the convicts, they nothing loath. The girl, with whom I lived, for I was as bad on this point as the others, was named Sarah Whitelam. She was a native of Lincoln, a girl of modest reserved

turn, as kind and true a creature who ever lived.
I courted her for a week and upwards and would have
married her on the spot, had there been a clergyman
on board . . . I had fixed my fancy upon her from the
moment I knocked the rivet out of her irons upon my
anvil and as firmly resolved to bring her back to
England when her time was out, my lawful wife . . .
She bore me a son on the voyage out. What is become
of her, whether she is dead or alive, I know not.[3]

The settlers in Sydney were initially unimpressed by the
arrival of another two hundred convicts, all of whom
were women, when they were so desperate for additional
provisions. As Judge Collins commented:

In the distressed situation of the colony, it was not a
little mortifying to find on board the first ship that
arrived, a cargo so unnecessary and so unprofitable
as two hundred and twenty two females, instead of a
cargo of provisions; the supply of provisions on board
her were so inconsiderable as to permit only the
addition of one pound and a half of flour being made
to the weekly ration.[4]

Arthur Phillip and his colleagues were to learn from the
Lady Juliana that the other three ships would be bringing
more than a thousand new convicts – and supplies. They
were also told that the Second Fleet would bring a new
force, the New South Wales Corps under the command
of Major Francis Grose, to relieve and replace the entire
Marine Corps. The marines who wished to stay in the
colony would be allowed to sign up with the new corps or
could accept land grants and stay on as farmer settlers.

When the women convicts were unloaded from the
Lady Juliana, many were found to be old, weak or ill and
unlikely to be of much use in working for the new colony.

Even so, the convicts were in relatively good shape compared with those who would arrive on the other three transports – the *Surprize*, the *Neptune* and the *Scarborough* – a few weeks later.

The next ship to reach Sydney was the supply ship the *Justinian* on 20 June. The convict transport the *Surprize* followed five days later. Three weeks after the arrival of the *Lady Juliana*, on the morning of 23 June, a lookout at South Head reported seeing a sail that then disappeared from sight in the wild seas and high winds. Two days later the *Surprize* came through the heads and anchored at Sydney with two hundred and eighteen male convicts and a detachment of the New South Wales Corps on board.

The settlers were in for a rude shock. Forty-two convicts had already died on the *Surprize* during the voyage, and more than half of the survivors were ill or dying.

The Reverend Richard Johnson was the first to go down into the holds of the *Surprize* amid the stench of the dead and dying. He described what he saw in a private letter he sent to a friend, Mr Thornton, in England. Such honesty and anger would never have appeared in any official report:

> Was the first on board the *Surprize*. Went down among the convicts, where I beheld a sight so truly shocking to the feelings of humanity, a great number of them laying, some half and others nearly quite naked, without either bed or bedding, unable to turn or help them selves. Spoke to them as I passed along but the smell was so offensive that I could scarcely bear it.[5]

The following day the other two transports, the *Neptune* and the *Scarborough*, arrived, having anchored the night before off Garden Island in Port Jackson. On both ships the convicts were in an appalling condition: 'I then went aboard the *Scarborough*; proposed to go down amongst them, but was dissuaded from it by the captain. The *Neptune* was still more intolerable, and therefore never attempted it.'[6]

Johnson tried to help save some of the convicts but was warned of the danger of entering the transports, 'where the air must be always putrid from the breath of a crowd of passengers'. He then described the terrible scenes when it came to unloading the dreadful human cargo:

> The landing of these people was truly affecting and shocking; great numbers were not able to walk, nor move a hand or foot, such were slung over the ship side in the same manner as they would sling a cask, a box or anything of that nature. Upon their being brought up to the open air some fainted, some died upon the deck and others in the boat before they reached the shore. When come on shore many were not able to walk, to stand, or to sit themselves in the least, hence some were led by others. Some crept on their hands and knees and some were carried on the backs of others.

The bodies of the dead continued to be thrown overboard until the Reverend Johnson complained to Phillip, after which point they were taken over to the north side of Port Jackson to be buried.

Judge David Collins also recorded the scene, noting that even those who were not sick were close to death from starvation:

> The appearance of those who did not require medical attention was lean and emaciated. Several of those miserable people died in the boats as they were rowing on shore, or on the wharf as they lifted out of the boats; both the living and the dead exhibited more horrid spectacles than had ever been witnessed.[7]

Captain Tench, who was another who witnessed the arrival of the Second Fleet and its sorry cargo, was angry at the shipping contractors, who he believed were paid enough to deliver the convicts in reasonable condition but 'violated every principle of justice and rioted on the spoils of misery'.[8]

Arthur Phillip wrote a letter of complaint to London about the treatment of the convicts. He wrote that while he did not want to 'dwell on the scene of misery' that came with the Second Fleet, 'It would be a want of duty not to say that it was occasioned by the contractors having crowded too many on board those ships, and from their being too much confined during the passage.'[9]

In another letter Phillip pointed out that, in the month following the arrival of the Second Fleet, there were more patients receiving urgent medical treatment in Sydney (four hundred and thirteen) than those fit for work (three hundred and sixteen),[10] and in the following six weeks a further eighty-nine would die.

There were almost five hundred convicts too sick to stand and in need of hospitalisation, but John White's little hospital on the western side of Sydney Cove could only cater for fifty or sixty. It was totally inadequate to deal with a tragedy of this dimension. The situation was made even more desperate by the fact that most of the medical supplies that White had pleaded to be brought from England had been lost on the *Guardian* when it had hit the iceberg six months earlier.

The recently arrived *Justinian* had aboard a large number of tents, and a hundred were pitched for the sick. Still, there were no beds or bedding, and it was the beginning of winter. As Reverend Johnson described it:

> At first they had nothing to lay upon but the damp ground, many scarcely a rag to cover them. Grass was got for them to lay upon, and a blanket given

amongst four of them . . . The misery I saw among
them is inexpressible; many were not able to turn, or
even to stir themselves, and in this situation were
covered over almost with their own nastiness;
their heads, bodies, clothes, blanket, all full of filth
and lice.[11]

The convicts soon described the conditions on the ships
that had led to their terrible state. They were kept below
deck where the ceilings were too low for them to stand
and chained to each other for most of the voyage, even
when the ships were leaking and they were sitting under
water, often chained to the sick and the dying.[12]

The appalling story of the worst of all of the ships,
the *Neptune*, was reported in the *Dublin Chronicle* on
12 January the following year. The article was based on
the story of Thomas Evans, who described the convict
quarters as being seventy-five feet long by thirty-five feet
at the widest point (22.8 by 10.6 metres) and the height
five feet seven inches (1.7 metres) at the lowest point.
Within this space were the 'miserable apartments for
confining, boarding and lodging' four hundred and
twenty-four male convicts. Each cabin was six feet
square, giving each man only thirty-seven cubic feet of
airspace – about the size of two coffins.

It appears that before leaving London the navy agent
on board the *Neptune*, Lieutenant Shapcote, had ordered
that all convicts 'except those of good character or ill
health' be put in irons. Many died before the ship had
even left the port, only to be 'thrown overboard unham-
mocked and unweighted'. During the voyage fifty or sixty
convicts at a time were allowed up on deck for two hours
but were never released from their chains.

On all the ships the water and food rations were
limited and soon 'a violent epidemic fever' and scurvy
broke out. Sometimes deaths were concealed so the other

convicts could draw on the extra food ration – until the stench of the corpse revealed its presence to the ship's surgeon.

Some of the details of what happened on the *Surprize* were recorded in a letter written by Captain Hill, a second captain of the New South Wales Marine Corps, to his friend Samuel Wathen, a philanthropist, Gloucester county sheriff and friend of William Wilberforce, the anti-slavery campaigner. The long letter, sent after the ship arrived in Sydney Cove, gives an account of the 'villainy, oppression and shameful peculation' during the voyage:

> The bark I was on board of was indeed unfit for her make and size to be sent so great a distance. If it blew but the most trifling gale she was lost in the waters . . . the unhappy wretches, the convicts were considerably above their waists in water . . . In this situation they were obliged for the safety of the ship to be penned down but when the gales abated no means were used to purify the air by fumigations, no vinegar was applied to rectify the nauseous steams issuing from their miserable dungeon. Humanity shudders to think that of nine hundred male convicts embarked on this fleet, three hundred and seventy are already dead and four hundred and fifty are landed sick and so emaciated and helpless that very few if any of them can be saved.[13]

Hill said that the maltreatment had been made worse because of the tight chains with short bolts that pinned the convicts to the floor below the decks, which meant 'it was impossible for them to move but at the risk of both their legs being broken'.[14]

The Times newspaper pointed out that the Second Fleet shipowners were paid for each convict loaded, not landed, and the greater the number that died, the lower their costs in feeding and clothing them:

It may be proper to observe, that the sum allowed by the government for each convict to Botany Bay is fully adequate – but it unfortunately happens, that the owners farm the benefit to the owners of the ship, and therefore the more that die on the passage, the greater his gain . . . As the matter now stands, the less of his cargo the Captain brings into port, the more profit he makes.[15]

The Second Fleet was the beginning of a program of transportation that would continue for another fifty years and involve the shipment of thousands more convicts. The government had written to Phillip in December 1789 to warn him that many more would be coming:

From the current crowded state of the hulks and the increase which might be expected of the number of felons under sentence of transportation, not only in this kingdom but in Ireland, after the next Spring Assizes, it is intended that about one thousand men shall be sent abroad, and preparations must be made for their reception.[16]

There was a very big difference between the treatment of the convicts on the First Fleet and of those on the Second Fleet. On the First Fleet it was the responsibility of the officers to inspect the quality of food and ensure that the convicts received their rations from the contractors. On the Second Fleet the responsibility for the distribution of provisions rested entirely with the master of the contracted ship.

Captain Tench contrasted the record of the First Fleet with that of the Second, where two hundred and seventy-three died before they reached Sydney and a further four hundred and eighty-six were sick on arrival:

On our passage from England, which had lasted more than eight months and with nearly an equal number of persons, only twenty-four had died, and not thirty were landed sick. The difference can be accounted for, only by comparing the manner in which each fleet was fitted out and conducted. With us, the provisions served on board were laid in by a contractor, who sent a deputy to serve them out and it became a part of duty for the officers of the troops to inspect their quality, and to order that everyone received his just portion. Whereas the fleet now arrived, the distribution of provisions rested entirely with the masters of the merchantmen, and the officers were expressly forbidden to interfere in any shape farther about the convicts than to prevent their escape.[17]

Tench hoped that the government would intervene to stop it happening again: 'No doubt . . . a humane and liberal government will interpose its authority to prevent the repetition of such flagitious conduct.'[18]

The *Neptune*'s captain, Donald Trail, and his chief mate, William Elerington, were charged when they returned to England with wilful murder. However, *The Times* was later to report that both men were ultimately acquitted:

Yesterday the Admiralty sessions finished at the Old Bailey . . . Captain Donald Trail late commander of the *Neptune* Botany Bay ship and William Elerington the chief mate were indicted for the wilful murder of one of the convicts on the passage over, after a trial that lasted three hours they were both honourably acquitted.[19]

On a less troublesome note the Second Fleet was also to provide a solution to Arthur Phillip's strained relationship with the marines and their commander Robert Ross. Lord Grenville informed Phillip:

> The discontents which have prevailed in the marine detachments and the desire expressed by most of the officers and men to return home as soon as they have performed the tour of duty they have undertaken, have led to the making arrangements for relieving them. With that view his Majesty has ordered a corps to be raised for that particular purpose, consisting three hundred rank and file and a suitable number of officers under a major commandant.[20]

The new marine corps would be led by Captain Nicholas Nepean, the brother of the undersecretary of the Home Office, Evan Nepean, until the arrival of their commanding officer Major Francis Grose on the *Pitt* in February 1792.

Also arriving with the Second Fleet was 23-year-old Lieutenant John Macarthur, who would play a major role in the military, commercial and political life of the colony over the next forty years. This would include the overthrow of Governor Bligh in 1808 in what would be Australia's only military coup.

Macarthur was controversial from the start. Before leaving England on the *Neptune*, he fought a duel with the master of the ship and later had a disagreement with his successor, Donald Trail. He is said to have quarrelled so much with Trail on the voyage that he transferred with his wife Elizabeth and young son Edward to the *Scarborough* even before reaching the Cape of Good Hope.

The Second Fleet also brought Phillip new instructions for the management of the colony from King George III that effectively changed its destiny from a penal colony to a permanent settlement:

> It is probable . . . that some of these people will
> be desirous of continuing there as settlers of that
> description will be of great utility, not only for the
> purposes of protecting and defence but for the culti-
> vation of the land, it is thought advisable that every
> reasonable encouragement should be held out to
> them to remain there . . . It is therefore Our Royal
> Will and Pleasure that you do issue your warrant to
> . . . such non-commissioned officers and men as
> shall be disposed to become settlers within your
> Government . . . the proportion of land herein
> mentioned.[21]

The instructions specified that non-commissioned officers
could take up to one hundred acres (about forty hectares)
and the privates fifty acres (about twenty hectares). An
extra four acres was given for each child. Those who
enlisted in the new corps were given a bounty of three
pounds and would receive double the land grant after five
years.[22]

The new instructions also asked that land be granted
to any settlers who emigrated from Britain, as 'every
encouragement' was to be given to them to become
farmers in the new colony. Phillip was told he could
allocate convicts as labourers to the new farmers 'on
condition of their maintaining, feeding and clothing such
convicts'.

After the return of the ships of the Second Fleet to
England the colony would again begin to struggle, as the
consumption of food outstripped what they could harvest
or catch.

Captain Watkin Tench was to complain that by late in
the year 1790 there had been very little rain and 'all the
showers of the last four months put together would [not]
make twenty four hours rain'.

Our farms, what with this poor soil, are in wretched
condition. My winter crop of potatoes, which I planted
in days of despair (March and April last), turned out
very badly when I dug them about two months back.
Wheat returned so poorly last harvest, that very little
besides Indian corn had been sown this year.[23]

On 9 July the following year the first convict transport
ship of the Third Fleet, the *Mary Ann*, arrived with one
hundred and forty-one women convicts and six children
on board. The *Mary Ann* had reached Sydney remarkably
quickly, in only four months and twelve days, and the
ship arrived with the convicts in near perfect health. Only
three had died on the entire voyage. With the *Mary Ann*
came the news that another ten ships were on their way
with more than two thousand more convicts for the
colony.

Over the next three months the *Matilda*, the *Atlantic*,
the *Salamander*, the *William and Ann*, the *Gorgon*, the
Active, the *Queen*, the *Albemarle*, the *Britannia* and the
Admiral Barrington arrived.

The voyage of the Third Fleet had not been without
incident. Before reaching the Canary Islands, some convicts
on the *Albemarle* broke into open mutiny. The ship's
captain managed to shoot one of the ringleaders, William
Siney, in the shoulder as he was about to cut down the
helmsman and take possession of the wheel of the ship. The
ship's crew and the marine escort then managed to wound
a number of the mutineers and force them down into the
hold before locking them in the prisoners' deck.

One of the mutineers, Thomas Pratt, confessed and
gave evidence against his colleagues. The captain,
Lieutenant Parry Young, had the two ringleaders, William
Siney and Owen Lyons, hanged on the fore yardarm as an
example and deterrent to the others. When the *Albemarle*
arrived in Sydney and Phillip was told of the event, he

was to write to the secretary of the navy board, Phillip Stephens, commending Lieutenant Young for his professional handling of the crisis.

On the voyage of the Third Fleet a total of one hundred and ninety-four men, women and children had died, and hundreds more landed 'so emaciated, so worn away from want of food' that it would take many months for them to recover. Phillip thought some of them would never recover and would permanently be a 'dead weight' on the stores.[24]

In April 1791 the food ration was again reduced. Shortages of food would occur again and again and would be met with reduced rations, but the British Government's announcement to Phillip that a fleet of convicts would in future be sent twice a year guaranteed the arrival of at least some fresh supplies and was to finally remove the threat of starvation.

17

ESCAPE

Several convicts got away from this settlement on board of the transports, which it will be impossible to prevent unless the masters of those ships . . . are prosecuted with severity . . .

Attempted escapes from the New South Wales settlement were commonplace from the outset, despite the fact that the convicts had little idea of where they were. Perhaps the first to successfully escape upon arrival in the new colony was a French-born convict named Peter Parris. According to Surgeon White Parris escaped when he was hidden on one of the French ships, either the *Astrolabe* or the *Boussole*, by sympathetic French sailors. Many of those who initially escaped, however, were not successful in the long run. Some eventually returned to the settlement starving and emaciated, while others disappeared into the countryside never to be seen again.

Other success stories were those who escaped on the convict transports after they had unloaded their cargoes and were released from government service to return to England. While all of the transports were thoroughly searched before being cleared to leave Sydney, it was extremely difficult to be sure that no one was hidden somewhere deep below the decks inside the ship.

Thomas Gilbert, the captain of the *Charlotte*, one of the first transports to return to England, described how his ship was searched for convicts by Lieutenant William Bradley of the *Sirius*:

> Before I left England I had entered into the usual obligation, binding myself to the forfeiture of a very considerable sum not to suffer any of the convicts under my charge to escape, nor to bring any with me; it cannot therefore be supposed that with such a risk I should permit any of them to come aboard and being equally conscious of not having given any room for such a suspicion with regard the seamen, I immediately assembled the officers of the ship . . . and . . . requested that a thorough search be made. This being done and the lieutenant not being able to find any, departed.[1]

Bradley obviously wasn't convinced, because soon afterwards he returned 'accompanied by some of his own petty officers' to make another search but 'with no better success'.

Several weeks after leaving Sydney, Gilbert recorded that two deserters from the *Sirius* were on the *Charlotte* and must have been there when the ship was searched before they left.

Arthur Phillip believed some of the masters of the ships may have collaborated in some of the convict escapes and wrote to the British Government asking that action be taken against the offenders:

> Several convicts got away from this settlement on board of the transports, which it will be impossible to prevent unless the masters of those ships . . . are prosecuted with severity for the convicts can . . . be secreted on board in such a manner as to render any search ineffectual . . .[2]

Only a day after writing this, Phillip was able to give details of a case in which a convict had been discovered on the *Neptune* shortly before it set sail for home. The convict admitted he had been carried out from shore on one of the ship's boats and secreted by the quartermaster in a concealed section of the *Neptune*'s hold:

> Since my letter yesterday was closed, several convicts being missing, a search was ordered to be made on board the *Neptune* . . . and one convict, Joseph Sutton was found concealed in the hold . . . Now, sir, if the master of the *Neptune* is not prosecuted . . . every ship that stops here on her way to China will carry off some of the best convicts, which it will be impossible for any force in this country to prevent.[3]

The convict who escaped more times than anyone else was almost certainly John Caesar. 'Black' Caesar, as he was known, was to become infamous in the first decade of the colony and is recognised as Australian's first bushranger.

It is believed that he was born in Madagascar and came to England from the West Indies, where he had worked as a slave on a sugar plantation. He was 23 and working as a servant in Deptford when he was charged with having broken into a house owned by Robert Reed and stealing twelve pounds and four pence. He appeared in the Kent Assizes and was sentenced to seven years' transportation in 1786, being sent with the First Fleet on the *Alexander* early the following year.

According to Judge David Collins:

> His frame was muscular and well calculated for hard labour; but in his intellects he did not widely differ from a brute; his appetite was ravenous, for he could in any one day devour the full rations for two days. To

gratify this appetite he was compelled to steal from others, all of his thefts were directed to that purpose.[4]

Caesar's lust for food was to get him into endless trouble. He was first convicted in the colony in 1789 for stealing four pounds of bread from the tent of another convict, Richard Partridge.

A few weeks later he made his first escape, taking with him some provisions and a cooking pot. However, unlike the Aboriginal people, Black Caesar had difficulty surviving in the Australian bush and for the next month lived on the outskirts of the settlement, periodically stealing any food he could find.

In May 1789 he robbed the small brickmakers' village of Brickfield, which was about two kilometres upstream from the settlement of Sydney. Despite being pursued by a detachment of marines, he managed to get away and back into the cover of the bush.

Two weeks later he was captured by another convict, William Saltmarsh, while trying to steal food from the shack of the assistant commissary for stores, Zachariah Clark.

Caesar was to be executed, but Phillip spared him with a pardon and he was instead sent in chains to tend the vegetables on Garden Island in the middle of Port Jackson harbour.

When he was released from his irons to work, however, Caesar again made his escape, this time by canoe, taking with him provisions along with 'an iron [cooking] pot and a musket, and some ammunition'[5] he had stolen from a marine private, Abraham Hand. Bradley takes up the story in his journal:

> The account [Caesar] gives of his subsisting himself for so long a time was, that when he saw a party of natives with anything on, or about their fire, that he

frightened them away by coming suddenly on them
and swaggering with his musket, then helping himself
to whatever they had left. In this way he made out
very well without ammunition, sometimes robbing
gardens. When he lost the musket he found it impossible to subsist himself. He was then attacked by the
natives and wounded in several places and escaped
from a party of them through very thick brush when
he surrendered himself.[6]

At this time Governor Phillip was preparing to send more
than two hundred convicts from Sydney to Norfolk
Island, where Lieutenant King had found the soil more
fertile.

It may be that Phillip saw the Norfolk Island venture
as an opportunity to be rid of the problem of Black
Caesar, as he was included in the contingent. On Norfolk
Island there was nowhere for him to escape to, and he
was forced to live under the martial law that had been
introduced by Major Robert Ross almost immediately
after he landed on the island.

Caesar was returned from Norfolk Island to Sydney
three years later, at the end of 1793, and again resorted
to his former practice of living on the outside of the
settlement while plundering the farms and huts on
the edge of town.

When caught and severely flogged, Caesar remained
defiant of authority and indifferent to punishment; he was
reported by Judge Collins to have said of the whipping
that 'all that would not make him better'.[7]

A little over a year later he fled the settlement again
and this time teamed up with other escaped convicts to
form a gang of bushrangers. By then Captain John Hunter
had returned from England to replace Arthur Phillip as
governor of the colony, and Caesar, now armed, had
gained the reputation of being public-enemy number one.

With practically every theft in the colony during 1795 being blamed on Black Caesar,[8] Governor Hunter offered a reward of five gallons of rum – the currency of the day – to anyone who could stop him:

> The many robberies which have lately been committed render it necessary that some steps should be taken to put a stop to the practice so destructive of the happiness and comfort of the industrious. And it is well known that a fellow known as Black Caesar has absented himself for some time past from his work, and has carried with him a musket, notice is hereby given that whoever shall secure this man Black Caesar and bring him in with his arms shall receive as a reward five gallons of spirits.[9]

Only a fortnight after the reward was posted, on Monday 15 February 1796, Caesar was shot dead on the Liverpool Plains, near current-day Strathfield, by a bounty hunter named Wimbrow. As Judge David Collins was to recall:

> Information was received that Black Caesar had that morning been shot by one Wimbrow. This man and another, allured by the reward, had been for some days in quest of him. Finding his haunt, they concealed themselves that night at the edge of the brush, which they perceived him enter at dusk. In the morning he came out, when, looking around him and seeing his danger, he presented his musket but before he could pull the trigger Wimbrow fired and shot him. He was first taken to the hut of Rose, a settler at Liberty Plains, where he died in a few hours. Thus ended a man, which certainly, during his life, could never have been estimated at more than one remove above the brute, and who had given more trouble than any other convict in the settlement.[10]

There is only one known case where convicts of the First Fleet escaped the settlement and reached England, and that is the remarkable story of Mary Bryant. Mary, who was married to another convict on the First Fleet, William Bryant, escaped with her husband, two young children and seven other convicts early in 1791. Stealing a boat from the settlement, they successfully sailed more than five thousand kilometres in sixty-nine days along the Australian coast to Dutch Timor.

Mary Bryant (née Broad, or Braund) was a 21-year-old who, in 1786, was convicted in the Devon court with two other women for highway robbery. She had stolen a silk bonnet and other goods valued at a little more than eleven pounds and twelve shillings. She was condemned to be hanged but the sentence was later commuted to seven years' transportation.[11]

William Bryant was an experienced fisherman from Cornwall who had been convicted in 1784 for forgery. Like his wife he had been sentenced to be hanged and the sentence was commuted to seven years' transportation. He was originally to go to America, but the War of Independence prevented him from being sent so he sat with many others in the increasingly overcrowded prisons and prison hulks until the decision was made to send convicts to New South Wales.

Both Mary Braund and William Bryant were put on the *Charlotte*, which carried both men and women convicts. During the voyage to New South Wales Mary gave birth to a daughter, whom she named Charlotte after the ship. It is not clear who the father was. Since the baby was born in September, a few weeks before the fleet reached Cape Town, she probably became pregnant in early January 1787 before she was put aboard the *Charlotte* in Plymouth.

Mary and William were married in Sydney, and Mary was to give birth in April 1790 to a second child, whom

they named Emanuel. William Bryant became a trusted
convict and, given his experience as a fisherman, was put
in charge of the governor's fishing boats. Making the most
of this opportunity, William was selling fish on the side –
fish that should have been put with all the other public
stores. When caught, he was given one hundred lashes.

In 1791 William Bryant's term was almost completed,
but he was one of a number of convicts whose records
were not sent to Australia and therefore, according to
Phillip, could not be released. It must have seemed
to them they might never be free.

Early that year there were only two ships in Sydney
Harbour: the *Supply*, which had recently returned from
Batavia carrying the much-needed food supplies, and the
Waaksamheyd, which had been contracted in Batavia to
carry additional supplies to the colony. After they
unloaded their cargo, both ships left, the *Waaksamheyd*
to return to Batavia and then on to England, and the
Supply to Norfolk Island. The colony then had no ships
in its harbour.

This left William Bryant and the other escapees in a
position to make an escape from Sydney in the governor's
small, single-masted, six-oared fishing boat with no risk
that they could be chased down and recaptured by a
larger ship.

On the night of 27 March, the same day the *Waaksamheyd* left, the Bryants made their escape. William and
Mary, their children Emanuel and Charlotte and seven
other convicts boarded the little cutter, which made off
down Sydney Harbour and out into the ocean. Among the
escapees were First Fleeters Samuel Bird and William
Morton, who was an experienced navigator. The
remaining five, Nathaniel Lilley, Samuel Broom (alias
John Butcher), James Cox, James Martin and William
Allen, had arrived on the Second Fleet in 1790. Of the
eleven who escaped, six would die over the next year and

only five would survive and eventually reach England.

According to escapee James Martin the convicts took provisions, which included 'one hundredweight of flour, one hundredweight of rice, fourteen pounds of pork, eight gallons of water, a compass, quadrant and chart'.[12] The details are obscure but it seems that Bryant was able to acquire the quadrant, the compass and a chart of the east coast of Australia and the Torres Strait from the captain of the *Waaksamheyd*, Ditmar Smith, before he left.

According to marine sergeant James Scott a longboat was launched in pursuit of the escapees at six o'clock the following morning, but by that time the Bryants and their colleagues were long gone.[13]

After leaving Sydney they headed north on one of the most extraordinary voyages in seafaring history. The little boat was to travel five thousand kilometres along the eastern coast of Australia, past the Great Barrier Reef and through the Torres Strait to the Dutch-controlled port of Koepang on the island of Timor.

Initially they kept fairly close to the coast, landing where it was possible and eating fish and edible palms. Two hundred miles north of Sydney and roughly off the coast from Port Stephens, the escapees' little boat was blown out to sea. For several weeks in heavy rain they were only rarely able to reach shore to light a fire.

James Martin also described how on one occasion they were forced to hastily return to the open sea when confronted by hostile Aboriginal people:

> There came natives in vast numbers with spears and shields . . . we . . . made signs to pacify them . . . we fired a musket thinking to afright them but they took not the least notice.[14]

As they reached the Torres Strait, they were chased by hostile natives in canoes before they finally reached the open sea, sailing across the Gulf of Carpentaria and into the Timor Sea, a journey that took four and a half days, 'having aboard little fresh water and no wood to make a fire'.[15]

When they reached Koepang, they successfully masqueraded as shipwrecked travellers and were given clothes while they waited for the next passing ship that could take them back towards England. According to James Martin the convicts were treated well until two months later William Bryant revealed their true identity:

> We went on shore to the Governors house where he behaved extremely well to us . . . filled our bellies and clothed double . . . [We] were very happy . . . for two months before Will Bryant had words with his wife, went and informed against himself, wife and children and all of us, which was immediately taken prisoner and was put in the castle.[16]

The convicts were also unlucky that the next English officer to arrive at the port of Koepang was to be Captain Edward Edwards, the cruel master of the *Pandora*. The *Pandora* had been sent out from England in November 1790 following the arrival of the news of the mutiny on the *Bounty*, to hunt down the mutineers. The pursuers reached Tahiti in 1791 and captured fourteen of the mutineers, whom Edwards ordered to be caged in a box on the deck of the *Pandora*. He did not find the other mutineers, who had sailed with Fletcher Christian on to Pitcairn Island, where they sank the *Bounty* and remained undetected by the British.

Returning to England with the captured mutineers, the *Pandora* smashed onto the northern end of the Barrier Reef in the Torres Strait. The ship was lost and thirty-one crew and four of the convicts drowned, although the others made it to shore. Edwards, pitiless even in a time of crisis, would not allow the mutineers to shelter in the tents, leaving them at the mercy of the sun. It was treatment such as this that fuelled his reputation for cruelty.

Following the shipwreck Edwards and the surviving crew and convicts embarked on their own epic voyage in three small open boats for some three thousand kilometres, heading westward to Koepang. They arrived nearly three weeks later in September 1791, about three months after the Bryants and their fellow escapees, who had then been in custody for a month in the port's prison.

Edwards 'clapped in irons' the convicts from New South Wales. He chartered a Dutch East Indiaman, the *Rembang*, to take them to Batavia, along with the captured mutineers and his surviving one hundred and twenty crew from the *Pandora*. They arrived there in December. The convict escapees were placed in prison while Edwards awaited a ship to take them on the final leg of the journey to face justice back in England. Shortly before Christmas William Bryant and his son, Emanuel, died of a fever in the disease-ridden prison.

Edwards then took Mary Bryant, her daughter, Charlotte, and the other surviving convicts on to Cape Town, during which time another three died: James Cox, Samuel Bird and the navigator William Morton.

At Cape Town Mary and Charlotte and the remaining four convicts – James Martin, William Allen, Samuel Broom and Nathaniel Lilley – were transferred to an English ship, the *Gorgon*. The *Gorgon* was on its way back to London with the First Fleet marine detachment from Sydney, having delivered a new marine corps to relieve them.

According to James Martin, 'We was well known to all the marine officers [on board] which was all glad we had not perished at sea.'[17]

The marine captain Watkin Tench was also on his way home to England on the *Gorgon* and had been impressed by the escape the year before:

Among them were a fisherman, a carpenter, and some
competent navigators, so that little doubt was entertained that a scheme so admirably planned would be
adequately executed . . . After the escape of Captain
Bligh, which was well known to us, no length of
passage or hazard of navigation seemed above human
accomplishment.[18]

When Tench saw the six surviving escapees being brought
aboard the *Gorgon*, he remembered Mary Bryant and one
of the other convicts and was moved to express sympathy
for their plight:

I confess that I never looked at these people without
pity and astonishment. They had miscarried in a
heroic struggle for liberty and having combated every
hardship and conquered every difficulty. The woman
and one of the men had gone out to Port Jackson in
the ship, which had transported me thither. They had
both of them been always distinguished for good
behaviour and I could not but reflect with admiration
at the strange combination of circumstances which
had again brought us together.[19]

On 5 May 1792, only a month before the *Gorgon* was to
reach England, Mary Bryant's daughter, Charlotte, died
and was buried at sea.

Back in London the story of the escape captured the
public imagination. There was considerable public
sympathy, which led to the eventual pardon of Mary
Bryant and the four others in May 1793, although by that
time their original sentences had either been served or
were nearly expired.

The well-known London diarist James Boswell had
taken up Mary Bryant's cause and campaigned for her
release. There were rumours that Boswell and the

ex-convict were lovers, perhaps not helped by the fact that he had agreed to pay her an annuity of £10. Whatever the truth of it, she went to live back with her family in Cornwall.

Of the other pardoned convicts, Samuel Broom (alias John Butcher) immediately enlisted as a volunteer with the New South Wales Corps and returned to the colony the same year. Two years later, in 1795, he was granted twenty-five acres (about ten hectares) of farming land in Petersham, now one of Sydney's inner-western suburbs.

One of the most bizarre escapes of the early settlement occurred in November 1791 when a large group of twenty convict men and a pregnant convict woman made their escape from Rose Hill taking with them food, clothing, bedding and some working tools. They planned to head overland for China!

A detachment of troops was sent in pursuit but, after a difficult march, returned without having seen the party. Over the next few weeks a number of the escapees progressively returned to the settlement, desperate for food. Two had been killed and a number of others wounded by Aboriginal people.

When questioned in the hospital by Captain Tench, the recovering survivors said they thought China was only a hundred miles away:

> I asked these men if they really supposed it possible to reach China. They answered that they were certainly made to believe (they knew not how) that a considerable distance to northward existed a large river, which separated this country from the back part of China and that when it should be crossed, (which was practicable) they would find themselves among copper coloured people, who would receive them and treat them kindly.[20]

18

THE DEPARTURE OF PHILLIP

I cannot conclude this letter without assuring you
[Arthur Phillip] how much I lament that the ill state
of your health deprives his Majesty of your further
services in the Government of New South Wales . . .

After three years in New South Wales many of the naval
officers, sailors, marines and civil officials who had come
out with the First Fleet began to return to England.

At the end of their sentence, or if they were pardoned,
the convicts were also legally free to go home. However,
the practical realities of trying to secure a passage aboard
a ship bound for England – bearing in mind they lacked
both money and sailing experience – combined with
official opposition, made it virtually impossible. Very few
ex-convicts realised their dream of making it home again.

By March 1791 the population of the colony had
doubled to a little over two thousand people, with about
two-thirds living in Sydney and the remainder on Norfolk
Island. About three-quarters were convicts and one
hundred and nine were children.[1]

The first group from the First Fleet to return
to England included Captain John Hunter and many of
the naval officers and crew of the sunken *Sirius*.
Phillip extended the charter of the Dutch vessel the

Waaksamheyd, which had followed the *Supply* back from
Batavia with supplies, so the ship could be used to carry
the crew of the *Sirius* back to England. A total of eighty-
five officers and crew boarded the *Waaksamheyd* for the
long journey home. On board, in addition to the captain
and crew of the *Sirius*, were a number of people who had
both shaped and recorded the story of the First Fleet,
including Lieutenant William Bradley, Jacob Nagle and
Captain Watkin Tench. Bradley, who had painted and
drawn many features of the colony of Sydney and
Norfolk Island, would also produce a range of drawings
and charts of the voyage home.

Under the charter arrangements the *Waaksamheyd* was
to have an awkward line of command. The ship's captain
was the Dutchman Ditmar Smith, but Captain John
Hunter decided where they went, and it was the British
officers aboard, rather than the Dutch, who possessed the
navigation skills required for the course they were to take
in the largely uncharted waters north of New Guinea.
Further tension arose from the fact that the English
officers regarded themselves as more refined than the
uncouth Dutchmen.

According to Jacob Nagle it had originally been
planned to sail the *Waaksamheyd* south under Tasmania
then west across the Great Southern Ocean to the Cape of
Good Hope, but after struggling into a headwind unsuc-
cessfully for several weeks the plans were changed:

> We steered to the South and when we got off Van
> Diemans land we found the wind continued from the
> westward, and we beating for three weeks in vain, we
> bore up and steered to the north and east for the
> middle passage.[2]

Only two weeks out from Sydney Lieutenant George
Maxwell, one of the marines, died and was buried at sea.

Maxwell had been one of two original lieutenants on the *Sirius*, but he had displayed the first signs of insanity more than two years earlier and had been an invalid in the colony ever since. He died after lying in his cabin for several days 'in a dreadful condition, constantly delirious and insensible to anything whatsoever'.[3]

The longer route taken north of New Guinea allowed the *Waaksamheyd* to chart areas beyond those already mapped by earlier explorers, but it also meant the ship would take six months to reach Batavia. Running low on food, they stopped for fresh supplies near Balut Island south of the Philippines, where the crew narrowly avoided being massacred. A few hundred natives had brought food aboard and were trading with the Europeans when Captain Smith's Malaysian mistress overheard the outline of a plan to kill all the Europeans aboard and take the ship. Jacob Nagle described the incident:

> About this time there was between two and three hundred on board with a pretence of trade, the Dutch Captain had a Malay girl sitting on the quarter deck which he kept as a miss, and she was very fond of him. She, understanding the language heard . . . they were then determined to massacre all the whites on board . . . The girl informed the Captain and he sent the mates below for an armful of cutlasses . . . The king [of the natives] finding they were discovered made a spring on the gunnels of the vessel and from thence into his boat . . . Though the decks were full of Malays and all armed with dirks, and seeing the king and general fly, they all jumped overboard and swam to the canoes, which were numerous, laying off waiting for the massacre.[4]

In late August, five months after leaving Sydney, the ship passed below Makassar Strait, where they saw a number of local Malay boats before reaching Batavia on 27 September. The *Waaksamheyd* was in poor shape by this point and needed several weeks of repairs before it could embark on the next leg of the journey.

While in Batavia, the British decided to buy the ship outright and discharged the Dutch captain. With the 'English colours and pennant hoisted',[5] the vessel came under the full command of Captain John Hunter for the remainder of the journey back to England.

They were in Batavia for nearly two months, and when they left there was evidence among the crew of the notorious fever for which that port was renowned. Lieutenant Bradley described the port as the 'grave of Europeans',[6] and Jacob Nagle claimed that 'when we arrived we had not a sick man on board, and when we left it, we had not a well man on board'.[7]

After the *Waaksamheyd* left Batavia for the Cape of Good Hope, Hunter's log contains regular reports of crew who died from fevers caught in the Dutch provincial city. When they reached the Cape in December 1791, many of the crew were still ill and several died. A number of the seriously ill were laid in wagons and taken to the local hospital, while others were nursed back to health on the boat. Even by the time the *Waaksamheyd* was to leave Table Bay, a number of the crew were still too ill to travel and would be left behind, while many of those who sailed would still not have entirely recovered from the illnesses contracted in Batavia.[8]

While in Table Bay, the ship experienced the same hostile winds that earlier captains had complained of. On one occasion the *Waaksamheyd* was blown off its anchor and out to sea. It was to take two days to sail back into the port.

One night when Captain Hunter was on shore, Lieutenant Bradley gave the crew a party, or 'frolic', to celebrate the fact that after nearly five years they would

soon be back in England. There was much noise from the
'drink and carousing' on the quarterdeck, which led
the captain of the English ship the *Swan*, also anchored
in the bay, to fear a mutiny was in progress and send a
boat with armed officers and men over to restore order.
When Bradley assured them that everything was fine,
'they all drinked hearty and laughed till we sent them
back nearly as well intoxicated as we were on board'.[9]

It was while the *Waaksamheyd* was in Cape Town that
John Hunter met Captain William Bligh for the first and
probably the only time. Bligh was in command of the
HMS *Providence* and, with the HMS *Assistant*, was on
his second attempt to collect tropical breadfruit from the
south Pacific for replanting in the West Indies.

His first attempt, two years prior, had ended in mutiny,
when the crew of the *Bounty* had risen up against him in
April 1789.

On Captain Cook's voyage more than eighteen years
earlier the English had observed the breadfruit growing
on trees in Tahiti and other places, and how it formed a
staple part of the native diet when simply roasted on a
fire. The British were keen to collect a large number of the
fruit plants for transplanting into the British-controlled
West Indies, where it was hoped they would provide a
cheap form of food for the slaves working on the sugar
plantations. The sinking of the *Bounty*, which the
mutineers subsequently scuttled at Pitcairn Island, and the
loss of all of the breadfruits that were thrown overboard
did not discourage the British. With Joseph Banks'
prompting, Bligh was sent again on the same mission, this
time with two ships.

Bligh was unimpressed with Hunter, who was highly
critical of the new colony he was now leaving. In a letter
Bligh sent to his friend and patron Joseph Banks, he wrote
that Hunter did not seem to have the leadership qualities
necessary for his current position: 'I may pronounce with

some certainty that the present second in command [of
New South Wales] . . . is not blessed with a moderate
share of good knowledge to give much stability to the new
settlement.'[10] Bligh, of course, had no idea that within
four years Hunter would become the governor of New
South Wales and that he himself would follow him into
the office ten years later.

The *Waaksamheyd* left the Cape on 18 January 1792
and sailed north-west with the prevailing winds to the
island of St Helena, some sixteen hundred kilometres
across the Atlantic. Two weeks later they sailed on and by
April were off the English coast, where they sailed
alongside a British frigate that was patrolling the English
Channel.

As they approached Portsmouth, they were told that
Lieutenant Ball had passed up the Channel on the *Supply*
just the day before and had asked about the *Waaksamheyd*. When told that the ship had not been seen, Ball,
who had left Sydney seven months later than the Dutch
ship, believed it must have been lost.

Immediately after the arrival in Portsmouth a court
martial was held on the *Brunswick* to try Captain John
Hunter and his crew for the sinking of the *Sirius*. Such a
trial was automatic following the loss of a navy ship, and
the court martial found that 'every thing was done that
could be done' to save the ship from being wrecked on the
Norfolk Island reef. Hunter and his crew were all
honourably acquitted.[11]

On reaching Portsmouth, too, the crew were paid off.
For Jacob Nagle this meant an unexpected windfall: he
received not only all the back pay owed to him but also the
money due to his fellow American Terrence Byrne, who
had died on the way home. Byrne and Nagle had signed on
with the First Fleet at the same time and had been on the
Sirius together for all of its adventures, including the
original voyage to Australia, the circumnavigation of the

globe to fetch food from the Cape and, finally, its sinking on Norfolk Island. The two men were single and had nominated each other as beneficiaries in their wills.[12]

Arthur Phillip had finally been able to release the *Supply* from the colony after being assured that regular convict convoys would be coming to Sydney. In addition to taking back official dispatches and letters, the *Supply* carried on board the first live kangaroo taken to England, as a gift for King George III.

After leaving Sydney in November 1791, Lieutenant Ball headed south and east below New Zealand to return via Cape Horn. He was well aware of what to expect on the route, which Captain Hunter had taken on the *Sirius* to fetch food from Cape Town two years earlier. By Christmas Day they were almost fifty-eight degrees south, below Cape Horn, in squalls, hail and snow. They were out of fresh food and reduced to a diet of portable soup, essence of malt and 'sour krout', which was thought to be anti-scorbutic.

By 6 January they were making good time, and after only six weeks' sailing they saw Cape Horn. At this time Hunter and the *Waaksamheyd* were still at the Cape of Good Hope, coming the other way. A month later, on 3 February, those aboard the *Supply* reached Santa Cruz, where they stayed for only four days to load up with fresh food and water before heading off to the north-east across the Atlantic.

At about noon on 20 April they saw the Lizard peninsula on the Cornish coast, which had been the last sighting the First Fleet had had of England five years earlier. They arrived in Portsmouth a few days later.

On reaching England, the now 36-year-old Ball returned to naval duty. He was promoted to captain in 1795 and served on a number of ships over the next twenty years before being appointed vice-admiral in the blue in 1814. Ball married Charlotte Foster in London in

1802. Sadly, she died the following year, and he was married again seven years later to Anne Johnston. When he died in 1818 aged 62, he was survived by his wife as well as a daughter, Anna Maria, in Sydney, whose mother was the convict Sarah Partridge.

Despite being the smallest ship of the First Fleet, the *Supply* had achieved a great deal. It had been the first to reach Botany Bay; it had taken Philip Gidley King and his small party to colonise Norfolk Island; it had sailed to Batavia for vitally needed food for the starving settlers in Sydney; and it had brought back the shipwrecked crew of the *Sirius*. Until the arrival of the Second and subsequent convict fleets it was for a time the only ship available to the new colony and the only contact the settlers had with the outside world. However, the *Supply* was to have an inglorious ending. After it returned to England, the navy sold the ship. It was renamed the *Thomas and Nancy* and carried coal on the River Thames until 1806, after which it disappeared from the official records.

The next group from the First Fleet to return home were the marines. They left Sydney on the *Gorgon* after almost four years in the colony, sailing out on 18 December 1791, nine months after the *Waaksamheyd* and less than two months after the *Supply*.

Of nearly two hundred and fifty marines and their officers who had come with the First Fleet, sixty-three decided not to go home but to stay as farmer settlers on either Norfolk Island or Rose Hill. The British Government was disappointed that so few had chosen to stay on, having authorised Arthur Phillip to make land grants and cash bonuses to the marines to encourage them to stay when their term of duty expired.[13] Captain Watkin Tench said that only some of them were sufficiently skilled to succeed as farmers and that most of those who stayed did so because they were attracted to female convicts, which would promise 'neither honour, nor tranquillity'.

Others, he said, were comfortable enough to stay because they had recently been paid almost four years' dues, with money that had arrived in Sydney on later ships.

The *Gorgon* had arrived in Sydney the previous September, bringing out convicts and supplies as one of the eleven ships of the Third Fleet and also carrying on board Lieutenant Philip Gidley King. King had been sent to London in 1790 by Arthur Phillip to report on the fortunes of the First Fleet; he returned to the colony with his new wife, whom he had married while in London.

The captain of the *Gorgon*, John Parker, had also brought his wife, Ann, along. She would go on to write *A Voyage Around the World in the Gorgon,* an account of the trip, which was published in London four years later.

Among the marines returning to England was their commander, Robert Ross. Apart from later being given command of a troop of marines at Chatham College and seeking to be paid a higher pension, Ross would all but disappear from the pages of history when he arrived back in England. He lived for only another two and a half years and died on 9 June 1794 at Brompton in Kent, aged 54.

Also on board was William Dawes, the marine officer who had established an observatory on Dawes Point, now the site of the southern approach to the Sydney Harbour Bridge. Soon after he returned to England, Dawes went to Sierra Leone and was three times appointed governor there over the next ten years. Back in England in 1804 he helped to train missionaries for the Church Missionary Society. From 1812 he embraced the campaign against slavery and died in Antigua in 1836. He had first married in 1800 and had two sons, one of whom, William Rutter, became an astronomer like his father. In Antigua he had married again, this time a woman called Grace Gilbert, who survived him.

When the *Gorgon* reached the Cape of Good Hope, it picked up the escaped convict Mary Bryant, her daughter,

Charlotte, and the other four surviving escapees from Sydney who had been taken back into custody in Koepang several months earlier. The *Gorgon* also took aboard the ten surviving mutineers from the *Bounty* who had been recaptured by Captain Edwards of the *Pandora* so they could be taken back to England and put on trial.

Captain Watkin Tench was also on the *Gorgon*. Shortly after arriving back in England, he was promoted to brevet-major and, with the outbreak of war with France, was soon at sea again. In November 1794 he was on the seventy-four-gun *Alexander* when it was captured by the French, and he would spend the next six months as a prisoner before being released as part of a prisoner exchange. He spent the remainder of the war in the Channel Fleet and was promoted to lieutenant-colonel in 1798. From 1802 he served on shore depots and finally retired, by this stage a major-general, in 1816. However, he was active again in 1819 and retired again as lieutenant-general in July 1821. Tench married Anna Maria Sargent of Devonport after returning to England, and while they had no children of their own they adopted the four orphaned children of Tench's sister and her navy husband Captain Bedford. Watkin Tench died in 1833 in Devon, aged 75.

Governor Arthur Phillip was one of the last officers of the First Fleet to leave New South Wales. On 11 December 1792 he sailed on the *Atlantic* with the last of the remaining First Fleet marines who did not wish to stay as settlers in the colony.

Phillip had wanted to leave earlier, having first requested to be relieved on 15 April 1790. He had written a private letter to Lord Sydney with the request, not realising that Sydney was no longer the minister for the Home Office and that Lord Grenville had taken over nine months earlier. Phillip gave no sound reason for wanting to be relieved but acknowledged that even if his request was approved it would be at least another year before it could take effect.[14] In a separate letter to Evan Nepean of the Home Office, Phillip made a very rare reference to his wife, saying that he thought she was dying and that other of his affairs needed attending to.[15]

Arthur Phillip had sent his request to go home at a time when the colony was suffering great hardship and was chronically short of food. However, he denied that he was trying to leave at the worst time. In a letter to Lord Sydney he insisted that the problems of the colony would be 'done away with before this letter reaches your Lordship'.[16]

Whatever the truth of the matter, Lord Grenville denied the request. In a short letter written almost a year after Phillip's letter to Lord Sydney, Grenville made it clear to Phillip that his private problems were less important than his public responsibilities to the colony:

Lord Sydney has transmitted to me a private letter which his Lordship has received from you by Lieutenant King, wherein you have expressed a desire to be permitted to return to England. I am much concerned that this situation of your private affairs should have been such as to render this application necessary at a time when your services in New South Wales are so extremely important to the public.

I cannot, therefore refrain from expressing my earnest hope that you might have it in your power so as to arrange your private concerns that you may be able, without material inconvenience, to continue in your Government for a short time longer. From the zeal which you have at all times manifested for the public service, I am inclined to believe that you will readily accede to this proposal, and I shall therefore only add, that as soon as your presence in the Colony can be dispensed with, you will be assured that everything on my part will be done to contribute to your accommodation.[17]

Phillip's permission to return home was not granted until Grenville had been succeeded by William Dundas. In a letter on behalf of the British Government Dundas referred to Phillip's health as a factor in the decision:

> I cannot conclude this letter without assuring you how much I lament that the ill state of your health deprives his Majesty of your further services in the Government of New South Wales and I have only to hope that, on quitting the settlement, you will have the satisfaction of leaving it in a thriving and prosperous situation.[18]

Judge David Collins was one of the few officials to stay longer than Phillip, and he would later return to Australia and become the governor of Tasmania. He recorded Phillip's departure:

> He was now about taking leave of his own government. The accommodations for his Excellency and the officers who were going home in the *Atlantic* being completed ... at six o'clock in the evening of Monday the 10th Governor Phillip quitted the charge with which he had been entrusted by his Sovereign, and in the execution of which he had manifested a zeal and perseverance that alone could have enabled him to surmount the natural and artificial obstacles which the country and its inhabitants had thrown in his way.
>
> His Excellency, at embarking on board the *Atlantic*, was received near the wharf on the east-side (where his boat was lying) by Major Grose, at the

head of the New South Wales corps, who paid him, as
he passed, the honours due to his rank and situation
in the colony . . . At daylight on the morning of the
11th, the *Atlantic* was got under way, and by eight
o'clock was clear of the Heads, standing to the E.S.E.
with a fresh breeze at south. By twelve o'clock she had
gained a considerable offing.[19]

The *Atlantic* would take six months to reach England,
arriving in May 1793. Phillip took with him two convicts
he had pardoned and two Aboriginal people, Bennelong
and Yemmerrawanne, who were to attract a lot of interest
in London.

Chief Surgeon John White was another of the few senior
members of the First Fleet who returned to England after
Phillip. After several years working under stressful and
difficult circumstances tending the sick in the colony – not
to mention the large numbers of sick convicts who came
on the Second and Third Fleets – he had applied for leave
in England in December 1792, when Phillip himself was
returning. White had to wait more than a year for
approval and finally sailed home on the *Daedalus* in
December 1794.

White married in 1800 and had three children. He had
also had a son, Andrew, with a convict woman from the
First Fleet, Rachel Turner. Andrew had been born in
Sydney in 1793 and he later also went to England. He was
to join the Royal Engineers and fought at the Battle of
Waterloo in 1815 before going back to Sydney in 1823 to
reunite with his mother, whom he had not seen since he
was an infant.

John White finally resigned his post rather than have
to return to Sydney after his leave finished. For three years
he served as surgeon on a number of navy ships then on
shore before retiring in 1820, aged 63. He spent his

retirement years on the south coast of England and died at Worthing, aged 75, in 1832.

White had kept a journal from the first month of his appointment to the First Fleet. Covering the voyage to New South Wales and the early years in the colony, it was published in London in 1790.

In 1792 – two years before he went home – a recently arrived convict artist, Thomas Watling, had been assigned to White, and the two men went on to develop an effective creative partnership. A keen naturalist, White recorded the bird and animal life of the colony, with illustrations by Watling. It is widely believed that some of the drawings and paintings in White's published book were Watling's work.

Watling was a 26-year-old Scottish coach painter when he was sentenced to fourteen years' transportation in 1788 for forgery. He left England on the convict transport *Pitt* in July 1791 and escaped in Cape Town but was recaptured by the Dutch, imprisoned and subsequently handed back to the English. He was then put on the *Royal Admiral* and reached Sydney in October 1792, when he began working with White.

Not a great deal is known about Watling's life after White went back to England. He was pardoned by Governor Hunter in 1797, and it is believed that in 1801 he went to live in Calcutta with his young son, thought to have been born to a convict woman in Sydney. In India he worked as a miniature portrait painter for some time before returning to Scotland. Once there, he was charged with forgeries committed in 1804 but discharged with the Scottish verdict of 'not proven'. He later moved to London, where he managed to obtain some financial support from the Royal Academy. It is not known how, when or where he died.

Judge David Collins had also requested to return to England, citing 'very urgent private and family affairs'. His leave was approved, but successive governors kept

him in the colony for another four years before he finally
went back on the *Britannia* in August 1796.

In 1802 Collins was chosen to establish a new colony
north of Bass Strait near what was later to become
Melbourne. However, a shortage of water and timber
forced him to shift to Hobart in Tasmania, where he
remained until he died in 1810, aged 54.

After Phillip left Sydney in December 1792, there would be
a period of almost three years before the appointment of
the next governor of New South Wales. In the meantime
the affairs of the colony were left in the hands of
Lieutenant-Governor Major Francis Grose, and later, for a
period of nine months, of Captain William Patterson.

When he arrived in the colony in 1791, Grose was to
express some surprise to see so many crops growing,
because he had heard so much about famine and food
shortages before he arrived. In a letter to a friend that was
published in the *Gentleman's Magazine* in February 1793,
Grose painted the colony as a land of milk and honey –
although he had arrived in late summer when the local
scene would have looked its best:

> Landed with my family at this place on 14th February
> and to my great comfort and astonishment, I find
> there is neither scarcity that was represented to me,
> nor the barren sands I was taught to imagine I would
> see. The whole place is a garden, on which fruit and
> vegetables of every description grow in the greatest
> luxuriance. Nothing is wanting here but oxen and
> black cattle, within five miles of my habitation there
> is food in abundance for thousand head of cattle . . .
> There is a good house as I desire.

The 39-year-old Grose had come from a well-to-do
family, and his grandfather had been a well-known

antiquarian during the reign of King George II. Young Francis had been commissioned as an ensign in the army in 1775 and fought in the American War of Independence before being wounded and sent home in 1779.

In his two years as acting governor of New South Wales he appointed a number of marines and former marines to important positions in the colony. He also granted land to serving marines and allocated convicts to work their farms. Grose believed the colony would develop more by encouraging private initiative rather than by relying on the public enterprise and encouraged the marine officers to engage in trade. It was under the watch of Grose that military control of the colony's economy began to be established.

After two years Grose resigned, claiming his old wounds from the American wars were causing him much pain. At the end of 1794 he returned to England. For the next nine months he was replaced by Captain William Patterson, who had arrived with the New South Wales Corps of marines in 1791. Patterson was to be the colony's administrator until the arrival of the new governor, Captain John Hunter.

Like his immediate predecessor, the 39-year-old Patterson had joined the army at an early age and had served in Cape Town in 1777, India in 1781, received his commission as a lieutenant in 1787 and was promoted to captain in 1789 when he volunteered to join the New South Wales Corps.

During the nine months he was in charge, Patterson granted more land than Arthur Phillip had done in five years as governor, and, like Major Francis Grose, he did nothing to check or control the increased involvement of the military in the farming and commerce of the colony. This gradually became a major problem, one that would dog the colony's administration for many years, eventually coming to a head with the overthrow of Governor William Bligh more than ten years later, in 1808.

While Grose and Patterson were administrating the colony in the absence of a new governor, Captain John Hunter was pressing his claim to the governorship. Hunter's reputation – and no doubt the feeling that he was governor material – had been further enhanced by the publication of his *An Historic Journal of the Transactions at Port Jackson and Norfolk Island* in London in 1793.

By 1795 Hunter had been back in England for three years, having arrived home in April 1792 to find England again at war with France. He immediately joined as a volunteer on the *Queen Charlotte* and met up with his old commander and mentor Sir Roger Curtis, whom he had sailed with in the north Atlantic and the West Indies during the 1780s. Also on the *Queen Charlotte* was his old patron Admiral Lord Howe, who along with Curtis was to support Hunter's claim to succeed Phillip as governor of New South Wales.

The unmarried Hunter sailed back to New South Wales in September 1795, celebrating his 58th birthday a few weeks before reaching Sydney and assuming the office of governor on his arrival. While his first reports to London were favourable, he was soon to privately complain that he was facing a difficult time in the job.

Hunter was to have the same problem as most of the other naval officers who were appointed governor. He was accustomed to the discipline of the quarterdeck, where the commander was the absolute and total master. Like Phillip before him and King and Bligh after him, he had no experience and little aptitude for dealing with the entrenched commercial interests and disobedience of the military.

Hunter moved to reduce the influence of the military in the colony. Government control of wages, prices and hours of work had become ineffective, and the mark-up on imported supplies by the military merchants reached as high as seven hundred per cent.

By 1798 and after three years of Hunter's government, more of the settlement's economic activity had shifted to the fertile soils around Parramatta. Here, most of the harvest came from private farms and not those cultivated by the government.

In the absence of a large program of free settlers it had been the marines who had become the farmers. Many had also become merchants, building up an effective monopoly in the selling of supplies – especially grog – at the huge mark-ups already mentioned.

One such successful former military officer was John Macarthur, who was to become one of the richest and most powerful men in the colony. Macarthur had been a captain in the New South Wales Corps, which arrived in 1791 to replace the original Marine Corps. Over the next few years he became a successful farmer before taking the appointment of inspector of public works.

After four years as governor Hunter's reputation in London was being undermined by increasing complaints, many of which were being sent by his enemies in Sydney. His position was further weakened by the discovery that some of his own staff were corrupt, including his steward Nicholas Franklyn, who committed suicide after being accused of being at the centre of an illegal trading operation in rum.

Eventually, and probably unfairly, Hunter was abruptly recalled. His former colleague and friend Philip Gidley King, who had successfully manoeuvred himself into the job while he had been back in England, carried the dispatches outlining Hunter's formal sacking from England to Sydney.

A devastated Hunter left Sydney on the *Buffalo* and arrived back in England in May 1801, demanding an inquiry into his management of the colony. He was not only denied the chance to clear his name but was given the official cold shoulder and denied an audience with the secretary of state.

He was, however, able to attract some sympathy and an element of vindication with the publication in London in 1802 of his account of the colony, *Governor Hunters Remarks on the Causes of the Colonial Expense of the Establishment of New South Wales. Hints for the Reduction of Such Expense and for the Reforming the Prevailing Abuses*. Hunter was subsequently granted a pension of £300 per annum and, in 1804, despite being nearly 67 years old, was given command of the *Venerable*, a seventy-four-gun warship in the Channel Fleet. In 1807 he was appointed rear-admiral and in 1810, when he was 73, vice-admiral. In his last years he lived alone in Hackney in London and died in 1821, aged 84.

For Philip Gidley King the voyage to Sydney in 1800 to take up the position of governor was his third trip to New South Wales.

After arriving originally with the First Fleet, King had spent almost all of his two years in the new colony establishing the little settlement on Norfolk Island before leaving for England in 1790. King was 32 years old when he arrived back in London for the first time, to discover that while he was sailing for England a letter confirming his promotion and pay increase had been sent to Sydney. Governor Phillip had recommended his promotion, but lack of seniority had been a problem until the British Government announced he was to be given the title of lieutenant-governor of Norfolk Island, on a salary of £250 a year.

King spent only three months in England before his second trip to New South Wales. While in England, he was also promoted in the navy to the rank of commander. Only three days before his departure he married Anna

Josepha at St Martin-in-the-Fields in London, then sailed
with his new wife and new commission back to New
South Wales on the *Gorgon* in March 1791.

When the ship stopped at Cape Town on its way to
Sydney, King heard of continuing shortages of food in
New South Wales and bought more livestock to take on
to the colony. His unauthorised spending would result
in protracted correspondence later, and many of
the cattle died before reaching Sydney anyway. The
Gorgon arrived in Sydney on 21 September 1791, and
King and his wife spent five weeks there before sailing
on to Norfolk Island. There, six weeks later, Anna
would deliver the first of their three children, Phillip
Parker.

In the twenty months that King had been away from
Norfolk Island, it had changed dramatically. The island
now had a population of nearly a thousand people and,
after a long period of martial law under Major Robert
Ross, there was widespread disaffection among the
settlers.

During his second term on Norfolk Island King tried
again to grow flax, which had been the original reason
why the British Government had wanted to colonise an
island that had no natural harbour. While he had been in
London, King had persuaded the government to authorise
bringing Maori flax-makers from New Zealand to
Norfolk Island to help get the industry off the ground.
Captain Vancouver on the *Daedalus* duly brought two
Maoris to the island, but it was then discovered that they
knew nothing about flax-making. King used the return of
the Maoris to their homeland as an excuse to undertake
an unauthorised visit to New Zealand and wrote up an
account of his journey, which was first published in
London in 1794.

After nearly four years back on Norfolk Island King
had developed a reputation for tempestuousness and

heavy drinking. In 1796, suffering from gout and other illnesses, he was given permission by Governor John Hunter to return for the second time to England.

King was not yet 40 and had been commander of Norfolk Island for a total of nearly six years. By this stage the little island colony was not only self-sufficient in grain but also able to export pigs and other produce to Sydney, which was still dependent on imported food for its survival.

Back in London for the second time King found he still had supporters, including former governor Arthur Phillip, who was back in England and would actively promote King as the future governor of New South Wales. In a letter to the home secretary, William Dundas, Phillip said he wanted to render 'justice to an officer of merit' and that King was 'the most likely to answer the intentions of the Government in the present state of the colony'.[20] King also had the support of Joseph Banks, to whom he had regularly sent botanical specimens.

The representations on King's behalf were successful, and in 1798 he was given a dormant commission as governor of New South Wales in the event that John Hunter died or was absent from the colony. At the time of this appointment there was no question of John Hunter's not continuing as governor, however.

King's departure from England for his third voyage to New South Wales was delayed for some months, and when he finally left Portsmouth on the *Speedy* in August 1799, the British Government had given him the dispatch recalling Hunter. King travelled with his wife, Anna, and youngest daughter, Elizabeth, while his two oldest children, Phillip and Maria, stayed with friends to be schooled in England.

During the next six years Governor King encountered the same resistance from the military that Hunter had faced when trying to make them relinquish their control over all facets of the colony's economy. In 1806 King handed over the governorship to William Bligh and sailed home for the third and last time, sick and exhausted. He arrived in England in November 1807 and died less than a year later, aged only 50.

When he returned to England, Arthur Phillip had been away for five years and seven months and was 55 years old. He did not go into retirement but, immediately on arrival, attended to a number of personal matters, including making a successful request to Home Secretary William Dundas that he keep being paid a salary even after retirement. He also sought medical treatment for the pain in his side that had troubled him for some years. In February 1794, a little more than a year after arriving back in England, he married Miss Isabella Whitehead, a 41-year-old from Preston in Lancashire.

Phillip had returned to a turbulent Europe. While he was still sailing home aboard the *Atlantic*, there were massacres in Paris, and the Tuileries Palace was stormed. In the month he reached England, Louis XVI was executed, and soon England was again at war with France.

In March 1796 Phillip was recalled to the navy as commander of the seventy-four-gun warship the *Alexander* and spent several months patrolling from Plymouth to Portsmouth. In July he was made commander of a fleet of nineteen British ships that were bound for the East Indies. He took the convoy as far as Tenerife, where he handed over to two other British warships. For the rest of the year he appears to have been on routine patrol work based at Cawsand Bay, near Plymouth.

He then served for two years as commander of the *Swiftsure* but shortly after being transferred to the *Blenheim* was relieved as commander to make way for another captain. He was humiliated, saying that he had been forced ashore in the 'most mortifying circumstances'.[21]

The *Blenheim* was to be his last ship. For the next three years he was alternately on half-pay and not working or doing shore work with the navy, which included being commander of the Hampshire Sea Fencibles at Lymington, not far from his old home at Lyndhurst. The Sea Fencibles was made up of naval officers and volunteers and was established as an anti-invasion coastal force during the revolutionary and Napoleonic wars with France.

In 1799 he was promoted to admiral in the blue and in 1804 was still inspecting the Fencibles' detachments along the Sussex coast, ensuring they were in readiness for an invasion from Napoleon's France. Later in 1804 he was promoted again to admiral of the white and in 1805 to rear-admiral of the red, after which he retired from the navy.

At that time Phillip was 67 years old and had left New South Wales almost twelve years earlier. He would spend the next nine years living mostly in Bath, where he was regularly visited by many of his former colleagues from New South Wales, including his friend Philip Gidley King.

Phillip died on 31 August 1814 and was buried at St Nicholas' Church in Bathampton. His wife Isabella died nine years later and was buried with him.

There were just over four thousand two hundred people in the colony when Phillip left. A little more than three thousand one hundred were in Sydney or at Parramatta and Toongabbie west of Sydney, and just over one thousand one hundred were on Norfolk Island. Over three thousand were convicts, forty-seven were part of the civil establishment and five hundred and two were military. The balance of the population was made up of emancipated convicts, a few free settlers and children.[22]

There were now more than two hundred and fifty children, compared with the thirty-six that had landed with the First Fleet five years earlier. The great majority of the new offspring had been born to convict parents, and many were illegitimate.

Phillip had been extremely sparing in the exercise of his powers to emancipate convicts. According to the commissary's report of December 1792 a little more than a month after Phillip left only twelve men and three women had been officially freed, although there would have been many more who had served their sentences by that time.

Within the first five years, too, not many major buildings had been built in Sydney Cove. Apart from the two-storey, six-room, stone governor's residence, which was the only building in the colony with a set of stairs, there was the commissary's office and the more modest houses of Judge Advocate David Collins, Reverend Richard Johnson and his wife, and the surveyor-general, Augustus Alt. There was the dry store and a smaller house and some stores and sheds nearer the water's edge. Across the stream on the western side of Sydney Cove was the 'commodious' one-storey house of Lieutenant-Governor Francis Grose, the military barracks, the spirit store and, further towards Dawes Point, the hospital and the residences of Surgeon John White and his assistants. Scattered over the slopes were a total of one hundred and sixty wattle-and-daub convict huts, which housed as many as ten convicts each.[23]

A little over a month before Phillip departed for England, in October 1792, an official survey revealed that only one thousand seven hundred acres (less than seven hundred hectares) of ground was under cultivation.[24] Of this about a thousand acres was 'public farming' and the remaining seven hundred acres was split between a total of sixty-seven 'settlers and others', the 'others' being individual ex-convicts who had been given small grants of land. The survey also showed that almost all of the farming was now around Parramatta and nearby Toongabbie, about twenty-five kilometres west of Sydney, and that very little was taking place around Sydney itself.

During his time as governor Phillip had relied on state-owned farms and done little to promote the development of private farming. The public farms, however, had only limited success and Phillip repeatedly complained that the convicts did not make good farm workers and he lacked the supervisors to make them work better.

While he was governor, Phillip had the power to grant land to convicts who had served their sentences. However, he did so sparingly, and during his entire term only four thousand acres were given to individuals. At no stage had he ever seen the convicts as forming the foundations of the new country that was being established in Australia. From the earliest days of his appointment until he left to return to England, he only ever regarded them as a source of farm labour to free settlers for the duration of their incarceration. Within six months of arriving, he had pleaded for free settlers to develop the new colony, saying that fifty farmers would be more productive than a thousand convicts in 'rendering the colony independent of the mother country as to provisions'.[25]

Nearly two years later he was still arguing with the British Government that the colony's lack of progress on the agricultural front was due to the convicts, who he consistently complained were incapable of providing the foundation for viable food production in the colony:

> [I]t has never been possible to direct the labour of more than a small part of the convicts to the principal object. A civil and military establishment forms a considerable part of our numbers, which is increased by women and children, all of whom are undoubtedly

necessary, but are deadweight on those who have to render the colony independent for the necessities of life . . . Settlers will secure themselves and their provisions in a short time and everyone they feed will then be employed in cultivation.[26]

He had already proposed that the most fertile lands west of Sydney should be earmarked for free settlers, rather than being wasted as grants to incompetent convict farmers:

The land . . . twenty miles to the westward of Rose Hill, that is, to the banks of the Nepean, is as fine land for tillage as most of England . . . I propose that tract of land for those settlers which may be sent out . . . I think each settler should not have less than twenty men on his farm, which I suppose to be from five hundred to one thousand acres; it will be necessary to give that number of convicts to those settlers who come out, and support them for two years from the public stores; in that time if they are in any ways industrious – and I do not think they will be able to do it in less time – at the expiration of two years they may return half the convicts they have been allowed and would want no further assistance from the Government.[27]

Before Phillip returned to England, he called together the convicts whose terms he had recognised as expired and outlined their options. First, they could accept a land grant and endeavour to make a success of farming on a small plot of land. Second, if they didn't want to take the chance on their own, they could continue to work as labourers and draw the normal rations. Third, they were at liberty to return home, which most still dreamt of doing. It was made clear, however, that the government would provide no assistance to them and they would have

to arrange their own passage on one of the ships returning
to England.

As a result very few of the convicts ever reached home,
which is as the government designed it. As Lord Grenville,
the home secretary, had made clear to Phillip, as far
as Britain was concerned the convicts were beyond
correction, and even where they had served a seven- or
fourteen-year sentence, they were expected to stay away
until they died:

> The return of the [convicts] to this country cannot
> legally be prevented, provided they can engage the
> masters or owners of any vessels arriving in New
> South Wales to transport them from thence. But as
> there is little reason to hope that any persons of that
> description will apply themselves here to the habits
> or pursuits of honest industry, it will be extremely
> desirable that every reasonable indulgence should
> be held out to them with a view of inducing them
> to remain in New South Wales and that it should
> be distinctly understood that no steps are likely to be
> taken by Government for facilitating return.[28]

Contrary to Phillip's vision, then, it was the convicts and
their offspring who would remain in Sydney and unwill-
ingly form the backbone of what was to become the
nation of Australia. When the idea of transportation to
New South Wales had been conceived, the British
Government had expressed little hope in the colony's
becoming anything more than a dumping ground for its
human refuse. The story of the First Fleet, however,
turned out to be one of success against the odds. In an
expedition remarkable for its courage, hardship, famine
and misadventure, perhaps the most remarkable thing is
that this new colony and its people survived at all.

CHRONOLOGY

1717 The British Parliament passes legislation for the overseas transportation of convicts to America. Over the next sixty or so years more than forty thousand British convicts are sent.

1760 George III ascends to the British throne and begins a fifty-year reign. He will authorise the colonisation of Australia before becoming insane and being replaced by the Prince Regent in 1811.

1770

> **April** Captain James Cook charts the east coast of Australia and anchors in what he names Botany Bay.

> **May** After leaving Botany Bay, Cook sails north past another harbour, which he names Port Jackson. Eighteen years later this will become the settlement of Sydney.

1776 The American War of Independence means the British can no longer export their surplus convicts to the American colonies. The prison population grows rapidly in Britain, accelerated by an increase in convictions and a decrease in executions.

1777 The British Parliament passes the *Hulk Act* to allow the increasing number of convicts to be housed on decommissioned naval vessels on the Thames and in other ports. A Bill is also passed in the British Parliament authorising the resumption of overseas transportation of convicts, but no country of destination is prescribed in the legislation.

1779 A British House of Commons committee examines a number of possible overseas destinations for the transportation of convicts, including Gibraltar and the west coast of Africa. Eminent botanist Joseph Banks recommends Botany Bay as a site.

1781–2 A number of attempts to establish convict settlements on the west coast of Africa fail.

1783

August American James Matra proposes that the British Government establish a colony in New South Wales for American loyalists following the loss of the colonies in the American War of Independence.

1784 A further Bill is passed in the British Parliament calling on the government to resume overseas transportation of convicts.

1785

April Another House of Commons committee is established to examine where to transport convicts. The committee baulks at the high estimated costs of transporting convicts to New South Wales.

August The navy sloop *Nautilus* is sent to survey the west African coast and later reports it unsuitable for the establishment of a convict colony.

1786

March The nation is shaken by the news of a prison riot on a hulk in Plymouth. Forty-four convicts are shot, eight of them fatally.

18 August Lord Sydney announces that King George III has authorised the establishment of a penal colony in New South Wales.

31 August Lord Sydney instructs the British Admiralty to arrange enough shipping to take seven hundred and fifty convicts plus marines, officers and some civilian officials to establish a settlement in Botany Bay.

September The British Government announces that Captain Arthur Phillip has been appointed as leader of the expedition and first governor of New South Wales.

October The Admiralty confirms it will assign two navy ships, the *Sirius* and the *Supply*, and will arrange the charter of other, privately owned, vessels to carry the First Fleeters and their supplies to Botany Bay.

Other key personnel are appointed to the venture, including commander of the Marine Corps Major Robert Ross, the Reverend Richard Johnson, Chief Surgeon John White and Judge David Collins.

November The Admiralty stipulates that only forty of the wives of the two hundred and fifty marines will be allowed to accompany their husbands to Botany Bay.

December The first convicts are transferred from the hulks and prisons to the convict transport ships on the Thames prior to being ferried to Portsmouth, where the First Fleet is being marshalled.

1787

11 January Arthur Phillip complains of overcrowding on the transports, and the ninth chartered ship is added to the fleet. The six convict transport ships are the *Alexander*, the *Charlotte*, the *Scarborough*, the *Lady Penrhyn*, the *Friendship* and the *Prince of Wales*. The three ships to carry food, equipment and supplies are the *Fishburn*, the *Borrowdale* and the *Golden Grove*.

February While the fleet is being loaded in Portsmouth with convicts, equipment and two years' supplies, Phillip writes his 'vision' for the establishment of the penal colony.

18 March Convicts begin to die on the transports while the fleet is still at Portsmouth, and Phillip is given permission to temporarily unload them into barges while ships are smoked and fumigated.

2 April Arthur Phillip is issued with his commission and detailed instructions for the establishment of the colony.

5 May Phillip is authorised to buy a large quantity of rum en route to Botany Bay for the marines, who have previously been told they would not have a grog ration in the new colony.

13 May The First Fleet leaves Spithead, outside Portsmouth, for the voyage to New South Wales with almost fifteen hundred people crowded onto the eleven small ships. More than a thousand will be landed to establish the settlement in Sydney, and more than four hundred seamen are expected to eventually sail back with their ships.

20 May Arthur Phillip sends his first report back from the *Sirius* with the navy escort the *Hyaena* – which is returning to Portsmouth – saying that an attempted mutiny by convicts has been thwarted.

2 June The fleet arrives in the Spanish port of Santa Cruz, Tenerife, in the Canary Islands and stays for a week to take aboard fresh water and a limited amount of seasonal fruit and vegetables.

19 June The fleet reaches Port Praya in the Cape Verde Islands off the west coast of Africa. Phillip decides against trying to land because of adverse currents and winds, and leaves immediately to head across the Atlantic to Rio de Janeiro.

11 July The fleet crosses the equator, and water rationing is introduced.

6 August After two months' sailing the fleet reaches the Portuguese port of Rio de Janeiro and scurvy breaks out among the convicts. The officers find abundant fresh oranges and other fruit and load on board fresh food, sixty-five thousand litres of rum and a variety of plants for cultivation in the new colony.

4 September After a month in the port the fleet leaves Rio and heads east back across the Atlantic on the prevailing winds to Table Bay at the Cape of Good Hope.

6 October A week out from the Cape a well-organised plot by convicts to seize the *Alexander* is uncovered.

13 October The fleet reaches the Dutch port of Table Bay after forty days' sailing. Initially the Dutch authorities are uncooperative, but over the next month fresh food and plants are purchased and loaded aboard the fleet, including more than five hundred cows, chickens, geese, pigs, horses, sheep and food for the animals for the next leg of the voyage.

13 November The fleet leaves Table Bay for the longest leg of the journey, to the south of Tasmania.

25 November Arthur Phillip transfers from the flagship *Sirius* to the smaller, faster *Supply* and takes it and the three other fast ships ahead in an attempt to reach Botany Bay well in advance of the bulk of the fleet, in order to lay the foundations of the colony before the others arrive.

1788

18 January After the most difficult sailing of the whole voyage the *Supply* arrives in Botany Bay.

19 January The other fast ships, the *Alexander*, the *Scarborough* and the *Friendship*, also reach Botany Bay.

20 January To everyone's surprise Captain John Hunter arrives and anchors the seven slowest ships (the *Borrowdale*, the *Prince of Wales*, the *Lady Penrhyn*, the *Charlotte*, the *Fishburn*, the *Golden Grove* and the *Sirius*) in Botany Bay within forty hours of the *Supply*.

21 January After an examination Botany Bay is found to be unsuitable for settlement. Arthur Phillip takes John Hunter and other officers in small boats to explore alternative sites for the settlement in Port Jackson, twelve kilometres to the north.

23 January Phillip returns, having found fresh water and a sheltered harbour in what he is to name Sydney Cove in Port Jackson. The fleet is ordered to immediately abandon Botany Bay.

24 January As the fleet prepares to leave Botany Bay for Sydney Cove, it sees two ships trying to enter the heads. They are the French exploration ships the *Astrolabe* and the *Boussole*, commanded by Captain La Perouse, which left France three years earlier.

25 January Some of the ships of the First Fleet are damaged as they struggle against fierce headwinds to get out of Botany Bay. The French ships then struggle to get in.

26 January Arthur Phillip arrives in Sydney Cove on the *Supply* before the rest of the fleet and conducts a small ceremony on what will become Australia Day. The rest of the fleet arrive and anchor in Sydney Cove on the evening of the 26th.

27 January The unloading of the fleet, the clearing of land and the pitching of tents for more than a thousand settlers begin. For the next few years most of the settlers will live in tents or crude shacks with little or no furniture.

February Unable to harvest sufficient local fresh food, the settlers are beset by scurvy and other illnesses. Chief Surgeon John White reports that by mid-year more than a hundred and fifty marines and convicts are infirm.

2 February Lieutenant Philip Gidley King returns to Botany Bay in a small boat and spends three days visiting La Perouse and the French. He is told some of the convicts have already walked overland to ask the French to help them escape.

6 February The bulk of the women convicts are finally unloaded from the ships and the sailors bring grog ashore, which leads to a night of wild debauchery.

14 February Philip Gidley King is sent on the *Supply* with a party of twenty-three settlers to establish a colony on Norfolk Island in the Pacific Ocean, about fifteen hundred kilometres to the north-east of Sydney.

27 February Thomas Barrett becomes the first convict hanged in the new colony, for stealing food from the public store.

10 March La Perouse and the French ships leave Botany Bay heading north. The ships are later lost and never heard from again.

13 March The first reduction is made to the food ration.

5–6 May The first three of the privately owned chartered ships of the fleet, the *Charlotte*, the *Lady Penrhyn* and the *Scarborough*, leave Sydney to return to England via China, where they will pick up a cargo of tea for the East India Company. A number of convicts are thought to have successfully escaped by hiding in the departing vessels with the support of sympathetic sailors.

15 May Arthur Phillip sends back his first report on the colony with the returning ships and hints at the problems that lie ahead when he admits that the clearing of land has been slow, very little grain has been sown and more supplies need to be sent from England.

The foundation stone is laid for the two-storey governor's house, which was designed and built by convict brickmaker James Bloodsworth and finished in June 1789.

4 July Chief Surgeon John White appeals to Arthur Phillip for more fresh food in the diet of the settlers to offset widespread sickness.

5 July Arthur Phillip asks the British Government to send clothing to cover the naked Aboriginal people.

9 July Lieutenant Ball returns from the tiny Lord Howe Island without success at catching the huge turtles it was hoped would supplement the diet of the settlers.

Arthur Phillip sends a more pessimistic report to London in which he says the colony's first harvest has totally failed, most of the livestock brought from the Cape has died or been lost in the bush and that the colony will remain dependent for much longer than planned on food and supplies sent from England.

13–14 July The next four privately chartered ships of the fleet – the *Alexander*, the *Friendship*, the *Prince of Wales* and the *Borrowdale* – leave on their ill-fated return to England.

28 September Phillip reports to London that the settlers' shoes have worn out and that many of the convicts are now in rags, as there is not enough thread to repair their clothing.

1 October Captain John Hunter is sent on the *Sirius* via Cape Horn to the Cape of Good Hope for food, although Phillip notes that the amount the ship will be able to hold will not sustain the colony for long.

19 November The last of the privately contracted ships, the *Fishburn* and the *Golden Grove*, depart for England, leaving the colony with only the two navy ships, the *Sirius* and the *Supply*.

31 December The settlers forcibly abduct a local Aboriginal man named Arabanoo (whom they rename Manly) in an attempt to bridge the language and cultural gap that exists between the newcomers and the locals.

1789

1 January The *Sirius* reaches Robben Island off Table Bay with most of the crew stricken with scurvy and the following day anchors in Table Bay, where it will stay for forty-nine days. Four of the crew desert in the port.

20 February Hunter sails for Sydney on the *Sirius* with a shipload of food.

March The government receives the first report of the colony from the returning ships the *Prince of Wales* and the *Borrowdale*. The reports give them comfort enough to confirm New South Wales as the Second Fleet's destination. If the reports had been negative, the fleet would have been sent to Nova Scotia instead. An order is also given to the Admiralty to immediately send a ship to the colony with relief supplies of food. The *Guardian* is loaded with supplies in Portsmouth.

April An outbreak of smallpox in New South Wales kills an estimated half of the local Aboriginal population but only one white man. It is a mystery how the disease was unleashed more than a year after the arrival of the First Fleet.

Arabanoo, who has become liked and trusted by the settlers, dies while treating the sick among his people.

2 May The *Sirius* is first sighted in Port Jackson returning from the Cape of Good Hope with food. Different accounts are given in the journals as to when it anchored in Sydney Cove. (Collins says it was 6 May; Hunter says the evening of 9 May.)

29 July The *Lady Juliana*, the first ship of the Second Fleet, leaves Plymouth with two hundred and twenty-six convict women on what will be a year-long voyage to Sydney.

12 September The *Guardian*, under the command of Captain Edward Riou, finally leaves Portsmouth more than three months later than planned, with over nine hundred tons of urgent relief supplies for New South Wales.

October The food ration is further reduced in the colony.

1 November Following an assessment of existing stores everyone is reduced to two-thirds of the established ration.

24 November The *Guardian* arrives at the Cape of Good Hope having taken the most direct route south along the African coast. The *Lady Juliana*, which left England a month earlier, is still in Rio de Janeiro with its cargo of women convicts.

24 December Thirteen days and more than a thousand kilometres out of the Cape of Good Hope, and having topped up with supplies, the *Guardian* crashes into an iceberg. Half the crew attempt to abandon ship and the rest stay on the submerged and stricken vessel.

1790

4 January Survivors on only one of the *Guardian*'s five lifeboats are picked up by a passing French ship four hundred kilometres east of Natal and taken back to Cape Town.

21 February Nearly two months after it began sinking, the *Guardian* is seen in the Indian Ocean south of Madagascar by a passing Dutch packet and towed back to Table Bay, where the ship is later destroyed and its remaining cargo salvaged.

28 February The *Lady Juliana* sights land approaching Cape Town.

5 March Arthur Phillip sends more than two hundred settlers on the *Sirius* and the *Supply* from Sydney to Norfolk Island, where their prospects for survival are thought to be better. He also sends the marine commander Major Robert Ross, who has become his nemesis.

19 March After unloading the settlers, the *Sirius* is caught and wrecked on the reef on Norfolk Island.

20 March Major Robert Ross declares martial law on Norfolk Island. Captain John Hunter and his crew from the *Sirius* are stranded on the island with the other settlers for the next eleven months.

9 April Back in Sydney the Reverend Richard Johnson complains that he and fellow settlers' 'hopes are almost vanished' and that they are being 'buried alive' in the colony.

11 April The standard food ration in Sydney is reduced to 'less than half'. Pork is expected to completely run out in July, rice by September and flour by November. Later in the month settlers begin to starve to death. Marine captain Watkin Tench records seeing a man fall dead from hunger before him.

15 April Arthur Phillip writes and asks London to be relieved of his post.

17 April The tiny *Supply*, now the only ship left in the colony, is sent north to Batavia for food. On board is Lieutenant Philip Gidley King, who is being sent back to England by Arthur Phillip to report directly to the British Government on the colony. King will board a succession of ships after Batavia to reach England.

Chief Surgeon John White writes to a friend in England angrily suggesting that the colony has been a failure and should be abandoned.

May Arthur Phillip is seriously wounded by an Aboriginal man who throws a spear that pierces the governor's shoulder and comes out of his back.

3 June The *Lady Juliana*, with its cargo of female convicts, arrives after more than a year at sea. The ship also brings food for the starving colony.

20 June The terrible story of the Second Fleet arrives with the *Justinian*, followed by the *Surprize*, *Neptune* and *Scarborough*. More than a quarter of the convicts died in the appalling conditions aboard the ships and hundreds more are sick and dying when they arrive in Sydney.

19 September The *Supply* returns from Batavia with food.

17 December The Dutch ship *Waaksamheyd* arrives in Sydney with more food, having been chartered for the purpose several months earlier in Batavia by Lieutenant Ball of the *Supply*.

1791

12 February The *Supply* finally brings Captain Hunter and the crew of the *Sirius* back to Sydney, after they have been stranded for nearly a year on Norfolk Island following the sinking of the *Sirius*.

27 March Captain John Hunter and most of the crew of the *Sirius* are the first group from the First Fleet to go home to England on the chartered *Waaksamheyd*, after more than three years in the colony.

Late at night, after the *Waaksamheyd* has left Sydney, eleven convicts, including Mary Bryant and her two children, make a daring escape from the colony and embark on a remarkable journey in a small boat to Timor. Eventually Bryant and the other escapees are recaptured. Bryant and four other convicts reach England, but the others all perish.

9 July The *Mary Ann*, the first convict transport ship of the Third Fleet, arrives in Sydney with one hundred and forty-one women convicts and six children on board.

21 September Philip Gidley King arrives back in Sydney from

England on the *Gorgon* and is immediately sent to Norfolk Island to replace marine commander Major Robert Ross, who is being recalled with the marines to England.

27 September After six months' sailing, and with many of the crew stricken with scurvy, the *Waaksamheyd* reaches Batavia, where Captain Hunter buys the ship for the rest of the journey back to England. They arrive in April the following year.

November The last ship of the First Fleet, the *Supply*, finally leaves Sydney with its crew to return to England, carrying with it the first live kangaroo exported from Australia, as a gift for King George III. The ship reaches Portsmouth the day before the *Waaksamheyd*, which had left Sydney seven months earlier.

18 December Major Robert Ross and his Marine Corps, recalled after nearly four years in the colony, sail back to England on the *Gorgon*, which arrived as part of the Third Fleet. The soldiers are replaced by a new marine force, the New South Wales Corps.

1792

11 December Arthur Phillip is one of the last officials of the First Fleet to leave, after nearly five years in the colony. He sails on the *Atlantic* back to England, taking with him two Aboriginal men, Bennelong and Yemmerrawanne, who are an attraction in London society and are taken to meet George III.

1795

7 September Captain John Hunter returns to Sydney to take up his appointment as second governor of New South Wales. The governorship has been in the hands of caretakers Grose and Patterson since the departure of Arthur Phillip nearly three years earlier.

1796

October Suffering ill health, Philip Gidley King returns to England for the second time, after serving five years as lieutenant-governor of Norfolk Island.

1800

    22 September Philip Gidley King returns to Sydney on the *Speedy* to take over as governor from an embittered John Hunter, whom he has been sent to replace. King serves six years as governor before relinquishing the post to William Bligh.

1814

    31 August Arthur Phillip dies in England aged 75. After returning to England, Phillip had served again in the navy before retiring in 1805.

NOTES

1. ENGLAND

[1] In 1761 the first entirely manufactured canal was built, to carry coal to Manchester; in 1768 Arkwright invented his spinning machine; and in 1767 James Watt developed his steam engine.

[2] George III's father had died nine years earlier, in 1751.

[3] The three kings reigned for almost a hundred years. George I was king from 1714 to 1727, George II from 1727 to 1760 and George III from 1760 to 1811.

[4] McAlpine and Hunter, pp. 56–61.

[5] Colquhoun, p. 53.

[6] Letter from Walpole to Mann, in Dover (ed.), p. 9.

[7] Radzinowicz, p. 4.

[8] Ibid., p. 29.

[9] Ibid.

[10] Hall, p. 254.

[11] Radzinowicz, p. 147.

[12] Howard, pp. 8–9.

[13] Ibid., p. 7.

[14] Ibid., p. 17.

[15] Ibid.

[16] Ibid., p. 23.

[17] *An Act for Punishment of Rogues, Vagabonds and Sturdy Beggars, 1597*, Eliz. 39. See Hughes, p. 40.

18   Radzinowicz, p. 120.
19   *1421: The Year China Discovered the World.*
20   Tasman's 1644 map of his voyages is stored in the Mitchell Library, Sydney.
21   Dampier, p. 464.
22   Manning Clark, p. 191.

2.   THE BOTANY BAY DECISION
1   *Journal of the House of Commons*, Public Records Office, RB F342.4206/1. See also Currey.
2   Ibid.
3   Ibid.
4   Ibid.
5   De Brosses, p. 29.
6   Banks, April–May 1770.
7   The *Guardian*, which was sent to New South Wales in 1790, was to have sheds installed on the instruction of King George III, following representations from Banks.
8   George III, Vol. 6, p. 415.
9   James Maria Matra, 'A Proposal for Establishing a Settlement in NSW to Atone for the Loss of the American Colonies', 23 August 1783, *HRNSW*, Vol. 1, Pt 2, p. 2.
10   Ibid., p. 5.
11   Ibid., p. 7.
12   Matra Note, *HRNSW*, Vol. 1, Pt 2, p. 8.
13   UK National Archives HO47/3 Pt 5.
14   *Journal of the House of Commons*, Vol. 40, Col. 1161, 20 April 1785.
15   Letter from Auden to Sydney, 13 January 1785, *HRNSW*, Vol. 1, Pt 2, p. 10.
16   Sir George Young's Plan, 13 January 1785, *HRNSW*, Vol. 1, Pt 2, p. 10.
17   Ibid., p. 12.
18   *Annual Register 1786*, Vol. 28, p. 198.
19   Manning Clark, p. 67.

20 Letter from Sydney to the Treasury, 18 August 1786, *HRNSW*, Vol. 1, Pt 2, pp. 14–16.

21 Manning Clark, p. 68.

22 Letter from Sydney to the Treasury, 18 August 1786, *HRNSW*, Vol. 1, Pt 2, pp. 14–16.

23 Ibid.

24 *Parliamentary Register*, 23 January 1787, Vol. 26, p. 211.

25 *The Times*, 21 October 1786.

3. ARTHUR PHILLIP

1 McIntyre, p. 79.

2 Ibid., p. 80.

3 Mackaness, pp. 3–4.

4 Ibid., p. 4.

5 Ibid., p. 6.

6 Ibid., p. 7.

7 *London Observer*, 15 December 1793.

8 McIntyre, p. 25.

9 Ibid., p. 64.

10 The story was recorded by Mackaness, pp. 54–7. McIntyre says that if it happened, it was likely to be during the transfer of prisoners between Rio de Janeiro and Colonia (p. 110).

11 McIntyre, p. 101.

12 Spain, p. 37.

13 Letter from Howe to Sydney, 3 September 1786, *HRNSW*, Vol. 1, Pt 2, p. 22.

14 *Royal Australian Historical Society Journal*, p. 264.

15 Phillip's Views on the Conduct of the Expedition and the Treatment of Convicts, February 1787, *HRNSW*, Vol. 1, Pt 2, p. 50.

16 Ibid.

17 Ibid.

18 Ibid.

19 Ibid., p. 51.

20 Ibid., p. 52.

21 Ibid., p. 53.
22 Ibid., p. 54.

4. PREPARATION FOR THE VOYAGE
1   Letter from Sydney to the Treasury, 18 August 1786,
    HRNSW, Vol. 1, Pt 2, p. 14.
2   Ibid.
3   Letter from Sydney to the Admiralty, 31 August 1786,
    HRNSW, Vol. 1, Pt 2, p. 20.
4   Heads of a Plan, 18 August 1786, *HRNSW*, Vol. 1, Pt 2,
    p. 17.
5   Estimates of Ordnance Stores, *HRNSW*, Vol. 1, Pt 2, p. 33.
6   Heads of a Plan, 18 August 1786, *HRNSW*, Vol. 1,
    Pt 2, p. 20.
7   Ibid.
8   Ibid., p. 18.
9   Phillip's Instructions, 25 April 1787, *HRNSW*, Vol. 1, Pt 2,
    p. 90.
10 Heads of a Plan, 18 August 1786, *HRNSW*, Vol. 1, Pt 2,
    p. 19.
11 Governor Phillip's First Commission, 12 October 1786,
    HRNSW, Vol. 1, Pt 2, p. 24.
12 From the mid-eighteenth century ships of the Royal Navy
    were rated into six categories according to the number of
    cannons or guns that they carried. The largest of the
    warships, first rate, carried a hundred or more guns;
    second rate eighty-four; third rate seventy; fourth rate fifty;
    fifth rate thirty-two; and sixth rate thirty-one guns or
    fewer.
13 Letter from the Admiralty to Sydney, 12 October 1786,
    HRNSW, Vol. 1, Pt 2, p. 24.
14 The wale, or gunwale/gunnel, is the top ridge on the side
    of a ship.
15 Philip Gidley King, p. 5.
16 Ibid., p. 19.
17 Hunter, p. 5.

18 *The Times*, 31 October 1786.

19 Philip Gidley King, p. 5.

20 *The Times*, 14 September 1786.

21 Letter from Middleton to Nepean, 11 December 1786, *HRNSW*, Vol. 1, Pt 2, p. 35.

22 Return of the Botany Bay Detachment of Marines and Return of the Male, Female and Children Convicts Embarked for Botany Bay, 15 April 1787, *HRNSW*, Vol. 1, Pt 2, p. 79.

23 Letter from Rose to Stephens, 21 October 1786, *HRNSW*, Vol. 1, Pt 2, p. 26.

24 Letter from Walshe to Sydney (undated but thought to be written at the end of 1787), *HRNSW*, Vol. 1, Pt 2, p. 119.

25 Bateson, p. 39.

26 Ibid., p. 38.

27 'Rations provided for the marines during their passage to Botany Bay', in a letter from the Admiralty to Sydney, 21 November 1786, *HRNSW*, Vol. 1, Pt 2, p. 29.

28 Letter from Phillip to Nepean, 11 April 1787, *HRNSW*, Vol. 1, Pt 2, p. 77.

29 Letter from the Admiralty to Sydney, 21 November 1786, *HRNSW*, Vol. 1, Pt 2, p. 29.

5. THE CONVICTS

1 Based on the records of convictions of the First Fleet convicts. See Cobley.

2 Ibid.

3 Ibid., p. 85.

4 Ibid., p. 36.

5 Ibid., p. 227.

6 Tench, *Expedition*, Ch. I.

7 See www.oldbaileyonline.org, ref: t17830910-41.

8 Ibid.

9 Cobley, p. 241.

10 Ibid.

[11] See www.oldbaileyonline.org, ref: t17860222-131.

[12] See www.oldbaileyonline.org, ref: t17831210-19.

[13] Ibid.

[14] Holden, p. 73.

[15] Nicol, p. 83.

[16] See www.oldbaileyonline.org, ref: t17840114-40.

6. PORTSMOUTH

[1] *London Chronicle*, 28 September 1786.

[2] Ibid.

[3] *The Times*, 19 October 1786.

[4] Ibid., 11 October 1786.

[5] Ibid., 21 October 1786.

[6] Ibid., 29 December 1786.

[7] Hunter, p. 4.

[8] *The Times*, 2 March 1787.

[9] Letter from Phillip to Nepean, 11 January 1787, *HRNSW*, Vol. 1, Pt 2, p. 46.

[10] White, March 1787.

[11] Ibid.

[12] Letter from Phillip to Nepean, 18 March 1787, *HRNSW*, Vol. 1, Pt 2, p. 58.

[13] Ibid.

[14] Letter from Ross to Stephens, 13 April 1787, *HRNSW*, Vol. 1, Pt 2, p. 78.

[15] Letter from Ross to Nepean, 14 March 1787, *HRNSW*, Vol. 1, Pt 2, p. 57.

[16] Letter from Ross to Stephens, 9 July 1788, *HRNSW*, Vol. 1, Pt 2, p. 156.

[17] *The Times*, 21 December 1786.

[18] Bowes Smyth, April 1787.

[19] Ibid.

[20] Tench, *Expedition*, Ch. I.

[21] *The Times*, 23 October 1786.

[22] Letter from White to Nepean, 27 February 1787, *HRNSW*, Vol. 1, Pt 2, p. 48.

23 Philip Gidley King, p. 6.

24 Nagle, p. 8.

25 Ibid., p. 70.

26 Ibid., p. 77.

27 Nagle (Dann (ed.)), p. xiii.

28 See Lambert.

29 Ibid.

30 Ralph Clark, May 1787.

31 Letter from Phillip to Nepean, 11 April 1787, *HRNSW*, Vol. 1, Pt 2, p. 77.

32 Letter from Phillip to Nepean, 4 January 1787, *HRNSW*, Vol. 1, Pt 2, p. 44.

33 Letter from Phillip to Sydney, 12 March 1787, *HRNSW*, Vol. 1, Pt 2, p. 56.

34 Letter from Sydney to Phillip, 20 April 1787, *HRNSW*, Vol. 1, Pt 2, p. 82.

35 Letter from Ross to Nepean, 27 April 1787, *HRNSW*, Vol. 1, Pt 2, p. 93.

36 Memorial from the Marines, 7 May 1787, *HRNSW*, Vol. 1, Pt 2, p. 101.

37 Letter from Phillip to Nepean, 2 December 1786, *HRNSW*, Vol. 1, Pt 2, p. 28.

38 Letter from Phillip to Sydney, 8 May 1787, *HRNSW*, Vol. 1, Pt 2, p. 102.

39 Letter from Sydney to Phillip, 5 May 1787, *HRNSW*, Vol. 1, Pt 2, p. 99.

40 Letter from Phillip to Stephens, 12 May 1787, *HRNSW*, Vol. 1, Pt 2, p. 103.

41 Collins, *English Colony in New South Wales*, p. liv.

42 Ibid.

43 Philip Gidley King, p. 7.

44 White, May 1787.

45 Letter from Phillip to Nepean, 11 May 1787, *HRNSW*, Vol. 1, Pt 2, p. 103.

46 Mackaness, p. 47.

7. THE VOYAGE

1   Nagle, p. 85.
2   Tench, *Expedition*, Ch. II.
3   Collins, *English Colony in New South Wales*, p. lvi.
4   White, May 1787.
5   Hunter, p. 5.
6   Collins, *English Colony in New South Wales*, p. lvii.
7   Ralph Clark, 16 May 1787.
8   Letter from Phillip to Nepean, 20 May 1787, *HRNSW*, Vol. 1, Pt 2, p. 105.
9   Ibid., p. 106.
10 Hunter, p. 6.
11 Letter from Phillip to Nepean, 5 June 1787, *HRNSW*, Vol. 1, Pt 2, p. 108.
12 Nagle, p. 86.
13 White, May 1787.
14 Ibid., June 1787.
15 Hunter, p. 8.
16 White, June 1787.
17 The others included Robert Ross, John Hunter, Philip Gidley King, John White, David Collins and marine officers James Campbell and Watkin Tench.
18 Philip Gidley King, p. 9.
19 Tench, *Expedition*, Ch. III.
20 White, June 1787.
21 Letter from Phillip to Nepean, 5 June 1787, *HRNSW*, Vol. 1, Pt 2, p. 107.
22 Hunter, p. 24.
23 Letter from Johnson to Fricker, 30 May–8 June 1788, in Johnson.
24 Nagle, p. 87.
25 Hunter, p. 10.
26 Letter from Phillip to Nepean, 2 September 1787, *HRNSW*, Vol. 1, Pt 2, p. 112.
27 Scott, June–July 1787.
28 White, June 1787.

29 Ralph Clark, July 1787.
30 White, June 1787.
31 Ibid., July 1787.
32 O'Reilly, p. 186.
33 White, July 1787.
34 Ralph Clark, July 1787.
35 Ibid., August 1787.
36 Ibid., September 1787.
37 Cobley, p. 35.
38 Hunter, p. 5.
39 Ralph Clark, September 1787.
40 White, July 1787.
41 Collins, *English Colony in New South Wales*, p. lxix.
42 Ibid.
43 Phillip, p. 28.
44 Hunter, p. 18.
45 Ibid., p. 19.
46 Letter from Phillip to Nepean, 2 September 1787, *HRNSW*, Vol. 1, Pt 2, p. 113.
47 Letter from Phillip to Stephens, 2 September 1787, *HRNSW*, Vol. 1, Pt 2, p. 114.
48 Mackaness, p. 16.
49 Nagle, p. 89.
50 Bowes Smyth, August 1787.
51 White, August 1787.
52 Bowes Smyth, August 1787.
53 White, August 1787.
54 Ibid.
55 Bowes Smyth, August 1787.
56 Nagle, p. 89.
57 White, August 1787.
58 Cobley, p. 17.
59 Hunter, p. 19.
60 White, August 1787.
61 Collins, *English Colony in New South Wales*, p. lxxx.

62 Letter from Phillip to Nepean, 2 September 1787, *HRNSW*, Vol. 1, Pt 2, p. 112.

63 Ibid., p. 113.

64 Letter from Ross to Stephens, 10 July 1788, *HRNSW*, Vol. 1, Pt 2, p. 173.

65 Scott, June 1790.

66 Letter from Phillip to Nepean, 2 September 1787, *HRNSW*, Vol. 1, Pt 2, p. 114.

8. LEAVING CIVILISATION

1 White, September 1787.

2 Letter from Phillip to Nepean, 2 September 1787, *HRNSW*, Vol. 1, Pt 2, p. 114.

3 Easty, September 1787.

4 Bowes Smyth, September 1787.

5 White, September 1787.

6 Ralph Clark, September 1787.

7 Philip Gidley King, p. 19.

8 Bowes Smyth, October 1787.

9 Nagle, p. 90.

10 Ralph Clark, October 1787.

11 White, October 1787.

12 Hunter, p. 40.

13 Letter from Phillip to Stephens, 10 November 1787, *HRNSW*, Vol. 1, Pt 2, p. 118.

14 Phillip, p. 18.

15 Bowes Smyth, October 1787.

16 White, October 1787.

17 Ibid.

18 Ibid.

19 Ibid., November 1787.

20 Ibid., October 1787.

21 Ibid.

22 Letter from Southwell to his uncle, 12 July 1788, *HRNSW*, Vol. 1, Pt 2, p. 666.

23   Collins, *English Colony in New South Wales*, p. lxxx.

24   White, November 1787.

25   Worgan, *Letter*.

26   White, November 1787.

27   Collins, *English Colony in New South Wales*, p. lxxxvi.

28   Ibid., p. lxxxvii.

29   Ralph Clark, November 1787.

30   White, November 1787.

31   Ibid.

32   Ralph Clark, November 1787.

33   Philip Gidley King, p. 24.

34   Letter from Phillip to Nepean, 1 March 1787, *HRNSW*, Vol. 1, Pt 2, p. 55.

35   Letter from Nepean to Phillip, 27 April 1787, Vol. 1, Pt 2, p. 55.

36   Letter from Sydney to the Admiralty, 5 May 1787, *HRNSW*, Vol. 1, Pt 2, p. 94.

37   Philip Gidley King, p. 27.

38   Easty, November 1787.

39   Philip Gidley King, p. 29.

40   Ibid.

41   Hunter, p. 33.

42   Ibid., p. 34.

43   White, December 1787.

44   Scott, December 1787.

45   Bowes Smyth, January 1788.

46   Letter from Newton Fowell to John Fowell, 12 July 1788, in Fowell.

47   Hunter, p. 36.

48   Bowes Smyth, January 1788.

49   White, January 1788.

50   Bowes Smyth, January 1788.

51   Ibid.

52   Ibid.

53   Ibid.

54   Letter from Phillip to Sydney, 15 May 1788, *HRNSW*,
     Vol. 1, Pt 2, p. 121.

9.   ARRIVAL
1   Philip Gidley King, p. 32.
2   Ibid.
3   Ibid.
4   Bowes Smyth, January 1788.
5   Ibid.
6   Letter from Phillip to Sydney, 15 May 1788, *HRNSW*,
     Vol. 1, Pt 2, p. 123.
7   Cook, April 1770.
8   Letter from Phillip to Sydney, 15 May 1788, *HRNSW*,
     Vol. 1, Pt 2, p. 123.
9   Tench, *Expedition*, Ch. VIII.
10   Bowes Smyth, January 1788.
11   White, January 1788.
12   James Cook named Port Jackson in honour of Sir George
     Jackson (1725–1827), a member of parliament, the judge
     advocate of the fleet and a friend and patron of Cook's.
     Cook was also to name Jackson Head and Jackson Bay on
     the south island of New Zealand after him.
13   Cook, May 1770.
14   Nagle, p. 94.
15   Letter from Phillip to Sydney, 15 May 1788, *HRNSW*,
     Vol. 1, Pt 2, p. 124.
16   Phillip, p. 25.
17   Letter from Phillip to Sydney, 15 May 1788, *HRNSW*,
     Vol. 1, Pt 2, p. 124.
18   White, January 1788.
19   Ibid.
20   Tench, *Expedition*, Ch. VIII.
21   Worgan, *Journal (January 20–July 11, 1788)*.
22   Philip Gidley King, p. 36.
23   Ibid.

24   Worgan, *Journal (January 20–July 11, 1788)*.
25   Ralph Clark, January 1788.
26   Ibid.
27   Bowes Smyth, January 1788.
28   Bradley, January 1788.

10. STRUGGLE
1   White, January 1788.
2   Collins, *English Colony in New South Wales*, p. 4.
3   Ibid., p. 5.
4   Tench, *Expedition*, Ch. IX.
5   Worgan, *Letter*.
6   Scott, January 1788.
7   Worgan, *Journal (January 20–July 11, 1788)*.
8   Bowes Smyth, February 1788.
9   Tench, *Expedition*, Ch. IX.
10   Ralph Clark, February 1788.
11   Collins, *English Colony in New South Wales*, p. 6.
12   Ibid.
13   Bowes Smyth, February 1788.
14   White, February 1788.
15   Ralph Clark, February 1788.
16   Philip Gidley King, p. 37.
17   Collins, *English Colony in New South Wales*, p. 4.
18   Philip Gidley King, p. 38.
19   Ibid., p. 39.
20   Ibid.
21   Hunter, p. 76.
22   Collins, *English Colony in New South Wales*, p. 13.
23   Letter from Phillip to Nepean, 9 July 1788, *HRNSW*, Vol. 1, Pt 2, p. 152.
24   Worgan, *Journal (January 20–July 11, 1788)*.
25   Ralph Clark, February 1788.
26   Tench, *Settlement*, Ch. XVII.
27   Ibid.

28 Letter from Phillip to Sydney, 15 May 1788, *HRNSW*, Vol. 1, Pt 2, p. 127.

29 Tench, *Settlement*, Ch. IV.

30 White, March 1788.

31 Letter from Phillip to Sydney, 15 May 1788, *HRNSW*, Vol. 1, Pt 2, p. 128.

32 Ibid., p. 124.

33 White, March 1788.

34 Opinion of Joseph Banks, 14 May 1789, *HRNSW* (Banks Papers), Vol. 1, Pt 2, p. 232.

35 White, March 1788.

36 Phillip's Instructions, 25 April 1787, *HRNSW*, Vol. 1, Pt 2, p. 84.

37 Tench, *Expedition*, Ch. XIII.

38 Collins, *English Colony in New South Wales*, p. 79.

39 Ibid., pp. 258–9.

40 Ibid., p. 14.

41 Small, pp. 1–15.

42 Tench, *Settlement*, Ch. XIII.

43 Letter from Phillip to Sydney, 15 May 1788, *HRNSW*, Vol. 1, Pt 2, p. 128.

44 Ibid., p. 136.

45 Worgan, *Journal (January 20–July 11, 1788)*.

46 *Sydney Gazette*, 4 April 1804.

47 Worgan, *Letter*.

48 Ibid.

49 Tench, *Settlement*, Ch. I.

50 Ibid., Ch. XIX.

51 White, August 1788.

52 Nicol, p. 88.

53 Tench, *Settlement*, Ch. XVIII.

54 White, March 1788.

55 Ibid.

56 Ibid.

57 Collins, *English Colony in New South Wales*, p. 26.

58 Davis.

11. FRICTION IN THE SETTLEMENT

1 Tench, *Settlement*, Ch. XVIII.
2 White, March 1788.
3 Letter from Phillip to Nepean, 9 July 1788, *HRNSW*, Vol. 1, Pt 2, p. 153.
4 Tench, *Expedition*, Ch. XVI.
5 Letter from Phillip to Lord Sydney, 28 September 1788, *HRNSW*, Vol. 1, Pt 2, p. 190.
6 Letter from Phillip to Nepean, 9 July 1788, *HRNSW*, Vol. 1, Pt 2, p. 153.
7 Ibid., p. 154.
8 Letter from Phillip to Nepean, 15 April 1790, *HRNSW*, Vol. 1, Pt 2, p. 329.
9 Letter from Phillip to Sydney, 15 May 1788, *HRNSW*, Vol. 1, Pt 2, p. 122.
10 Ibid.
11 Phillip's Instructions, 25 April 1787, *HRNSW*, Vol. 1, Pt 2, p. 84.
12 Philip Gidley King, p. 37.
13 'Government of Norfolk Island', letter from Phillip to King, 12 February 1788, *HRNSW*, Vol. 1, Pt 2, p. 137.
14 Ball named the island after Viscount Richard Howe, who was first lord of the Admiralty.
15 Philip Gidley King, p. 40.
16 Letter from Phillip to Sydney, 15 May 1788, *HRNSW*, Vol. 1, Pt 2, p. 125.
17 Letter from Phillip to Nepean, 9 July 1788, *HRNSW*, Vol. 1, Pt 2, p. 155.
18 Ibid., p. 151.
19 Letter from Ross to Stephens, 10 July 1788, *HRNSW*, Vol. 1, Pt 2, p. 173.
20 Letter from Phillip to Sydney, 28 September 1788, *HRNSW*, Vol. 1, Pt 2, p. 190.
21 Tench, *Expedition*, Ch. XVII.
22 Extract from an unsigned letter written by an officer of the

marines, dated Port Jackson, 18 November 1788 and included in the Joseph Banks Papers, *HRNSW*, Vol. 1, Pt 2, p. 221.

[23] Letter from Phillip to Sydney, 30 October 1788, *HRNSW*, Vol. 1, Pt 2, p. 208.

[24] Letter from Ross to Nepean, 16 November 1788, *HRNSW*, Vol. 1, Pt 2, p. 212.

[25] Letter from Ross to Stephens, 10 July 1788, *HRNSW*, Vol. 1, Pt 2, p. 171.

[26] Letter from Phillip to Sydney, 16 May 1788, *HRNSW*, Vol. 1, Pt 2, p. 139.

[27] Letter from Ross to Stephens, 10 July 1788, *HRNSW*, Vol. 1, Pt 2, p. 173.

[28] Ibid., p. 169.

[29] Collins, *Papers*, p. 53.

[30] Letter from Collins to Nepean, 15 November 1788, *HRNSW*, Vol. 1, Pt 2, p. 209.

[31] Letter from Clark to Campbell, 10 February 1791, in Ralph Clark.

12. THE FLEET GOES HOME

[1] Tench, *Settlement*, Ch. II.

[2] Letter from Phillip to Sydney, 9 July 1788, *HRNSW*, Vol. 1, Pt 2, p. 146.

[3] Gilbert, p. 2.

[4] Ibid., p. 4.

[5] Ibid.

[6] Ibid., p. 5.

[7] Ibid., p. 6.

[8] Ibid., p. 13.

[9] Ibid., p. 15.

[10] Ibid., p. 32.

[11] Ibid., p. 40.

[12] Ibid., p. 45.

[13] Ibid., p. 47.

14 Ibid., p. 50.
15 Ibid., p. 52.
16 Ibid., p. 57.
17 Ibid., p. 62.
18 Ibid., p. 74.
19 Ibid., p. 81.
20 Ibid., p. 85.
21 Watts, in Phillip, p. 153.
22 Ibid., p. 156.
23 Ibid., p. 160.
24 Ibid., p. 162.
25 Ibid., p. 164.
26 Shortland, in Phillip, p. 136
27 Ibid., p. 137.
28 Ibid., p. 143.
29 Ibid., p. 147.
30 Hunter, p. 114.
31 Ibid., p. 115.
32 Ibid., p. 113.

13. THE ABORIGINAL PEOPLE

1 Cook, April 1770.
2 Ibid.
3 Banks, 4 May 1770.
4 Banks, 'House of Commons Inquiry, 1779', *Journal of the House of Commons*, New South Wales State Library, RB F342.4206/1.
5 J. L. Kohen and Ronald Lambert, 'Hunters and Fishers in the Sydney Region', in Mulvaney and White (eds), p. 345.
6 Letter from Phillip to Nepean, 5 July 1788, *HRNSW*, Vol. 1, Pt 2, p. 142.
7 Phillip's Instructions, 25 April 1787, *HRNSW*, Vol. 1, Pt 2, p. 89.
8 Phillip's Views on the Conduct of the Expedition and the Treatment of Convicts, February 1787, *HRNSW*, Vol. 1, Pt 2, p. 53.

9 Letter from Phillip to Nepean, 5 July 1788, *HRNSW*, Vol. 1, Pt 2, p. 143.

10 Worgan, *Letter*.

11 Bowes Smyth, January 1788.

12 Nagle, p. 102.

13 Tench, *Expedition*, Ch. XI.

14 Ibid.

15 Ibid.

16 Ibid.

17 Ibid.

18 Ibid.

19 Tench, *Settlement*, Ch. XVII.

20 *The Times*, 2 December 1786.

21 White, May 1788.

22 Tench, *Settlement*, Ch. I.

23 Letter from Phillip to Sydney, 28 September 1788, *HRNSW*, Vol. 1, Pt 2, p. 192.

24 Letter from Phillip to Sydney, 30 October 1788, *HRNSW*, Vol. 1, Pt 2, p. 208.

25 Letter from Phillip to Stephens, 16 November 1788, *HRNSW*, Vol. 1, Pt 2, p. 214.

26 Tench, *Settlement*, Ch. II.

27 Ibid., Ch. III.

28 Ibid.

29 Ibid.

30 Ibid.

31 Ibid.

32 Ibid.

33 Ibid.

34 J. L. Kohen, 'First and Last Peoples: Aboriginal Sydney', in Connell (ed.), p. 76.

35 Letter from Phillip to Nepean, 13 February 1790, *HRNSW*, Vol. 1, Pt 2, p. 308.

36 Tench, *Settlement*, Ch. III.

37 Letter from Phillip to Sydney, 12 February 1790, *HRNSW*, Vol. 1, Pt 2, p. 299.

38 Tench, *Settlement*, Ch. IV.
39 Ibid.

14. CRISIS
1   Collins, *English Colony in New South Wales*, p. 20.
2   White, May 1788.
3   Tench, *Expedition*, Ch. XIII.
4   White, July 1788.
5   Letter from Phillip to Sydney, 9 July 1788, *HRNSW*,
    Vol. 1, Pt 2, p. 145.
6   Ibid., p. 146.
7   Letter from Phillip to Sydney, 28 September 1788,
    HRNSW, Vol. 1, Pt 2, p. 188.
8   Ibid.
9   Ibid., p. 192.
10 Letter from Phillip to Nepean, 9 July 1788, *HRNSW*,
    Vol. 1, Pt 2, p. 152.
11 Letter from Phillip to Stephens, 10 July 1788, *HRNSW*,
    Vol. 1, Pt 2, p. 168.
12 Letter from Phillip to Nepean, 28 September 1788,
    HRNSW, Vol. 1, Pt 2, p. 190.
13 Ibid., p. 193.
14 Mortality Bill, compiled by David Collins, 28 September
    1788, *HRNSW*, Vol. 1, Pt 2, p. 193.
15 Tench, *Settlement*, Ch. II.
16 Hunter, p. 89.
17 Ibid., p. 90.
18 Letter from Phillip to Sydney, 28 September 1788,
    HRNSW, Vol. 1, Pt 2, p. 185.
19 Letter from Hunter to Stephens, 3 January 1789, *HRNSW*,
    Vol. 1, Pt 2, p. 225.
20 Ibid.
21 Hunter, p. 101.
22 Ibid., p. 99.
23 Nagle, p. 106.
24 Ibid.

25 Ibid., p. 95.

26 Hunter, p. 112.

27 Ibid., p. 113.

28 Ibid., p. 116.

29 Nagle, p. 106.

30 Ibid.

31 Hunter, p. 117.

32 Ibid., p. 120.

33 Tench, *Settlement*, Ch. VI.

34 Collins, *English Colony in New South Wales*, p. 49.

35 Ibid., p. 48.

36 Ibid.

37 Tench, *Settlement*, Ch. VI.

38 *The Times*, 27 April 1790.

39 Collins, *English Colony in New South Wales*, p. 69.

40 Letter from Sydney to the Admiralty, 29 April 1789, *HRNSW*, Vol. 1, Pt 2, p. 230.

41 Superintendents on Board the *Guardian*, Whitehall, 24 August 1789, *HRNSW*, Vol. 1, Pt 2, p. 262.

42 Letter from Grenville to the Admiralty, 8 June 1789, *HRNSW*, Vol. 1, Pt 2, p. 248.

43 In a letter to Phillip on 20 June 1789 Nepean had said, 'The *Guardian* will sail in about a fortnight,' *HRNSW*, Vol. 1, Pt 2, p. 254.

44 Riou, p. 6.

45 Clements, p. 7.

46 Riou, p. 6.

47 Clements, p. 9.

48 Riou, p. 11.

49 Clements, p. 12.

50 Riou, p. 11.

51 Clements, p. 15.

52 Ibid., p. 16.

53 Riou, p. 16.

54 Clements, p. 19.

55 Ibid.

56 Letter from Riou to the Admiralty, 25 December 1789, *HRNSW*, Vol. 1, Pt 2, p. 286.

57 Ibid.

58 Clements, p. 23.

59 Riou, p. 32.

60 Letter from Riou to Stephens, 7 March 1790, *HRNSW*, Vol. 1, Pt 2, p. 317.

61 Clements, p. 35.

62 Ibid., p. 37.

63 *The Times*, 29 April 1790.

64 Letter from Riou to Stephens, 20 May 1790, *HRNSW*, Vol. 1, Pt 2, p. 336.

65 Letter from Lieutenant Shapcote, naval agent in charge of transports, to commissioners of the navy, 24 April 1790, *HRNSW*, Vol. 1, Pt 2, p. 334.

66 Letter from Riou to Stephens, 20 May 1790, *HRNSW*, Vol. 1, Pt 2, p. 337.

67 Ibid., p. 338.

68 Letter from Grenville to Phillip, 16 November 1790, *HRNSW*, Vol. 1, Pt 2, p. 414.

69 Letter from Phillip to Grenville, 17 July 1790, *HRNSW*, Vol. 1, Pt 2, p. 360.

70 Letter from Phillip to Sydney, 11 April 1790, *HRNSW*, Vol. 1, Pt 2, p. 326.

15. A Waiting Game

1 Letter from Phillip to Nepean, 12 February 1790, *HRNSW*, Vol. 1, Pt 2, p. 302.

2 Letter from Collins to his father, 23 March 1790, Mitchell Library, Sydney, microfilm CY2119.

3 Hunter, p. 173.

4 Nagle, p. 118.

5 Letter from Newton Fowell to John Fowell, 31 July 1790, *HRNSW*, Vol. 1, Pt 2, p. 380.

6 Letter from Ross to Phillip, 22 March 1790, *HRNSW*, Vol. 1, Pt 2, p. 319.

[7] Nagle, p. 121.

[8] Ibid.

[9] Nagle, p. 127.

[10] Letter from Grenville to Phillip, 24 December 1789, *HRNSW*, Vol. 1, Pt 2, p. 284.

[11] Tench, *Settlement*, Ch. VI.

[12] Letter from Phillip to Sydney, 11 April 1790, *HRNSW*, Vol. 1, Pt 2, p. 325.

[13] Tench, *Settlement*, Ch. VI.

[14] Ibid.

[15] Ibid.

[16] *Gentleman's Magazine*, January 1791.

[17] Letter from White to Skill, 17 April 1790, *HRNSW*, Vol. 1, Pt 2, p. 332.

[18] Letter from Johnson to Henry Fricker, 9 April 1790, Mitchell Library, Sydney, microfilm CY1397.

[19] Letter from Newton Fowell to John Fowell, 31 July 1790, *HRNSW*, Vol. 1, Pt 2, p. 373.

[20] Tench, *Settlement*, Ch. VI.

[21] Ibid., Ch. VII.

[22] Ibid.

[23] Nagle, p. 127.

[24] Ibid., p. 129.

[25] Tench, *Settlement*, Ch. VIII.

16. ARRIVAL OF THE SECOND FLEET

[1] *The Times*, 6 June 1788.

[2] *The Times*, 30 September 1788.

[3] Nicol, p. 84.

[4] Collins, *English Colony in New South Wales*, p. 96.

[5] Letter from Johnson to Thornton, July 1790, *HRNSW*, Vol. 1, Pt 2, p. 388.

[6] Ibid.

[7] Collins, *English Colony in New South Wales*, p. 99.

[8] Tench, *Settlement*, Ch. VII.

9 Letter from Phillip to Nepean, 13 July 1790, *HRNSW*, Vol. 1, Pt 2, p. 354.

10 Letter from Phillip to Grenville, 17 July 1790, *HRNSW*, Vol. 1, Pt 2, p. 362.

11 Letter from Johnson to Thornton, July 1790, *HRNSW*, Vol. 1, Pt 2, p. 388.

12 Ibid.

13 Letter from Hill to Wathen, 26 July 1790, *HRNSW*, Vol. 1, Pt 2, p. 366.

14 Ibid.

15 *The Times*, 18 November 1791.

16 Letter from Grenville to Phillip, 24 December 1789, *HRNSW*, Vol. 1, Pt 2, p. 286.

17 Tench, *Settlement*, Ch. VII.

18 Ibid.

19 *The Times*, 9 June 1792.

20 Letter from Grenville to Phillip, 20 June 1789, *HRNSW*, Vol. 1, Pt 2, p. 254.

21 Additional Instructions for Phillip, 'Given at our Court at St James', 20 August 1789, *HRNSW*, Vol. 1, Pt 2, p. 256.

22 Ibid., p. 257.

23 Tench, *Settlement*, Ch. X.

24 Letter from Phillip to Grenville, July 1791, *HRNSW*, Vol. 1, Pt 2, p. 538.

17. ESCAPE

1 Gilbert, p. 2.

2 Letter from Phillip to Nepean, 22 August 1790, *HRNSW*, Vol. 1, Pt 2, p. 393.

3 Letter from Phillip to Nepean, 23 August 1790, *HRNSW*, Vol. 1, Pt 2, p. 394.

4 Collins, *English Colony in New South Wales*, p. 58.

5 Ibid., p. 76.

6 Bradley, January 1790.

7 Collins, *English Colony in New South Wales*, p. 320.

8 Ibid., p. 378.

9 Ibid.
10 Ibid., p. 381.
11 Cobley, p. 36.
12 Martin.
13 Scott, March 1791.
14 Martin.
15 Ibid.
16 Ibid.
17 Ibid.
18 Tench, *Settlement*, Notes.
19 Ibid.
20 Ibid., Ch. XVI.

18. The Departure of Phillip

1 Bradley, March 1791.
2 Nagle, p. 131.
3 Ibid.
4 Ibid., p. 138.
5 Bradley, October 1791.
6 Ibid.
7 Nagle, p. 142.
8 Bradley, January 1792.
9 Nagle, p. 143.
10 Letter from Bligh to Banks, 17 December 1791, Mitchell Library, Sydney, microfilm CY3004/274.
11 Bradley, April–May 1792.
12 Nagle, p. 145.
13 Letter from Grenville to Phillip, 19 February 1791, *HRNSW*, Vol. 1, Pt 2, p. 458.
14 Letter from Phillip to Sydney, 15 April 1790, *HRNSW*, Vol. 1, Pt 2, p. 329.
15 Letter from Phillip to Nepean, 15 April 1790, *HRNSW*, Vol. 1, Pt 2, p. 330.
16 Letter from Phillip to Sydney, 15 April 1790, *HRNSW*, Vol. 1, Pt 2, p. 329.

17 Letter from Grenville to Phillip, 15 February 1791, *HRNSW*, Vol. 1, Pt 2, p. 463.
18 Letter from Dundas to Phillip, 15 May 1792, *HRNSW*, Vol. 1, Pt 2, p. 625.
19 Collins, *English Colony in New South Wales*, pp. 208–11.
20 Letter from Phillip to Dundas, 26 October 1796, *HRNSW*, Vol. 2, p. 75.
21 Mackaness, p. 401.
22 Collins, *English Colony in New South Wales*, p. 209.
23 Ibid., p. 172.
24 Ibid., p. 209.
25 Letter from Phillip to Nepean, 9 July 1788, *HRNSW*, Vol. 1, Pt 2, p. 151.
26 Letter from Phillip to Nepean, 17 June 1790, *HRNSW*, Vol. 1, Pt 2, p. 348.
27 Letter from Phillip to Sydney, 13 February 1790, *HRNSW*, Vol. 1, Pt 2, p. 306.
28 Letter from Grenville to Phillip, 19 February 1791, *HRNSW*, Vol. 1, Pt 2, p. 460.

BIBLIOGRAPHY AND FURTHER READING

PRIMARY SOURCES

Banks, Joseph, *The Endeavour Journals of Joseph Banks, 1768–1771*, Angus & Robertson, Sydney, 1963

Blackburn, David, *Papers and Letters of David Blackburn*, Mitchell Library, Sydney, MSS: ML Safe 1/120

Bowes Smyth, Arthur, *A Journal of a Voyage from Portsmouth to New South Wales and China in the Lady Penrhyn, Merchantman William Cropton Sever, Commander, by Arthur Bowes Smyth, Surgeon, 1787–1789*, P. G. Fidlon and R. J. Ryan (eds), Australian Documents Library, Sydney, 1979

Bradley, William, *A Voyage to New South Wales, the Journal of Lieutenant William Bradley RN of HMS Sirius, 1786–1792*, Trustees of the Public Library of New South Wales in Association with Ure Smith, Sydney, 1969

de Brosses, Charles, *Voyages to the Terra Australis*, Da Capo Press, New York, 1967

Clark, Ralph, *The Journal and Letters of Ralph Clark 1787–1792*, Australian Documents Library in association with the Library of Australian History, Sydney, 1981

Clements, Thomas, *Guardian: A Journal of the Proceedings on Board the Above Ship, Lieutenant Riou, Commander; as Delivered into the Admiralty Board by Mr. Clements*, Charles Stalker, London, 1790

Collins, David, *An Account of the English Colony in New South Wales*, Vol. 1, A. H. & A. W. Reed, Sydney, 1975
Collins Family Papers, Vol. 1, Mitchell Library, Sydney, MSS: ML 700

Colquhoun, Patrick, *A Treatise on Police of Metropolitan London*, Gillet, London, 1805

Cook, Captain James, *The Journal of HMS Endeavour, 1768–1771*, Rigby, Adelaide, 1977

Crittenden, Victor, *The Voyage of the First Fleet 1787–1788, Taken from Contemporary Accounts*, Mulini Press, Canberra, 1981

Currey, John, *Report of the Select Committee on Convicts, 1799*, Colony Press, Melbourne, 1982

Dalrymple, Alexander, *An Account of the Discoveries Made in the South Pacific Ocean, 1767*, Hordern House Rare Books for the Australian National Maritime Museum, Sydney, 1996

Dampier, William, *A New Voyage Around the World*, Oxford, 1703

Davis, *Memoranda by Convict Davis, Servant to Mr Foster, Superintendent of Convicts, Norfolk Island* (original manuscript held in the Dixson Library, State Library of New South Wales, Sydney, DLMS Q168)

Easty, John, *Memorandum of the Transactions of a Voyage from England to Botany Bay 1787–1793: A First Fleet Journal*, Angus & Robertson, Sydney, 1965

Fowell, Newton, *The Sirius Letters: The Complete Letters of Newton Fowell, Midshipman and Lieutenant Aboard the Sirius Flagship of the First Fleet on its Voyage to New South Wales, 1788–1790*, Fairfax, Sydney, 1988

George III, *George III 1738–1820: The Correspondence of King George the Third*, Sir John Fortescue (ed.), Macmillan, London, 1928

Gilbert, Thomas, *Commander of the Charlotte, Voyage from New South Wales to Canton, in the Year 1788: With Views of the Islands Discovered*, J. Debrett, London, 1789

Howard, John, *The State of Prisons in England and Wales: With Preliminary Observations, and an Account of Some Foreign Prisons and Hospitals*, William Eyres, Warrington, 1777

Hunter, John, *An Historic Journal of the Transactions at Port Jackson and Norfolk Island, Historical Records of Australia*, Series I, Vols 1–10

Johnson, Reverend Richard, *Some Letters of Rev. Richard Johnson, BA, First Chaplain of New South Wales*, collected and edited by George Mackaness, Review, Dubbo, New South Wales, 1978

King, Philip Gidley, *The Journal of Philip Gidley King: Lieutenant R.N. 1787–1790*, Australian Documents Library, Sydney, 1980

Martin, James, *James Martin's Memorandums* (part of the Bentham Papers held in the Special Collections of London University), republished in Mike Walker, *A Long Way Home*

Nagle, Jacob, *The Nagle Journal: A Diary of the Life of Jacob Nagle, Sailor, from the Year 1775 to 1841*, J. C. Dann (ed.), Weidenfeld and Nicolson, New York, 1988

Nicol, John, *The Life and Adventures of John Nicol, Mariner*, Farrer and Rinehard, London, 1936 (reprinted in R. J. Ryan, *The Second Fleet Convicts*)

O'Reilly, John Boyle, *Moondyne*, George Robertson, Sydney, 1880

Parker, Ann, *A Voyage Around the World in the Gorgon, Man of War*, Debrett, London, 1795

Phillip, Arthur, *The Voyage of Governor Phillip to Botany Bay: With an Account of the Establishment of the Colonies of Port Jackson and Norfolk Island: Compiled from Authentic Papers which have been Obtained from Several Departments, to which are Added, the Journals of Lieuts. Shortland, Watts, Ball and Capt. Marshall, with an Account of their New Discoveries*, Hutchinson of Australia, Richmond, Victoria, 1982

Riou, Edward, *The Journal of the Proceedings on Board His Majesty's Ship the Guardian, Commanded by Lieutenant*

Riou, *Bound for Botany Bay, from the 22nd of December, 1789, to the 15th of January, 1790*, Ridgeway, London, 1790

Scott, James, *Remarks on a Passage to Botany Bay, 1787–1792: A First Fleet Journal*, Trustees of the Public Library of New South Wales in association with Angus & Robertson, Sydney, 1963

Shortland, John Willoughby, *The Shortland Family of the Royal Navy and Australasia with Particular Reference to the 'First Fleet'*, John Willoughby Shortland, Miranda, NSW, c.2003

Spain, Edward, *The Journal of Edward Spain, Merchant Seaman and Sometimes Warrant Officer in the Royal Navy; Describing the Life at Sea During the American Revolution and the Wars with France*, St Marks Press, Bankstown, NSW, 1989

Tench, Watkin, *A Complete Account of the Settlement at Port Jackson, in New South Wales, including an Accurate Description of the Situation of the Colony*, G. Nicol and J. Sewell, London, 1793

—— *A Narrative of the Expedition to Botany Bay: With an Account of New South Wales. Its Productions, Inhabitants. Etc: to which is Subjoined a List of Civil and Military Establishments at Port Jackson*, Debrett, London, 1789 (reprinted by Angus & Robertson, in association with the Royal Australian Historical Society, Sydney, 1961)

Walpole, Sir Horace, *Letters of Sir Horace Walpole, Fourth Earl of Oxford, to Sir Horace Mann*, Vol. 3, Lord Dover (ed.), Dearborn, New York, 1833

Waterhouse, William, *Papers: Letters Received from William Waterhouse*, Mitchell Library, Sydney, MSS 6544

White, John, *John White: Surgeon General to the First Fleet*, Debrett, London, 1790 (reprinted by Australian Medical Publishing, Sydney, 1933)

Worgan, George B., *Journal of a First Fleet Surgeon*,

including *Letter, 12–18 June* and *Journal (January 20–July 11, 1788)*, Library Council of New South Wales in association with the Library of Australian History, Sydney, 1978

SECONDARY SOURCES

Bateson, Charles, *The Convict Ships 1787–1868*, Reed, Sydney, 1974

Beaglehole, John Cawte, *Exploration of the Pacific*, A & C Black, London, 1966

Bonwick, James, *Australia's First Preacher: The Reverend Richard Johnson, First Chaplain of New South Wales*, Sampson Low, Marston & Co., London, 1898

Chapman, Don, *1788: The People of the First Fleet*, Doubleday, Sydney, 1986

Clark, Manning, *A History of Australia*, Vol. 1, 'From the Earliest Times to the Age of Macquarie', Melbourne University Press, Melbourne, 1962

Cobley, John, *The Crimes of the First Fleet Convicts*, Angus & Robertson, Sydney, 1970

Connell, John (ed.), *Sydney: The Emergence of a Global City*, Oxford University Press, Oxford, 2000

Eldershaw, M. Barnard, *Phillip of Australia: An Account of the Settlement of Sydney Cove 1788–92*, Angus & Robertson, Sydney, 1977

Gillen, Mollie, *The Search for John Small, First Fleeter*, Library of Australian History, Sydney, 1985

Hall, Jerome, *Theft, Law and Society*, Little Brown, Michigan, 1937

Henderson, Graeme, *The Sirius Past and Present*, Collins, Sydney, 1988

Holden, Robert, *Orphans of History: The Forgotten Children of the First Fleet*, Text Publishing, Melbourne, 2000

Hughes, Robert, *The Fatal Shore: The Epic of Australia's Founding*, Harvill, London, 1996

Keneally, Thomas, *The Commonwealth of Thieves*, Random House Australia, Sydney, 2005

Kenny, John, *Before the First Fleet: Europeans in Australia 1606–1777*, Kangaroo Press, Kenthurst, NSW, 1995

King, Jonathan, *The First Fleet: The Convict Voyage that Founded Australia*, Macmillan, South Melbourne, 1982

Lambert, Andrew, *War at Sea in the Age of Sail, 1650–1850*, Cassell, London, 2000

Mackaness, George, *Admiral Arthur Phillip: Founder of New South Wales, 1738–1814*, Angus & Robertson, Sydney, 1937

Mackay, David, *A Place of Exile: The European Settlement of New South Wales*, Oxford University Press, Melbourne, 1985

McAlpine, Ida and Richard Hunter, *George III and the Mad Business*, Allen Lane, London, 1960

McIntyre, Kenneth Gordon, *The Rebello Transcripts: Governor Phillip's Portuguese Prelude*, Sovereign Press, London, 1984

Menzies, Gavin, *1421: The Year China Discovered the World*, Bantam, London, 2003

Mulvaney, D. J. and Peter J. White (eds), *Australians in 1788*, Fairfax, Syme & Weldon, Sydney, 1987

O'Brien, Eris, *The Foundations of Australia*, Angus & Robertson, Sydney, 1950

Radzinowicz, Leon, *A History of the English Criminal Law and its Administration from 1750*, Vol. 1, Stevens and Sons, London, 1948–50

Rawson, Geoffrey, *The Strange Case of Mary Bryant*, Robert Hale, London, 1938

Rees, Sian, *The Floating Brothel: The Extraordinary Story of the Lady Juliana and its Cargo of Female Convicts Bound for Botany Bay*, Hodder, Sydney, 2001

Ryan, R. J., *The Second Fleet Convicts*, Star Printery, Sydney, 1982

Small, John and Mary, *The Small Family in Australia*, William John Pollock (ed.), Star Printery, Erskineville, NSW, 1988

de Vries, Susanna, *Strength of Spirit: Pioneering Women of*

Achievement from First Fleet to Federation, Millennium Books, Alexandria, NSW, 1995

Walker, Mike, *A Long Way Home*, John Wiley & Sons, London, 2005

Watkins, David, *The Architect King: George III and the Culture of the Enlightenment*, Royal Connection, London, 2004

JOURNALS, PERIODICALS AND OTHER WORKS

The Advertiser

Annual Register (of a View of the History, Politics and Literature for the Year 1786), Dodsley, London, 1788

Felix Farley's Bristol Journal

General Evening Post

Gentleman's Magazine

Historical Records of Australia, Series I, Vols 1–10 (John Hunter, *An Historic Journal of the Transactions at Port Jackson and Norfolk Island*)

Historical Records of New South Wales (HRNSW), Vol. 1, Pt 1 (Cook 1762–80), Pt 2 (Phillip 1783–92), Vol. 2 (Grose and Patterson 1793–5), Vol. 3 (Hunter 1796–99), Vol. 4 (Hunter and King 1800, 1801, 1802), Vol. 5 (King 1803–05), Vol. 6 (King and Bligh 1806–07, 1808)

Journal of the House of Commons, Vols 37–40

London Chronicle

London Observer

Old Bailey trial records: www.oldbaileyonline.org

The Parliamentary Register, or *History of the Proceedings of the House of Commons*

Royal Australian Historical Society Journal, Vol. XXI, Pt IV

Sydney Gazette

The Times

Whitehall Evening Post

INDEX

Page references given in italics are to the Chronology section of the book.